AF361623

THE WAY OF HUMILITY

THE WAY OF HUMILITY

ST. AUGUSTINE'S
THEOLOGY OF PREACHING

Charles G. Kim, Jr.

The Catholic University of America Press
Washington, D.C.

Cataloging-in-Publication Data is available from the Library of Congress

ISBN: 978-0-8132-3739-8

eISBN: 978-0-8132-3740-4

For Abby

CONTENTS

ACKNOWLEDGEMENTS

"God resists the proud but gives grace to the humble."

Peter 5:5

A FAVORITE AND FREQUENTLY QUOTED VERSE from St. Augustine, this verse sums up the life of this proud sinner. It is only by the grace of a humble Savior that this project has come to completion. I began reading St. Augustine's *Confessions* in high school, alongside a study of the Latin language. I did not understand either very well but knew that there was deep wisdom in the thought of this great saint. I could never have predicted the twists and turns my life would take to get to this point, but I have written a dissertation on one of the most influential people in the Western world. His writings have also had the profound effect of reminding me again and again that anything worth being called true has its source in God. Whatever is true and good in the writings of St. Augustine are so only because they participate in our true and good God.

Fr. Meconi has shown me the grace of God in this project by encouraging me to study what I was passionate about. I will be forever grateful for him believing in me and my academic work. I am also appreciative of early comments on this dissertation from Drs. Carol Harrison and Daniel Smith. I know it was a lot of time and difficult being across the ocean for Dr. Harrison, but I am grateful for your notes and contributions. Later versions of this work were read and commented on by two anonymous reviewers provided through the publisher. My deep gratitude to them both for what made this a much better study. The editorial team at Catholic University of America Press has made this work much better than I could have imagined or done on my own. Thank you to John Martino and Trevor Crowell and their teams. I own all the faults that remain.

I owe tremendous thanks to the grace and encouragement of my parents. They have believed in me and encouraged me for my entire life. In the last several years, they have helped Abby and I with our son, Charlie, and my daughter, Ramona. I have always seemed to pursue things which were new to them, hockey, soccer, Latin, and Augustine. No matter what I was interested in, they learned about it and pushed me to do my best at whatever I found myself doing. I do not deserve your love and can only continue to say thank you.

Finally, I have truly known the redemptive, unconditional love of the God of second chances through my wife, Abby. She has suffered the most from the time I have spent reading and writing about someone and something else. She has worked tirelessly to birth and take care of Charlie and Ramona, go to work full time, and be the best wife to me. I cannot conceive of how she has the energy to do what she does, while suffering through various medical difficulties. It is only through the mercy of God, I am sure. I am grateful for the love of God which I see in her. Thank you. I love you.

THE WAY OF HUMILITY

Abbreviations	Latin Titles	English Titles	English Translation	Latin Editions	Date
ciu. Dei	*De ciuitate Dei*	*City of God*	William Babcock, (I/6-7) (New City Press, 2013).	CCSL 47–48	413–27
conf.	*Confessiones*	*Confessions*	Maria Boulding, (I/1), (New City Press, 1997).	CCSL 27	397–401
doc. Chr.	*De doctrina* Christiana	*Teaching Christianity*	Edmund Hill, *Teaching Christianity*	CCSL 32 (I/11) (New City Press, 1996)	396; 426/27
en. Ps.	*Enarrationes in Psalmos*	*Expositions of the Psalms*	Maria Boulding (New City Press) 6 vols: Ps 1–32 (III/15) 2000; Ps 33–50 (III/16) 2000; Ps 51–72 (III/17) 2001; Ps 73–98 (III/18) 2002; Ps 99–120 (III/19) 2003; Ps 121–50 (III/20) 2004	CCSL 38–40	392 (1–32) through 406/07 (119–33), sporadically up through 422
ep.	*Epistulae*	*Letters*	Roland Teske, *Letters* (New City Press) 4 vols: 1–99 (II/1) 2001; 100–55 (II/2) 2003; 156–210 (II/3) 2004; 211–70 and Divjak 1–29 (II/4) 2005	CSEL 34, 44, 57,58,88	cf. Fitzgerald, s.v., *Epistulae, Augustine Through the Ages,* 299–305
f. et symb.	*De fide et symbolo*	*On Faith and the Creed*	Michael Campbell, in *On Christian Belief* (New City Press, 2005) 155–176.	CSEL 41	Oct. 8, 393

continued

Abbreviations	Latin Titles	English Titles	English Translation	Latin Editions	Date
Jo. eu. tr.	*In Johannis euangelium tractatus*	*Tractates on the Gospel of John*	John Rettig, *Tractates on the Gospel of John* (Catholic University of America Press) 5 vols: 1 (1–10) 1988; 2 (11–27) 1988; 3 (28–54) 1993; 4 (55–111) 1994; 5 (112–24) 1995	CCSL 36	406/21?
ord.	*De ordine*	*On Order*	Robert Russell, FC 1, 239–334.	CCSL 29	Nov. 386– Mar. 387
s.	*Sermones*	*Sermons*	Edmund Hill, *Sermons* (Hyde Park: New City Press) 11 vols: 1 (1–19); 2 (20–50) 1990; 3 (51–94) 1991; 4 (94A–147A); 5 (148–83) 1992; 6 (184–229Z); 7(230–72B) 1993; 8 (273–305A); 9 (306–40A) 1994; 10 (341–400); 11 (Dolbeau's Newly-Discovered) 1997.	PL 38–40; CCSL 41, 41Aa, 41Ab, 41Ba, 41Bb	cf. *Aug. Through the Ages*, 774–89
sol.	*Soliloquia*	*The Soliloquies*	Kim Paffenroth, *Soliloquies* (Hyde Park: New City Press, 2000).	CSEL 89	Nov. 386- Mar. 387
Trin.	*De Trinitate*	*The Trinity*	Edmund Hill, *The Trinity* (I/5) (New City Press, 1991).	CCSL 50/50A	399–422/26

[1] This is an adapted list. The dates come from Allan Fitzgerald and John C. Cavadini, editors, *Augustine through the Ages* (Grand Rapids, MI: Eerdmans, 1999): xxxv–xliii.

LIST OF ABBREVIATIONS

AugR	Augustinianum (Roma)
BA	Oeuvres de Saint Augustin, Bibliothèque augustinienne (Paris, 1936–)
CCSL	Corpus Christianorum Series Latina (Turnhout, 1953–)
CSEL	Corpus Scriptorum Ecclesiasticorum Latinorum (Vienna, 1866–)
EAA	Collection des Études Augustiniennes, Série Antiquité
FC	The Fathers of the Church (New York/Washington, 1949–)
IP	Instrumenta Patristica (Mediaevalia)
LCL	Loeb Classical Library (New York/Cambridge, MA, 1912–)
MiAg	Miscellanea Agostiniana (Rome, 1930)
OCD	Oxford Classical Dictionary (Oxford, 2003)
OLD	Oxford Latin Dictionary (Oxford, 2012)
PL	Patrologiae Cursus Completus, Series Latina (Paris, 1844–65)
PLS	Patrologiae Cursus Completus, Series Latina Supplementa (Paris, 1958–)
REB	Revue Bénédictine (Paris)
REAug	Revue des Études Augustiniennes
SC	Sources Chrétiennes (Paris: Cerf, 1942–)
SPM	Stromata Patristica et Mediaevalia (1950)
WSA	The Works of Saint Augustine (Hyde Park, NY, 1990–)

INTRODUCTION

HUMILITY, BOTH IN WORD AND DEED, is central to the preaching of Augustine. To take just one example from the nearly 550 sermons from the collection known as the *Sermones ad Populum* "Sermons to the People," Augustine preached a common theme that the way of life in Christ consisted in humility.[1] He wrote, "If we are humble, we shall deserve to be given the bliss of seeing God fully face to face provided we deserve to be counted among the little ones."[2] All those seeking to see God, the beatific vision, must become humble. From the preacher leading the ecclesiastical community at Hippo, down to the lower status fisherman or farmer, all had to learn humility, and all desire to come to see the face of God. The preacher offers for his community an example through his words, what he learned from Christ. As Augustine says later in the same sermon, "Learn from Christ what you won't learn from man; in him is to be found the standard of humility."[3] The sermon through the words of the preacher offered to the people an example of humility, which Christ intends for the whole church to learn. The preacher trains the gathered church to see the humility of Christ; for humility is the ground of the virtues and necessary for a participation in the *totus Christus* (the whole Christ).

I will show through an analysis of the context of the preaching of Augustine and through three separate themes in the sermons of Augustine that humility and speaking humbly constitute an integral part of Augustine's life and theology of preaching to his congregations across North Africa. In this way, it is impossible to think of Augustine's theology of preaching without considering the virtue of humility. In so doing, this study will move

---

1 *s.* 68; Pierre-Patrick Verbraken, *Études critiques sur les sermons authentiques de saint Augustin* (Steenbrugis: Abbatia Sancti Petri, 1976) 70.

2 *s.* 68.7 [= Mai 126] (SL 41Aa.447; WSA III.3, 228).

3 *s.* 68.11 [= Mai 126] (CCSL 41Aa.447; WSA III/3, 231).

the conversation on Augustine's theology of preaching forward, by foregrounding how Augustine's emphasis on humility undergirds the task of preaching in the liturgy of the church.

Moreover, this study demonstrates that the character of Christian discourse through Augustine changed its cultural referents, and authorities, and the way the educated preachers communicated with their congregations by using an implicit argument from the lived virtue of the speaker and the participation of the hearer, rather than simply rhetorical persuasion and logical syllogism. The preaching of humility provides a window into how the preacher could model the virtue in words as it was expected to be lived out in everyday life, the *via humilitatis agendo*, "the way of humility through action."

From a theological angle, Augustine's theology is best understood as it is worked out before the church at Hippo. Although Augustine is known to history through his more famous literary works, like *The Confessions*, *City of God*, and *On the Trinity*, Augustine spent the majority of his life acting out his theology in the sermon. It is here we see the heartbeat of his theology in connection with the people to which he preached and loved so dearly. He desired that God work in all of them so that together they might catch a glimpse of the Beatific Vision, which all Christians are promised in the eschaton.

Shortly after Christmas and before Epiphany, Augustine preached a sermon in the year 425 on the way of life of his clergy for the people at Hippo.[4] Apparently, some concerns had arisen about how the monastery adjacent to the Basilica Pacis handled a large financial windfall.[5] Augustine wanted to calm the congregation's anxieties by sharing his outlook on the life of a bishop and the monastic community. The elderly bishop begins by saying:

> What I'm going to talk about is the matter for which I wanted your graces to come here today in greater numbers than usual, as I asked you to yesterday. We live here with you, and we live here for you; and my intention and wish is that we may live with you in Christ's presence forever. I think our way of life is plain for you to see; so that I too may perhaps make bold to say what the apostle said, though I can't of course be compared with him: 'Be imitators of me, as I too am of Christ' (1 Cor 11:1). And that's why I don't want any of you

---

4 Pierre-Patrick Verbraken, *Études critiques,* 148.

5 Augustine explains the situation in the most detail in *s.* 355.

to find an excuse for living badly. 'For we aim at what is good, 'says the same apostle, 'not only in the sight of God, but also in the sight of men' (2 Cor 8:21).[6]

Augustine recognizes that he is an example for his congregation as their preacher. He wants that example to be drawn from the biblical witness of Paul and of Christ. To consider oneself an example for others could be courting disaster. The monks in Augustine's monastery, attached to the basilica, in some cases did not always live up to their high calling, as happened in case of a certain Januarius who left money that the people feared was being held by the monks at the basilica.[7]

This introduction of the sermon from Augustine highlights the scrutiny with which he considered his words and his actions. The goal of his life in the community was that the people of Hippo would live in unity with Christ. Augustine offered his life for the people, desiring that they would not merely see him as the true example, but would find Christ in his words and in his actions. He says in a simple and memorable Latin phrase from the above sermon, "vobiscum hic vivimus, et propter vos vivimus" (we live here with you and we live because of you). The monks and leaders lived with them, and they lived for them. The conclusion indicates why they do it, "intentio votumque nostrum est, ut apud Christum vobiscum sine fine vivamus" (our intention and vow are that we should live with you all in the presence of Christ without end). The ecclesial community, and in this case the sermon, is one of the places where the *telos* (end) of their lives comes to the center. Christ meets them in the words and example of the bishop in the sermon which in turn comes from the humble scriptures witnessing to the advent and final vision of the humble Christ.

6 *s.* 355.1 (SPM 1.124; WSA III/10, 166): "Propter quod volui et rogavi hesterna die, ut hodie frequentior conveniret caritas vestra, hoc est quod dicturus sum. Vobiscum hic vivimus, et propter vos vivimus: et intentio votumque nostrum est, ut apud Christum vobiscum sine fine vivamus. Credo autem ante oculos vestros esse conversationem nostram; ut et nos dicere fortassis audeamus, quamvis multum illi impares, quod dixit Apostolus: Imitatores mei estote, sicut et ego Christi 1. Et ideo nolo ut aliquis de nobis inveniat male vivendi occasionem. Providemus enim bona, ait idem apostolus, non solum coram Deo, sed etiam coram hominibus."

7 F. van der Meer, *Augustine the Bishop: The Life and Work of a Father of the Church*, trans. Brian Battershaw and G.R. Lamb (London: Sheed and Ward, 1961) 199–234.

Augustine's earliest biographer encapsulates what made him such a persuasive figure in North African Christianity and in the Christianization of the late Roman Empire by writing, "No one can read what he wrote about divinity without profit. But, I think that those were able to profit still more who could hear him speak in church and see him with their own eyes.... Truly, he was indeed one of those of whom it is written, 'speak this way and act the same way'" (Jas. 2:12).[8] Possidius thus praised Augustine repurposing a phrase from the book of James, which brings together two critical aspects of the life of the preacher which cannot be separated: 1) the preaching itself and 2) the life of the preacher which practiced that message.

For Augustine, the speaking and acting of the preacher centered on the virtue of humility taught first by Christ. Preaching a virtue like humility requires great balance and self-awareness. If the preacher is not careful, he could very easily promote himself as the perfection of humility. This would in turn bring too much praise to himself and ultimately make the speaker too proud of his humility. This raises significant problems for the former illustrious orator. Augustine as a preacher remains in the general occupation of public speaking that once brought him great adulation as a rhetor and in turn made him proud. Possidius' remark appears to indicate that Augustine handled this conundrum with great aplomb, both acting and speaking in a way that did not betray his humility.

As to the quality of the speaking itself, Possidius lauds Augustine's ability not only to find moving words about God, but also to speak in such a way that hearing him "profited" the listener, even more than the one who simply read him. As readers of some remove from that time, there will always be elements of his preaching style and quality that will be left to the past. This study, aware of the limitation of time and distance, intends to pursue what Possidius hinted at in this provocative quote about the uniqueness of being present in the basilica to hear the bishop preach. Are there traces of that

---

8 Possidius, *Vita Augustini* 31.9: "quod agnoscunt qui eum de divinis scribentem legentes proficiunt. Sed ego arbitror plus ex eo proficere potuisse, qui eum et loquentem in ecclesia praesentem audire et videre potuerunt ... verum etiam ex iis ad quos scriptum est, Sic loquimini, et sic facite." in Possidius, *Vita Augustini: zweisprachige Ausgabe eingeleitet, kommentiert und herausgegeben,* ed. Wilhelm Geerlings (Paderborn: Ferdinand Schöningh, 2005), 104; translated in English, Frederick R. Hoare, *The Western Fathers* (New York: Sheed and Ward, 1954). Paulinus of Nola similarly praises Augustine in a letter to his son, calling him "the trumpet of the Lord," *ep.* 32 (WSA II/1, 110).

quality of the spoken word that survive in the written record of the perfor-
mances of that erstwhile rhetor turned bishop?

Turning to Augustine, we find the former imperial orator in Milan preaching regularly in a far-flung corner of the Roman empire in a smaller port city called Hippo Regius.[9] This destination would have been as good as exile to the young orator, but as a preacher rooted in the virtue of humility in the humble God, he found new purpose for his use of rhetoric. In a quint-essential passage, he preached, "[God] had come, you see, to teach humility and overthrow pride; God had come in humility.... And so it was safer and sounder for the Lord to gain an orator through a fisherman than a fisherman through an orator."[10] In a characteristically Augustinian turn of phrase, the great preacher raises the fisherman (*piscator*) to a more exalted place than the famed ancient orator, in imitation of the humble God.[11] Through this phrase we catch a glimpse of how Augustine taught the virtue of humility demon-strated to him through God's coming in that same humility. This juxtaposi-tion of the fisherman and the orator occurs more than 20 times throughout Augustine's preaching, along with several other references in letters and other written works.[12] It is not hard to hear Augustine critiquing his own past as an orator along with an admonition to the gathered faithful. If the Lord came to teach humility, it would be hypocritical to come with the pomp of a Roman official. The Lord thus chose to use humble *piscatores* (fishermen) to proclaim his advent, his new *via*, and his new medicine for the tumor of pride that had grown in so large in the human heart.[13]

9 The present-day city of Annaba, on the northern tip of Algeria.

10 *s.* 341.4 [Dolbeau 22.4] (EAA 147.556; WSA III/11, 286): "Venerat enim docere humilitatem, expugnare superbiam; venerat humilis Deus. Salubrius itaque lucratus est Dominus oratorem de piscatore, quam piscatorem de oratore."

11 Christine Mohrmann, "Das Wortspiel in den augustinischen Sermones," in *Études sur le latin des chrétiens*, Vol. 1 (Roma, Edizioni di Storia e Litteratura: 1961): 323–49.

12 *s.* 43 (CCSL 41.51), *s.* 51 (CCSL 41a.15), *s.* 68 [Mai 126] (CCSL 41A.445), *s.* 87 (PL 38.537), *s.* 198 [Dolbeau 26] (EAA 147 p. 414), *s* 223G [Wilmart] (MiAg 1.690), *s.* 229m [Guelferbytanus 15] (MiAg 1.488), *s.* 248 (PL 38.1158), *s.* 249 (PL 38.1161), *s.* 250 (SC 116. 310), *s. 252 (PL 38.1172), s.* 252A [Wilmart 13] (MiAg 1.712), *s.* 272A (RB 84.265), *s.* 298A (PLS 2.1161), *s.* 311 (PL 38.1416), *s.* 335C (PLS 2.753), *s.* 341 [Dolbeau 22] (EAA 147.554), *s.* 350E (WSt 122.199), *s* 360B [Dolbeau 25] (EAA 147.265), *s.* 361 (PL 39.1608), *s.* 381 (PL 39.1683).

13 *s.* 123.1

Augustine preaches about humility with many different metaphors exhorting his people to heal their proud souls, as he healed his own. If he were to speak to them only to show off his elocution, he would confound the aim of inculcating the virtue of humility. Contrary to his understanding as a Platonist seeking to ascend to God through philosophical inquiry, he learned a new *via,* a *via humilitatis.*[14] This new path opened the door for all people to draw near to God through the writings of scripture, including John the Evangelist, a simple fisherman. Throughout his corpus of sermons, Augustine uses the fisherman-orator comparison, among many others, to preach humility. These themes can be seen in sermons written in Carthage, as well as Hippo, and appear early in his preaching career up until right before his death. The humility of the advent of the Word on earth connects to Augustine's understanding of Christology. The Word of God on earth is seen in the *forma servi,* but for those with eyes to see, the *forma servi* points to the *forma Dei* in Christ.[15]

This contrast between the fisherman and the orator stands among many different leitmotifs of humility in the preaching of Augustine. On many occasions, Augustine reimagines the liturgical setting of the sermon as a classroom for Christ the teacher to educate the students in the school of Christ through the preacher. Augustine will call himself, even though the preacher, a *condiscipulus.* By employing this construct, Augustine imitates and exhibits the humility he learned from Christ for the gathered church. These references to the schoolroom and Christ the Teacher hint at the larger theological doctrine of the church for Augustine. Augustine called the church the *totus Christus.*

Furthermore, Augustine recognized that the language of fishermen and the model of Christ as teacher could demonstrate humility for his audience. He could not, however, on his own ability, make them humble. The preacher had to rely on God to work on the inside. In 1 Cor 3:7, Paul says that the preacher works on the outside like a farmer, but God gives the growth (*Incrementum dat deus*). When Augustine comes across a difficult passage of scripture, he admonishes his hearers to rely on God to provide what he lacks as speaker, and they might lack in grasping what scripture offers. They must in humility recognize their dependency on the grace of Christ to see. The grace to see is a way of talking about Augustine's theology of salvation.

14 *conf.* 7.9.13 (CCSL 27:101); *ciu. dei.* 2.7 (CCSL 47:39–40).
15 *cf.* Phil 2:7.

Insofar as these images undergird his theology of preaching, they constitute a significant feature of the entire preaching corpus. The preacher speaks in a humble fashion like a fisherman. The true teacher in the sermon is no longer the speaker, but Christ who speaks in the scripture proclaimed by the preacher. Finally, the people listening must actively participate by relying on God to give the increase. Through these three leitmotifs of humility, we can penetrate deeper into the theology of Augustine at work in the sermon as a sacramental encounter with Christ, as his body the Church learns the *via humilitatis* taught and offered to humanity through the Word made flesh. As Possidius says, Augustine the preacher could "speak this way and act the same way." The sermonic themes and the language of the sermons evidence the claim of Possidius about the content and character, the medium and the message, of the preaching of Augustine.

Augustine's Preaching in Previous Scholarship

In the last decade, the scholarship on Augustine's sermons has moved from a trickle to something of a stream. While it is still understudied compared to some facets of Augustine's theology and writings, more attention has turned to the sermons themselves. The most productive outgrowth of this research has been to incorporate social history and rhetoric into the analysis of Augustine's thought. We can learn a great deal about how Augustine communicated with his audience by situating it properly within its historical epoch. What follows will start with the broader question of social history and rhetoric as they have been incorporated into the broader study of Augustine, and then move to the narrower field of Augustine's sermons.

In this mode of study, many scholars have centered on discourse in late antiquity and asked the question whether a man of such sophistication like Augustine could even communicate with a broader audience. We see this in the writings of Ramsay MacMullen and Philip Rousseau, to whom we will return in chapter three. These scholars suggest that the speech of these preachers ignored their audience and stayed closer to the literate speech of their polytheistic rhetorical forebears. Averil Cameron and Peter Brown have both written significant works on the state of discourse in the late ancient Christian world. Brown, in *Power and Persuasion*, focuses much more closely on the Greek East rather than the Latin West. He lays out very thoroughly the place of *paideia* and the need to reinscribe the power that comes from the kind of education that most preachers had.[16] Brown only cites MacMullen on one occasion in the book but appears to use the work of MacMullen's essay to a great degree in arguing for the cultural divide between the preacher and congregation. More recently, it appears that Brown has reconsidered his argument concerning the firm distinction between the elite class and the uneducated, illiterate masses who made up the majority of the Christian population in North Africa.[17]

Averil Cameron's foundational book *Christianity and the Rhetoric of Empire* proposes language as the most important explanatory factor for the rise of Christianity in the Late Roman Empire. Contra MacMullen and other simply materialist notions about the rapid rise of Christianity in the late Roman empire, Cameron brings preaching and writing to the fore. Drawing on the phrase "totalizing discourse" from Michel Foucault, Cameron focuses on the language and symbolism of asceticism and virginity as a way to interpret and explain the way that Christianity subsumed the pagan past and transformed it into a total control of the newly Christian empire.[18] Much of Cameron's argument rests on the fact that Christianity encouraged a literary culture, and religion of the book, rather than an oral culture.[19] After the British historian Edward Gibbon popularized the notion of a "fall" of the Roman empire, many historians of late antiquity characterized Christianity as merely a superstitious and irrational religion that ushered in the poorly termed "dark ages," obscuring the bright light of ancient culture. Turning her historical study to a renewed focus on discourse, Cameron writes:

> It is best seen in the case of Christian preaching, the hidden iceberg
> of Christian discourse; Christians not only sought to teach but,
> through regular repetition and by continually drawing on and

---

16 Peter Brown, *Power and Persuasion in Late Antiquity: Towards a Christian Empire*, (Madison: University of Wisconsin Press, 1992), 76. A. G. Hamman also registers his surprise that Augustine's audience could even understand the great preacher, due to the rhetorical nature of the sermons in *La vie quotidienne en Afrique du Nord au temps de Saint Augustin* (Paris: Hachette, 1979), 132.

17 Peter Brown, "Augustine and a crisis of wealth in Late Antiquity," *Augustinian Studies* 36 (2005): 5–30.

18 For Cameron's specific assessment of Foucault, see: "Redrawing the Map: Early Christian Territory after Foucault," *The Journal of Roman Studies* 76 (1986): 266–71.

19 Averil Cameron, *Christianity and the Rhetoric of Empire: The Development of Christian Discourse* (Berkeley: University of California Press, 1991), 109.

reinterpreting an increasingly familiar body of texts, also constantly reaffirmed the essence of the faith and the constituents of member-ship of the Christian community.[20]

It is the "hidden iceberg" which this study hopes to bring above sea level, by recognizing how the preacher communicated with a largely illiterate, but not dull, congregation. Both Cameron and Brown share a fascination with the power of the elites over the unlettered masses, recognizing little accommodation from the preachers to the masses, without any investigation of the intellectual abilities of the illiterate.

We hope to show that despite the high illiteracy, the people to whom Augustine preached were not dull, but well-equipped in their own way to follow an oral message like a sermon. Stanley Rosenberg offers a contrary picture of the kind of relationship between the pastor and flock. Relying on the insight of Walter Ong, Rosenberg propounds a more intelligent congre-gation, even if largely unlettered, due to the difference of a culture in transi-tion from orality to textuality. In an oral culture, unlettered men and women can reason and engage a speaker without needing to rely on a primarily written text. In a thought-provoking line, Rosenberg reminds his readers, "Plato regarded the poets as corrosive and destructive precisely because their mimetic art invited the masses into their world. Preaching is also a mimetic art." For Rosenberg, this phrase "mimetic art" encapsulates the manner in which a highly literate preacher like Augustine draws his hearers into his world, in a way like the poets described by Plato. Although the listeners may not be literate, they can have access to knowledge and information contained in books by their ability to think along with an effective orator. Augustine preaches humility to invite his listeners to imitate the very virtue he humbly preaches in the sermon.

Following Rosenberg's approach of noticing the oral intelligence of North Africans, we can appreciate how Augustine forged the sermons in a specific way with a different kind of audience. The *City of God* had an intended audience of educated non-Christian Romans. The sermons offer a glimpse into how Augustine's theology penetrated a broader cultural matrix. In a sense, the sermons tell us something about Augustine himself as well as the people to whom he preached.

20 Cameron, *Christianity*, 79.

John Rist, Henry Chadwick, Roland Teske, John Peter Kenney, and many others have done well to incorporate the philosophical background of Augustine into his theology.[21] We have a better sense of how Augustine's thought utilized and conversed with Platonic thinkers. Several authors studied various aspects of Augustine's preaching from the culture at large and the philosophical categories which might have been similar. Paul Kolbet proffered the most significant study using the ancient language of "psychagogy" as the lens through which to view all the sermons delivered by the bishop. This is what the ancients called their practice of using words to bring an audience up into a new world through words. He warns that a good historian does not use terms from the present day to set the course of study, but rather culling methods that were already prevalent in the culture. Kolbet thus spends a great deal of time addressing what authors Augustine would have known who wrote in the psychagogic form, a cross between rhetoric and logical philosophy, attempting to lead souls of those whom the writers encountered to wisdom. Kolbet's work presented a more complicated picture of Augustine's preaching as both rhetorical and philosophical.

Recent scholarship has begun to emerge which leans on another angle, namely the rhetorical, in Augustinian thought. Understanding his rhetoric though does not simply involve how Augustine modeled himself after others, but how these models and forms were used to communicate a deeper truth of the Gospel. Michael Cameron provides a compelling lens through which to read Augustine's sermons. He too centers his study on psychagogy, but further develops the function this performs in the *totus Christus*. He helpfully suggests that Augustine did not preach like modern day thinkers suppose. Cameron uses rhetoric to explain how Augustine came to define the doctrine of the *totus Christus*. The doctrine is most evident, according to Cameron, in the *Expositions on the Psalms*. This is thus one important distinction between our study and his, where we will work through the unedited *Sermones ad Populum*.

21 Rist, John M., *Augustine: Ancient Thought Baptized* (Cambridge: Cambridge University Press, 1994); Teske, Roland J., *Paradoxes of Time in Saint Augustine* (Milwaukee: Marquette University Press, 1996); Chadwick, Henry, *Augustine of Hippo: A Life* (Oxford: Oxford University Press, 2009); and Kenney, John Peter, *Contemplation and Classical Christianity: A Study in Augustine* (Oxford: Oxford University Press, 2013), to name just a few.

Similarly, Mark Clavier and Brian Gronewoller have written monograph-length works which weave rhetorical theory into the broader thought of Augustine's treatises.[22] Not only does Clavier integrate the concept of delight with cosmology, but his deep analysis incorporated the way Marius Victorinus provided a middle step in the development of Christian rhetoric from Cicero to Augustine. Gronewoller too found the study of rhetoric as a useful lens for capturing Augustine's understanding of order and economy in the way God arranged history. What at first might seem like a philosophical question reveals upon closer examination a closer connection the rhetorical manuals of late antiquity and Quintilian. These scholars have shown that while Plato and philosophy were influential on Augustine, they were not alone in shaping his thought.

Augustine's self-conscious reflection on rhetoric and philosophy was not straightforward. In Augustine's own mind, rhetoric and rhetorical theory do not primarily concern themselves with the truth.[23] They might be a means of conveying the truth, and they might not. What the Christian preacher, like Augustine, can do is take the tools learned in their rhetorical education and apply them to the theological truths found in the scriptures.[24] That is, how does rhetoric connect to the truth of which it has to express? Though more on that will come, it is important to remember Augustine's own complicated relationship to his rhetorical background. This comes to the fore when

22 Mark Clavier, *Eloquent Wisdom: Delight in the Thought of Augustine of Hippo* (Turnhout, Belgium: Brepols Publishers, 2014) and Brian Gronewoller *Rhetorical Economy in Augustine's Theology* (New York: Oxford University Press, 2021).

23 *doctr. Chr.* 4.2.3 (CCSL 32:117).

24 Exactly what "rhetorical education" means in much of the theological literature is disputed. It is a broad term which I hope to clarify in the first chapter of the dissertation. The most comprehensive modern study of the ancient schools comes from Henri-Irénée Marrou, *A History of Education in Antiquity*, trans. George Lamb (New York: Sheed and Ward, 1956). I will supplement it with the work of Robert Kaster, *Guardians of Language* (Berkeley: University of California Press, 1988). Chapter 1 will also look at Quintillian's *Institutiones oratoriae, The Institutio oratoria of Quintilian* ed. and trans. H.E. Butler (Cambridge, MA : Harvard University Press, 1961–66), Cicero's *De Oratore*, ed. and trans. E.W. Sutton (Cambridge, MA : Harvard University Press, 1948), the late ancient grammars of Donatus' *Ars Maior* in *Grammatici Latini* 1.450.1–1.451–24, ed. Heinrich Keil (Leipzig: Teubner, 1855–80), and Diomedes *Ars Grammatica* in *Grammatici Latini* 1.395.14–24, ed. Heinrich Keil (Leipzig: Teubner, 1855–1880).

Augustine writes explicitly on preaching in the final book of *De Doctrina Christiana*, as we will explore more in chapter one.

In the years since my own research began, several useful works have been published which focus on the preaching of Augustine.[25] The renowned Augustinian scholar J. Patout Burns carefully worked through all the *Sermones ad Populum* to provide a sketch of not only what Augustine preached, but also how that preaching may have changed over time.[26] Although a helpful resource for those who may be unfamiliar with Augustine's sermons, there is little engagement with the secondary literature, except a brief citation in the introduction of one recent attempt at aggregating several studies of the dating of the sermons.[27] While questions remain about the dating of the sermons, Burns work functions more to provide topical groupings of sermons only occasionally referencing the changes over time.

While Burns work on Augustine's preaching still maintains an introductory character, Michael Glowasky's monograph on Augustine's preaching considers the Bishop of Hippo's homiletical strategy in closer detail.[28] Carefully looking at the *Sermones ad Populum* for evidence of how Augustine treated an audience individually, he finds a sophisticated strategy of preaching which prepares different Christians on their journey to contemplating God. As Glowasky notes, his is one of the first to do a scholarly study of the sermons.[29]

25 The first dedicated study in English to Augustine as preacher, written by Peter Sanlon, does very little to advance our understanding of the relationship between rhetoric and Augustine's sermons (*Augustine's Theology of Preaching* [Minneapolis: Fortress Press, 2014]. The study mainly finds several themes and mentions where they occur but do not give an account of why Augustine spoke the way he spoke or why he composed the sermons in the manner he did.

26 Burns, J. Patout, *Augustine's Preached Theology: Living as the Body of Christ* (Grand Rapids, MI: Eerdmans, 2022) 5.

27 It is a careful study of the text of the sermons but relies heavily on a still sketchy dating scheme for the sermons.

28 Glowasky's book was published just before Burns. Although Burns deemed the dates of the sermons sufficiently well established, Glowasky's judgment about the attempts at dating the sermons stands in contrast: "The trouble with relying too heavily on chronology as the organizing principle, however, is that most of the dates currently assigned to Augustine's sermons are tentative at best," (*Rhetoric and Scripture in Augustine's Homiletic Strategy* [Leiden: Brill, 2021], 9). Glowasky relies primarily on Hubertus Drobner for this judgment, which as best we can tell, might be the same source for Burns (Burns, *Augustine's Preached Theology*, 5).

29 Glowasky, *Rhetoric and Scripture*, 3.

Along similar lines, Lutz Mechlinsky takes a close look at the preaching of Augustine as it relates to the canons of rhetorical composition and order, but with less attention to the spiritual nature of the sermons. In his book *Der Modus Proferendi in Augustins Sermones ad Populum*, Mechlinsky focuses on how Augustine's work *On Teaching Christianity* contributes to ancient rhetoric in his understanding of the role of composing speeches.[30] This work is helpful insofar as it firmly establishes Augustine within the broader conversation about the techniques of composition in ancient rhetoric. Mechlinsky shows more than just how Augustine's rhetorical ornamentation drew from classical sources such as Cicero and Quintilian, but even his mode of organizing his material for delivery. Mechlinksy analyzes four sermons trying to discern how Augustine might have followed the pattern set out in *On Teaching Christianity* 4 for the *modus proferendi* (manner of speaking). He does a thorough job explaining the extent to which Augustine followed the form of *prooemium* (introduction), *propositio* (proposal), *narratio* (narration), *argumentatio* (argument), and *peroratio* (conclusion).[31] Although a helpful summary of how Augustine thoroughly applied his rhetorical training to organizing his sermons, it does little to consider the theological implications or the historical situation of Augustine's preaching.

Building on this research, the present book seeks to organize the *Sermones ad Populum* around the virtue of humility. Although in some respects more specific, Augustine considers this virtue, as we will see below, as foundational for the Christian life, and indeed, what Christ came to teach. In that respect, it is specific enough to create some cohesiveness to the study, but it is also broad in a way that can open many avenues to grasp what a sermon does theologically for Augustine. None of the previous studies work with humility, nor do they have a means to uncover the action of the sermon.

30 Lutz Mechlinsky, *Der Modus Proferendi in Augustins Sermones Ad Populum* (Paderborn: Ferdinand Schöningh, 2004).

31 These are found at the end of each of Mechlinksy's section on each sermon (*Der Modus Proferendi:* 40, 111, 173, and 231). These canons of rhetoric are a shortened form of Cicero's judicial *partes orationis* ("divisions of oration") found in his *De inuentione* 1.20–109. One might expect to see *refutatio* as well. Quintilian has a shorter five-part list which matches closer to Augustine at *Institutio oratoria* 3.9. Cf. George A. Kennedy's overview of this passage from Cicero in *Classical Rhetoric and Its Christian and Secular Tradition from Ancient to Modern Times*, 2nd ed. (Chapel Hill: University of North Carolina Press, 1999), 103–6.

All of this provides a kind of prelude to the emphasis and method of this present study. More than anything, we would do well to remember that Augustine was a rhetorician first by training, so it stands to reason that the rhetorical manuals and examples would influence his way of presenting what he has understood from the scriptures in his sermons. Cicero and Ambrose, both of whom we will look at in chapter 2, both impressed Augustine as rhetoricians first and foremost. He came to see the wisdom they had to offer only after more careful investigation. Moving to the sermons themselves, what we see is, in a way, theology broadly considered. The *vita activa* and the *vita contemplativa*, the active life and the contemplative life, are both integral facets of how Augustine conceives of the Christian life reflecting in a way who God is.

We find Augustine acting and thinking all at once before a gathered audience. In a way, the sermons present a case study in not only what Augustine gleaned from the scriptures, but how he can present them to the audience as truth. He will make advancements on the rhetorical manuals he studied as a student and teacher of rhetoric insofar as he knows that what he has to communicate is the truth itself, not just words used to defend any position he may like. He turns to the scripture to contemplate and search for wisdom in the Word, and as preacher, he is constrained to present that understanding for as broad an audience as possible. So it is that a preacher "does" theology in attempting to help the audience gain understanding as well as a model for how to live.

In a more specific way, we will drill into the sermons to find humility, not only as a concept, but also as a practice. It is not merely an intellectual virtue, but an active virtue. We have chosen this as our way to encapsulate Augustine's theology of preaching because of the centrality of humility in the thought of Augustine.

Defining Humility

Before defining our own approach, it is worth spending a few moments on Augustine's understanding and use of *humilitas* "humility" and other words in its semantic range. For the purposes of our study, it is important to establish where and how Augustine learns this humility as we will see the difference it makes in the lives of two of his exemplars, which we will explore below in chapter two.

The closest Augustine gets to a definition of humility comes in *Confessions* 7, where he contrasts it with the pride of the Platonists. In his study on

Augustinian humility, French scholar Pierre Adnès begins by admitting that it is quite difficult to even find a simple, satisfactory definition of humility in all the various works of Augustine. It is much easier to find a definition of pride, the opposite of humility.[32] As pursuers of wisdom, the Platonists and Augustine became puffed up with their confidence of their own ability to know without the need of another. He explains that God "heals their swollen pride and nourishes their love, that they may not wander even further away through self-confidence, but rather weaken as they see before their feet the Godhead grown weak."[33] The primary problem of pride is that it leads one to lean on oneself. It is this self-sufficiency, which is the problem with Platonic philosophy, though Augustine is willing to concede that their view has much to recommend it.[34] It is also worth noting how Augustine relates the sin of pride to love. Pride inculcates an inflated love of self.[35] The humility found in Christ demonstrates a love that in submission puts God at the center, rather than self, in addition to a magnanimous self-giving which raises up others.[36]

How better to show this love and humility than in the incarnation of the Word?[37] Augustine argues that to know God fully, one must humbly submit and trust their will to someone. He explains:

32 Adnès, "Humilité a l'École de Saint Augustin," *Revue d'ascetique et de mystique* 31 (1955) 28–46, 28–29: "It must be admitted, despite the esteemed place Augustine has for humility in his spirituality, and that he does so materially speaking in his sermons or in his writings, it is not easy to find in his works a definition of humility truly precise and which satisfies us entirely … it is the perfect antithesis of pride. The Augustinian definitions of pride, however numerous and well known, we can now grasp the true essence of humility." (translations my own, unless otherwise noted).

33 *conf.* 7.18.24 (CCSL 27:108; WSA I/1, 179).

34 *ciu.* 8.5–6 (CCSL 47:221–223).

35 David Meconi, *On Self-Harm, Narcissism, Atonement, and the Vulnerable Christ* (New York: Bloomsbury, 2019).

36 Matthew Wilcoxen, *Divine Humility: God's Morally Perfect Being* (Waco, TX: Baylor University Press, 2019): "Given Augustine's premise that the self-giving love of God exemplified concretely in Christ is the foundation of the eternal city, humility is not the embrace of what is lower, but what is higher. To be humble is not to be less, but to be more, because more like God," 66.

37 Deborah Wallace Ruddy, "A Christological Approach to the Virtue of Humility," PhD diss. Boston College, 2001, "humility is not simply a human attribute temporarily assumed for Christ's earthly mission. Rather, it is principally a divine attribute" (66).

You wanted to show me first and foremost how you thwart the proud but give grace to the humble, and with what immense mercy on your part the way of humility (*via humilitatis*) was demonstrated to us when your Word was made flesh and dwelt among men and women.[38]

The way of humility, the *via humilitatis*, is shown through the Word taking on flesh in coming to humanity. Augustine goes on to define the humility of Christ in its characteristic obedience and dependence, thus becoming the paradigm of humility. Paul says, as Augustine reads it in the Latin he quotes, in Philippians 2:7–11 that Christ took on the *forma servi* and:

'being made in the likeness of men was found in human form', that 'he humbled himself and was made obedient to the point of death, even death on a cross, which is why God raised him from' the dead, 'and gave him a name above every other name, so that at the name of Jesus every knee should bow, in heaven, on earth, or in the under-world, and every tongue confess that Jesus Christ is Lord, in the glory of God the Father.'[39]

How does Christ teach obedience? He submits himself to being a slave and suffering death that he did not deserve. Albert Verwilghen, a French Augustinian scholar, summarizes the importance of Phil 2:7–11 for Augustine by underlining how the movement from the *forma dei* to the *forma servi* becomes for all Christians the way of humility, which is a submission to the will of the Father.[40] It is not epistemic humility or recognition that one might be wrong. Deborah Wallace Ruddy contends, "For Augustine, humility is more fundamental than a virtue because it refers to the pattern of Christ's self-emptying which is an outward expression of the very pattern of God's love."[41] The importance for Augustine

---

38 *conf.* 7.9.13. (CCSL 27.101; WSA I/1, 170)

39 *conf.* 7.9.14 (CCSL 27.101–102; WSA I/1, 171): "In similitudine hominum factus et habitu inventus ut homo, humiliavit *se* factus oboediens usque ad mortem, mortem autem crucis; propter quod Deus *eum* exaltavit *a mortuis* et donavit *ei* nomen, *quod est* super omne nomen, ut in nomine Iesu omne genuflectatur caelestium, terrestrium et infernorum et omnis lingua confiteatur, quia Dominus Iesus in gloria est Dei Patris."

40 Albert Verwilghen, *Christologie et Spiritualité selon Saint Augustin* (Paris, France: Beauchesne, 1984) 293.

41 Ruddy, "A Christological Approach to Humility," 67.

is on the willingness to believe that the human person is not sufficient in themselves. The way of humility taught by Christ requires a radical dependence and then a recognition of the limits of the abilities of human knowing and agency. Further it is a reliance and participation in the salvific mediation of Christ's humble incarnation.

Building on Verwilghen, we might also note that there is a kind of ontological sharing in Christ's humility through the power of grace. We will work through this in the final chapter in which we discuss *incrementum dat Deus* ("God gives the increase"). At this point, it is sufficient to note that participation in Christ works a transformation in the Christian so that they have eyes to see. This is the process of salvation for Augustine. Fr. David Meconi summarizes this well: "Augustine understands that in the incarnation, the Word of God united to himself humanity and in so doing made possible the union of each human with the Word."[42] Meconi employs the language of union, which is but another way of putting the *via humilitatis* from Augustine's own phrasing.

That Augustine was an orator and lover of wisdom himself made it exceedingly difficult to trust another. He had depended on his own abilities to speak, teach, and know which had brought him all the way to Milan. His education and his examples had encouraged him not to trust another but to trust himself. This is the difficulty for Augustine when considering becoming a Christian. He admits:

> Not yet was I humble enough to grasp the humble Jesus as my God, nor did I know what his weakness had to teach. Your Word, the eternal Truth who towers above the higher spheres of your creation, raises up to himself those creatures who bow before him; but in these lower regions he has built himself a humble dwelling from our clay, and used it to cast down from their pretentious selves those who do not bow before him, and make a bridge to bring them to himself.[43]

The Word made flesh is the "bridge," the mediator, who shows the way which people must travel in order to return to their union with God. Meconi notes that Augustine uses participation only three times in the *Confessions* though this

---

42 David Meconi, *The One Christ: St. Augustine's Theology of Deification* (Washington, DC: The Catholic University of America Press, 2013) 194.

43 *conf.* 7.18.24 (CCSL 27.108; WSA I/1, 179).

is the key to his understanding of Christ and the incarnation. As he describes participation, "It would not be until he could conceive of participation differently than he originally discovered in the platonic books that he could properly understand the Incarnation."[44] The power of the incarnation is that in the person of Christ God is at once present to humans and *ubique totus* "everywhere whole."[45] Those who would desire to understand must first believe or trust in another. This is the foundation of theology, *Crede, ut intellegas* "believe, so that you might understand," as Augustine preaches.[46]

Even the ability to trust requires grace and the work of God. The way of humility requires that one receives this gift, which is not possible for a fallen human. Augustine quotes Proverbs, "God resists the proud but gives grace to the humble."[47] For most of his life, Augustine had been a self-made man rising through the ranks of rhetorical education on the promise of his speaking abilities. The son of a low-level magistrate had gone from rural Thagaste, to Carthage, to Rome, and finally to Milan. He had understood Cicero better than his teachers.[48] All of this ability did not ultimately make him happy, but it was also all he knew. When he encountered the way of the humble Christ in the scriptures written by fishermen, he faced a dilemma. He could read and understand the scriptures in the manner he was trained, but he was not willing to recognize his need for the gift of grace. To receive that gift required that he become humble like Christ and trust another to provide something beyond which he could summon for himself.

In a particularly good summary of this view of Christ as the way which leads Augustine to a new method of communicating with his people, Augustine preaches in *s.* 123: "This is the way. Walk by humility, so that you might come to eternity. Christ as God is the fatherland to which we are traveling. Christ the man is the way by which we travel. We travel to him. We travel by him. Why would we fear that we could go astray? Christ did not turn away from the Father, even when he came to us."[49] So Augustine's preaching of

---

44 David Meconi, "The Incarnation and the Role of Participation in St. Augustine's *Confessions,*" *Augustinian Studies* 29:2 (1998): 61–75.

45 Gerald Boersma, "Augustine on the Beatific Vision as *ubique totus,*" *Scottish Journal of Theology* 71 (2018): 16–32.

46 *s.* 43.7 (CCSL 41.511).

47 Prv 3:34; Jas 4:6; 1 Pt 5:5.

48 Cf. Chapter 2.

49 *s.* 123.3 (PL 38.685; WSA III/4, 246): "Ista est via: ambula per humilitatem, ut

humility is firmly Christological. He must teach the gathered Church who Christ is so that they might travel to him and by him in their lives as Christians imitating Christ. Not only does Christ lie at the end of the path, but by the grace of incorporation into the body of Christ, one can travel by Christ to Christ. It is the gift of grace which explains the phrase "we travel by him." The goal and the way are Christ and knowledge of him. Christ's way was humility, the *via humilitatis.*

Several contemporary scholars have explored the virtue of humility in Augustine. In defining humility, we already cited Adnès who has stated the difficulty of finding a precise definition for humility. The purpose of his essay was to trace humility throughout many different works of Augustine, both sermonic and otherwise. He summarizes his findings on humility by saying that humility is nearly the entirety of Christian teaching, which reflects Augustine's Letter 118 to a young pursuer of truth in philosophy, especially Cicero.[50] At the end of the essay, Adnès encapsulates one critical element to the *Confessions,* and thus how Augustine viewed the human life, saying that our rest is in God and nothing but humility can establish us in God.[51]

The works of Otto Schaffner and Notker Baumann build upon one another in trying to establish what humility means as a virtue, and its relationship to the history of the teaching of virtue in the classical world. Schaffner laid the foundation by calling Augustine the "teacher of humility," specifically by advocating for the relationship between self-knowledge and humility.[52] In his understanding, Schaffner does not go far enough for Baumann in trying to relate Augustine's concept of humility to its non-Christian heritage or philosophically by ignoring its position as the foundation of virtue.[53] In

---

venias ad aeternitatem. Deus Christus patria est quo imus; homo Christus via est qua imus. Ad illum imus, per illum imus; quid timemus ne erremus? Non recessit a Patre, et venit ad nos."

50 Adnes, "Humilité à l'Ecole de Saint Augustin," 42: "Yes! Humility is itself only nearly the whole Christian discipline." Cf. *ep.* 118.

51 Adnes, "Humilité à l'Ecole de Saint Augustin," 46: "For our rest is in God, and there is nothing, save for humility, which we have seen, who can make us attain to God and establish us in him."

52 Otto Schaffner, *Christliche Demut: des Hl. Augustinus Lehre von der Humilitas* (Würzburg: Augustinus-Verlag, 1959).

53 Schaffner, *Christliche,* 53–57. Notker Baumann, *Die Demut als Grundlage aller Tugenden bei Augustinus* (Frankfurt am Main: Peter Lang, 2009).

his review of the literature, Baumann follows Cornelius Mayer saying that Christians use humility in a specific way that had no previous counterpart in the ancient world. For them, Christians take the term humility which was specifically used in a negative meaning in the classical world and turn it into a virtue. The bulk of Baumann and Schaffner's studies elucidate how the virtue of humility works among other virtues and self-knowledge. Baumann carries the conversation forward by trying to show what he believes that Schaffner merely takes for granted, which is how humility forms the basis of all virtue. He traces this through four principles: creatureliness, sinfulness, confession, and grace.[54] The primary location for a positive evaluation for humility in classical literature outside of Christian literature is in Iamblichus (245–325), which Baumann explores briefly in this work.[55] Neither Baumann nor Schaffner concern themselves particularly with the preaching or with the broader rhetorical context of the virtue of humility. Both of their studies, however, do help to explain exactly what the virtue of humility means for Augustine across his more theological and philosophical treatises.

It is worth noting that neither of these studies references an essay by a classicist who argues that the virtue of humility did not originate with Jesus Christ. W. van den Boer, a scholar of classics, acerbically states, "The examples mentioned are clear. *Tapeinos* and *humilis* were clearly used in *bonam partem* in pagan literature. The general opinion, especially of theologians, that the Greeks (and the Romans as well) used ταπεινός (c.q. humilis) exclusively in *malam partem*, has to be revised."[56] Our study is not comprehensive enough to counter this claim, but the examples from non-Christian rhetorical literature will indeed show the difficulty of sustaining this judgment. Augustine himself would at least take issue with it, as we will show, but suffice it to say that someone who participated in the very education in question must be considered in this conversation.

On a more philosophical level, Kent Dunnington has tried to revive an Augustinian notion of the virtue of humility which has been lost over time. Dunnington argues that in fact contemporary notions of humility rest on the assumption that there are certain things one cannot know, and this

<hr>

54 Schaffner, *Christliche*, 75–132.

55 Baumann, *Die Demut*, 213–21.

56 "Tapeinos in Pagan and Christian Terminology," in *Tria Corda: Scritti in onore di Arnaldo Momigliano, Biblioteca di Athenaeum* 1 (Como: Edizioni New Press, 1983), 143.

constitutes humility. Dunnington adequately shows in an article and book on the topic that in fact Augustine does not think humility requires one to attempt to say that one knows nothing, but simply that submission should play a role. Summarizing his position, he argues, "for Augustine, humility is about desire."[57] The article and book are helpful for understanding how we came to this position and what that should mean for Christians who want to be humble in the Augustinian tradition.

The only other work dedicated to the virtue of humility which mentions Augustine is Matthew Wilcoxen's *Divine Humility: God's Morally Perfect Being*. We will note briefly that Wilcoxen takes a more dogmatic tack as he tries to understand how a virtue like humility can properly be ascribed to the divine Christ, given that many definitions of humility rely solely on submission as the explanation for how humility works. Wilcoxen carefully explicates the trinitarian complications of such a creaturely view of humility. Augustine, Wilcoxen claims, laid the foundation for later theological projects to see humility *ad intra*, though later theologians have needed to work out the precise trinitarian details.[58]

For the purposes of this study, we seek not to challenge the accepted scholarship on the centrality of humility within the thought of Augustine in his more systematic treatises. Rather, we want to explore how he practiced that virtue through his sermons. Most of Augustine's time as bishop was spent preaching to an audience on a routine basis, which would have been a primary place for them to encounter the humility of Christ in the scriptures and preaching. We will argue that Augustine found a way to use his speech to exhibit that virtue. A key component of learning virtue was through the means of an *exemplum*. The preacher provided a model of humility for those gathered through his words as action.

Overview of Texts

The primary source of investigation will be the *Sermones ad Populum*. As there is no single compilation of all the *Sermones* in one critical volume, I will include a chart with the date, location, Patrologia Latina reference, and an

---

57 Kent Dunnington, *Humility, Pride, and Christian Virtue Theory* (Oxford: Oxford University Press, 2019).

58 Wilcoxen, *Divine Humility*, 106–7.

updated edition where available.[59] As of the writing of this study, the Corpus Christianorum Series Latina has only published an edition of sermons 1–70a and 151–183.[60] Hubertus Drobner has produced ten volumes of critical editions and commentaries on the *Sermones ad Populum*.[61] Primarily, I will be investigating these sermons in the original Latin text. New City Press has also recently translated all the extent sermons, including the recently found *Vignt-Six Sermons au People d'Afrique* edited by Francois Dolbeau.[62]

Where necessary for the argument at hand, I will use Pierre-Patrick Verbraken's monumental study on the authentic sermons and their dating and critical editions.[63] Although Verbraken's study has been the standard, Robert Gryson has updated some of the dating and location of the

59 Hubertus Drobner warns scholars that no incontestable date can be given for any sermon, "The Chronology of St. Augustine's *Sermones ad populum*," *Augustinian Studies* 31:2, (2000) 212.

60 *Sermones de Vetere Testamento: I-L*, ed. Cyrillus Lambot, CCSL 41 (Turnhout: Brepols, 1961). *Sermones in Matthaeum I: LI-LXX*, ed. P.P. Verbraken, L. De Coninck, B. Coppieters 't Wallant, R. Demeulenaere, F. Dolbeau, CCSL 41 Aa (Turnhout: Brepols, 2008). Sermones in Epistolas Apostolicas I: CLI-CLVI, ed. Gert Partoens, CCSL 41 Ba (Turnhout: Brepols, 2008). *Sermones in Epistolas Apostolicas II: CLVII–CLXXXIII*, ed. Shari Boodts, CCSL 41Bb (Turnhout: Brepols, 2016).

61 *Sermones 1–5*, Patrologia Beiträge zum Studium der Kirchenväter, Band VII (Frankfurt am Main: Peter Lang, 2000). *Sermones 6–12*, Patrologia Beiträge zum Studium der Kirchenväter, Band X (Frankfurt am Main: Peter Lang, 2003). *Sermones 13–21*, Patrologia Beiträge zum Studium der Kirchenväter, Band XXV v.1 (Frankfurt am Main: Peter Lang, 2016). Sermones 22–34, Patrologia Beiträge zum Studium der Kirchenväter, Band XXV v.2 (Frankfurt am Main: Peter Lang, 2016). *Sermones 35–41*, Patrologia Beiträge zum Studium der Kirchenväter, Band XIII (Frankfurt am Main: Peter Lang, 2004). *Sermones 42–50*, Patrologia Beiträge zum Studium der Kirchenväter, Band XXIX (Frankfurt am Main: Peter Lang, 2013). *Sermones 94/A-97*, Patrologia Beiträge zum Studium der Kirchenväter, Band XIX (Frankfurt am Main: Peter Lang, 2007). *Sermones 148–150*, Patrologia Beiträge zum Studium der Kirchenväter, Band XXVI (Frankfurt am Main: Peter Lang, 2012). *Sermones 196/A-204/A*, Patrologia Beiträge zum Studium der Kirchenväter, Band XXII v.1 (Frankfurt am Main: Peter Lang, 2010). *Sermones 336–340/A*, Patrologia Beiträge zum Studium der Kirchenväter, Band IX (Frankfurt am Main: Peter Lang, 2003).

62 *Vingt-six sermons au peuple d'Afrique*, ed. Francois Dolbeau (Paris: Institut d'études augustiniennes, 2009) trans. Edmund Hill *The Works of Saint Augustine Sermons: Newly Discovered Sermons* v. III/11, (Brooklyn, NY: New City Press, 1997).

63 Pierre-Patrick Verbraken, *Études critiques sur les sermons authentiques de saint Augustin* (Steenbrugis: Abbatia Sancti Petri, 1976).

sermons.[64] Marie Hombert has also offered some updated work on the subject of dating Augustine's preaching.[65] Francois Dolbeau has his own summary of the research on the dating and location of the sermons in the *Augustinus-Lexikon*.[66]

Methodology

The goal of this study is to elucidate Augustine's theological understanding of preaching and exactly how Augustine preached the virtue of humility, offering through his words and deeds a sacramental encounter with Christ. This study will be an interdisciplinary study including rhetoric, history, philosophy, and theology. In order to fully appreciate Augustine's theology of preaching we will need to consider his audience, his language, his influences, his education, and the theological implications of the preached word. Through this study, we will piece together what we will call Augustine's theology of preaching, the *via humilitatis agendo* ("way of humility acted out"). The term *via humilitatis* comes from Augustine himself, which he says Christ demonstrated and taught his followers.[67] The preacher proclaims the truths found in the scriptural text and exemplifies the *via humilitatis* before the gathered church in his speech. The hearers learn to imitate from their preacher the virtue of humility and turn inwards themselves to find Christ the teacher. The preacher relies on God in the gift grace to work on the inside of the hearers through the words of Scripture and the preacher.

We call it the *via humilitatis agendo* which denotes that the way of humility is both spoken and performed by the preacher for the audience in the liturgy of the church. *Agere* in Latin implies both to act and to perform a speech.[68]

---

64 Robert Gryson, *Répertoire général des auteurs ecclésiastiques latins de l'Antiquiteé et du Haut Moyen Âge / Tome I, Introduction, Répertoire des Auteurs: A-H* (Freiburg : Verlag Herder, 2007) 231–67.

65 Pierre-Marie Hombert *Nouvelles recherches de chronologie augustinienne* (Paris: Institut d'Études Augustiniennes, 2000).

66 Francois Dolbeau, "Sermones" in *Augustinus-Lexikon* V. 5 fasc. 2–3 (Basel: Schwabe & Co. AG, 2019): 243–399.

67 Albert Verwilghen describes the importance of Christ's taking on the *forma servi* and the hymn to the Philippians in the entire corpus of Augustine's work in *Christologie et Spiritualité selon Saint Augustin: L'Hymne aux Philippiens*, (Paris: Beauchesne Editeur, 1985).

68 This is considered further in Chapter 1.

This conception resonates with the contemporary philosophical school of Speech Act Theory. Speech Act Theory (SAT) rests on the simple notion that human speech is more than simply a stating of facts.[69] Speech is also action. Whenever someone speaks, given the right condition, their speech can also become a form of action and interact with the hearers and the community in unique ways. This will be explored further in the first chapter, in addition to showing how this contemporary account fits with what Augustine says himself about the philosophy of language in *On Christian Teaching*.

Not only does SAT help us to think about language as a species of action, but it also posits a threefold account of how the action works. Speaking involves the locution, the phrase spoken; illocution, how the speaker intends the locution; and perlocution, how the audience receives and responds to the phrase intended by the speaker. We will take this threefold framework as basis for framing the three key elements of the *via humilitatis agendo* found in the *Sermones ad Populum* which comprise Augustine's theology of preaching. The locution involves the very language which must be spoken and its source. This is of course the scriptural text. The illocution is how the preacher performs that language in a manner consistent with the biblical message. Finally, the perlocution is the final part which is to some degree out of the preacher's control. For us it will be how God works on the hearer through the preacher's words.

We have already argued how the virtue humility becomes central for Augustine in the *Confessions* when he learns about Christ's humility in the incarnation. The next part of our method will be to see how Augustine imitated two models in his education and how he responded to that as a preacher. His rhetorical education made him hunger for the praise of people around him by following the authority of ancient examples of speech found especially in Cicero. This baggage stays with him throughout his preaching life. He learns to reject this goal of seeking praise for himself when he becomes a preacher of humility after the example of Ambrose, who taught him to listen humbly to Christ in the scriptural text as his primary teacher.

Finally, our method is theological in nature. It rests on the idea that Christ can be encountered sacramentally through the words of the preacher and the scriptural text. This will be found in the words of Augustine himself

69 The philosopher J L Austin first theorized about speech acts in J L Austin, *How to Do Things with Words* (Cambridge, MA: Harvard University Press, 1962).

which can be read for their examples of Latin rhetoric, but also for their deep theological truths. So, when we look at his sermons, we are looking for both. We are trying to see how his theology undergirded what he said to his people, many of whom had less formal education than he did. One French historian and theologian argues that to miss the theology in the words of his preaching is to make a grave mistake. Merely attending to the words themselves misses the profound theological and doctrinal character which Augustine very much intended.[70] As we shall discover in the section on Augustine's education, this would also miss the *pectus* of the words he spoke; just as Augustine's teachers did with Cicero himself. Thus, our study seeks to attend to both the words and what they mean theologically.

In an essay which creatively considered the character of Augustine's preaching, William Harmless offered a unique perspective on how to approach St. Augustine's preaching corpus.[71] Drawing on a couple of references from the renowned French scholar Henri-Irénée Marrou, Harmless contends that Augustine's writings and way of doing theology should be thought of more like a jazz improvisationalist. In his opening, Harmless writes:

> I will argue that if we want to understand Augustine's way of thinking theologically, we need to analyze him not architectonically, not the way one approaches the systematics of a Thomas Aquinas; we need, rather, to approach him musicologically, understanding his works in terms of musical modalities and performance practices. In particular, we need to savor the role that improvisation played.[72]

70 Pierre-Marie Hombert says, "However, when we look closely, we see that rare are the works which descend to the intimacy of the text, in the tight stitching of the words, the composition of phrases, and more still those which examine how the resources of invention, disposition, and the elocution serve a purpose specifically theological and doctrinal, not only to make it clearly understood, but by being in a fitting style with the object which it expounds." "Rhétorique et Théologie. La prédication sur le Verbe incarné dans les sermons d'Augustin pour Noël," in *Ministerium Sermonis. Philological, Historical, and Theological Studies on Augustine's Sermones ad populum*, ed. Gert Partoenes, Anthony Dupont, and Mathijs Lamberigts (Turnhoult, Brepols Publishers, 2012), 272.

71 William Harmless, SJ "A Love Supreme: Augustine's 'Jazz' of Theology," *Augustinian Studies* 43:1/2 (2012) 149–77.

72 Harmless, "A Love Supreme," 150.

What Harmless proposed is what many who have studied Augustine realize, namely that Augustine does not think as systematically as many later theologians would like. When we want to find out what Augustine thought about an idea or doctrine, it will not do to think of merely one phrase. Marrou called this the "caractère flottant" ("the floating character") of his language. Following this line of thought, Frederick Van Fleteren proposes in a piece on the beatific vision, that one must look for a host of similar terms and words for one concept. One recent study of Augustine's theology of prayer falls into this trap by over defining the terms Augustine used for prayer, without recognizing that sometimes Augustine just wanted a different word for the same idea.[73]

In the mold of looking for "musical modalities and performance practices" we propose to look through the preaching of Saint Augustine for common phrases which elicit principles about how he understood the preaching moment. On first blush, this sounds like the opposite of what was said above. Why would we go looking for the same phrases? We will go looking for these phrases because like a musician, Augustine liked to "play his hits." We will not be looking for some timeless theological doctrine like the beatific vision or his concept of prayer, but rather what words or phrases he seems to repeat which gives us a window into how he was heard by his congregation. In so doing, we will watch the preacher at work and draw from that some general principles about his theology of preaching. Along the way, we will get to see how much Augustine enjoyed "riffing" on themes or images to suit his particular audience.[74]

Overview of the Project

As a study organized around the theology of preaching of St. Augustine, each chapter will take its point of departure from a doctrinal category which corresponds to the topic in question. Each of these is grounded in the humble Christ, the *sine qua non* of Augustine's preaching.

73 We will discuss Jonathan Teubner's *Prayer After Augustine: A Study in the Development of the Latin Tradition* (Oxford: Oxford University Press, 2018) in chapter 6.

74 For a thorough study of all the different ways Augustine interacts with his audience recorded in the *Sermones ad Populum*, see: Deferrari, Roy J. "Verbatim Reports of Augustine's Unwritten Sermons," *Transactions and Proceedings of the American Philological Association* 46 (1915): 35–45 and "St. Augustine's Method of Composing and Delivering Sermons," *American Journal of Philology* 43 (1922): 97–123, 193–219.

This study will proceed in two parts, each consisting of three chapters. The first part deals with the various contextual elements to the preaching of Augustine, language, culture, and evangelism. The second part concerns the textual evidence of the preaching itself in the *Sermones ad Populum* and the doctrines of Christology, Ecclesiology, and Soteriology. It will be organized following the tripartite structure of SAT: locution, illocution, and perlocution.

The first chapter seeks to explain Augustine's theology of language, particularly in the context of the preached sermon. That is, the preacher takes as his source the scriptural text. Through prayerful meditation on the Word, the preacher offers his words as a kind of imitation of the humble word, which leads to vision of Christ. Finally, the preacher and the parishioners rely on grace to truly see the beatific vision.

Moving from language to culture, the second chapter looks at Augustine's development both within his rhetorical education and in the Church under the teaching of Ambrose. It is thus a reflection of Augustine's theology of culture. Mimesis and imitation are crucial as Augustine learns first from the writings of Cicero and later through the humble preaching of Ambrose. Both of these figures are repristinated in the ecclesial oratory of Augustine.

To round out the contextual elements of Augustine's preaching, the final chapter of this section looks at the question of the preacher's audience. In Hippo Regius, the orator-turned-preacher must communicate with a broad audience the truth of the Humble Word. As Augustine explains in *On the Catechizing of the Uninstructed*, he must not fear the pedantic grammarians in his explanations for the less educated. At the same time, he heeds to the deep truths of scripture. In so doing, he communicates to a broad cross section of the community of Hippo, and North Africa generally.

The second part of the dissertation moves to the contents of the sermons themselves and into the higher registers of theological sophistication. Chapter 4 focuses on Augustine's locution of the Word, and his Christology. This is explored in part through the words he chooses and why are these different from what he would have known as a classical orator. As a reflection of Augustine's Christology, the African bishop followed the lead of the *forma servi* ("form of the servant"), the humble God proclaimed in the words of a fisherman. This reflects the divinity and humanity of the Son of God.

The fifth chapter focuses on how Augustine performs these words for the *totus Christus* "the whole Christ". How does he try to embody the virtue of humility using his words as an example for the people as he listens with them to the humble Christ in the scriptures? From one vantage point, Augustine appears to be the teacher for the congregation. At a deeper level, the aim of Augustine is to lead the whole body of Christ in the Church, to a vision of the humble Christ, who is the true teacher. The language of school becomes critical for the gathered body in the moment of the sermon.

The sixth and final chapter ends where it could have begun, a gift of God. The chapter focuses on two metaphors from the sermons, the *incrementum dat Deus* "God gives the increase" and *deificati oculi* "deified eyes" both integral elements of Augustine's soteriology. God provides and undergirds the ability of the preacher to lead the *totus Christus* to see the *forma dei* in the *forma servi*. Though the point may be a subtle one, the importance of God's gift and the prayerful desire of the people to see provide a full account of the preaching of Augustine. God gives the increase and makes up for what the preacher cannot control on his own and offers to the people what they desire, a vision of God. The book ends with a conclusion that considers how contemporary people might think of rhetoric and a way to conceive of how important rhetoric can be to a preacher.

PART 1

AUGUSTINE'S THEOLOGY OF PREACHING IN CONTEXT

CHAPTER 1

AUGUSTINE'S THEOLOGY OF LANGUAGE

A Preacher's Action in Speech

Introduction

THE FIRST THREE CHAPTERS OF THIS STUDY will explore the context of the more theological chapters which are to follow. They situate the latter three chapters on specific leitmotifs within the sermons themselves. As the goal of this study is to show that Augustine preached the virtue of humility through word and deed, which he learned from Christ himself, we will begin with addressing how Augustine understood the language of the sermon to function philosophically. We will draw on the insights of SAT (Speech Act Theory) to provide a framework that, in some respects, Augustine's words were his deeds, and his deeds were his words. We can understand something about the example he provided for his people by looking at the bare record of his speech. He performs actions through his words which provide an example of humility for the gathered faithful in the liturgy of the Church. We begin with an example where Augustine highlights the importance of humility for other preachers and indicates how his words were actions.

In the second decade of the 5th century, Augustine preached three times on one Sunday.[1] These sermons were the only known sermons to have been preached at a smaller community near Hippo called Fussala, recently received into the Catholic Church though formerly part of the Donatists.[2] For the service of consecration of a new bishop, Augustine chose as his theme the most characteristic sin, pride.[3] It is almost as if Augustine knows beforehand that he has made a reckless choice. In his homily, he says "Now pride is a great vice, and the first of vices, the beginning, origin and cause of all sins."[4] He goes on to explain why this concerned him so greatly for this particular new ordinand, "That's why the apostle Paul, after mentioning, among other things in the reading we heard when it was read just now, the virtues required of a bishop, also added this: *Not a new convert, in case being lifted up in pride he should fall into the judgment of the devil* (1 Tm 3:6)."[5] Augustine fears for this new bishop that the position would give occasion for pride. Augustine must demonstrate for this new bishop how a bishop preaches humbly to avert the chief sin, pride. This is a particularly delicate task because it was quite common, as Augustine knew, to use an oration to gain fame and acclaim.[6]

Over the course of the next several movements of the sermon, Augustine will take Christ both as his example and as the cure for pride. He will show that the Son's coming to earth was in itself an example of humility for how the bishop must go about leading his flock. The preacher must condescend to speak in a way that all gathered may know the truth of the scripture. This sermon provides a window into the manner in which Augustine preaches humbly in imitation of his Lord. Through his words, Augustine displays the characteristic element of humility, which he believes is necessary for a bishop. The difficulty will be to unearth how Augustine can imitate the humility of his Lord, without drawing attention to himself and so be puffed up with pride. His language and action in his words must themselves become

---

1 Gryson, *Repertoire General es Auteurs Ecclesiastiques Latins*, 252.

2 van der Meer, *Augustine the Bishop*, 230–31.

3 See John Cavadini's entry on "Pride" in *Augustine Through the Ages*, 679–85. He writes, "Superbia, for Augustine, is the archetypal sin, the original sin from which all other sin proceeds as from a root" (684).

4 *s.* 340A.2 ([= Guelferbytanus 32] MiAg 1: 563; WSA III/9, 297).

5 *s.* 340A.2.

6 *conf.* 4.14.23 (CCSL 27:52).

a *via humilitatis agendo* (a way of humility acted out), for those gathered to hear from God.

Before laying out the various ways Augustine goes about showing humility in action, it is worth giving some historical context for the sermon. The town of Fussala and their church was previously a Donatist stronghold, which had recently returned to Catholic faith.[7] As such, Augustine and the North African clergy needed to install a Catholic bishop to lead the recently returned congregation. According to Peter Brown, it appears likely that this hill country town spoke predominately Punic and needed a bishop who could speak both Latin and Punic.[8] After his first candidate withdrew from consideration, Augustine scrambled to find a replacement. In his haste, he chose a young lector in his care at his monastery in Hippo whom he thought could come in at the last moment as a replacement.[9] This ill-advised choice proved to be a decision which Augustine would regret in less than a decade.[10] Nevertheless, this young man Antoninus was ordained in 411, and this was very likely the occasion for this ordination sermon.[11]

Taking a step back, this sermon serves an example to see how Augustine understood the way the preacher operated in the Christian worship service. The preacher, in the context of Christian worship, becomes a key part of the liturgy. When the Church gathers for its weekly service, the people come to participate in and to see the humble Christ.[12] Focusing on the sermon, the preacher brings the scriptures, and the Word who speaks through him, to life for the people. One commentator, Jennifer Herdt, calls the liturgy a "spectacle." She notes, "For Augustine, both pagan and Christian worship are best construed as spectacle, as the authoritative public presentation of attractive example before the eyes of a collected assembly."[13] She contrasts

---

7 *ep.* *20.3 ad Fabiolam (CSEL 88:95).

8 Peter Brown, *Through the Eye of a Needle* (Princeton, NJ: Princeton University Press, 2012) 338.

9 *ep.* *20.2 ad Fabiolam (CSEL 88.94).

10 *ep.* 209.10 ad Caelestinum (CSEL 57.347).

11 Hubertus Drobner, *Predigten zu Kirch- und Bischofsweihe (Sermones 336–340/A)* (Frankfurt am Main: Peter Lang, 2003), 114.

12 We will explore this further in Chapter 6.

13 Jennifer Herdt, "The Theatre of the Virtues: Augustine's Critique of Pagan Mimesis," *Augustine's City of God: A Critical Guide*, ed. James Wetzel (Cambridge: Cambridge University Press, 111–29), 111. Although Herdt speaks frequently about the

the spectacle of the theatre with that of the Church. Both spectacles offer a living example for the people, either one of pride or vice. For Augustine, the preacher must showcase humility. This puts a difficult weight on the preacher. He must find a way to exemplify the humble Christ to the people while recognizing the fact that he will, at some point, fail them. On those occasions he does not, he runs the risk of becoming proud, which is the focus of the sermon at the church in Fussala.

In the same article, Herdt goes on to describe pagan virtue in contrast with Christian virtue. She writes, "Those held up by pagan culture as shining models are finally examples of a pride that closes sinful humanity in on itself rather than opening it up to the love of God and neighbor."[14] As pagan culture showcased its models of pride at the theater, Christians have models of humility in the liturgy. The vanity on display in the theater, or indeed in certain orators, drew all attention to the individual. On the contrary, the end of the spectacle of the liturgy was to deflect the attention away from an individual to the love of Christ, which binds the community together as one.

The primary *exemplum* is the Word made flesh, proclaimed in the liturgy. Herdt continues, "only by accepting the love shown to us in Christ's self-emptying humility ... our eyes [are] opened to see the true exemplarity of Christ's humility."[15] This is where the preaching of the sermon plays its part. As the Church is the body of Christ on earth and the preacher stands in Christ's place on earth, he has the unique role of embodying the humble Christ as a spectacle for the gathered faithful. He must be humble and must be a means of exhibiting that humility to the people, while pointing them towards the humility of Christ. As we noted in the introduction, this is the *via humilitatis agendo*. The preacher acts through his speech to exhibit the way of humility originally shown in Jesus Christ, and in turn the love of Christ, the lifeblood of their unity.

This is exactly what Augustine does in *s.* 340A. Augustine embodies humility through the action of his words. He has already laid out his argument

---

"spectacle of Christian worship" she does not define exactly what part of the service should be considered as the spectacle. The position taken here is that the preacher is a critical part of that spectacle, which for Augustine was often the longest part of the gathering for worship.

14 Herdt, "Theater of the Virtues," 111.

15 Herdt, "Theater of the Virtues," 111.

that pride is their great temptation and sin. As he progresses, he will show humility in action. In another section of the homily, Augustine self-reflectively puts himself under the exhortation from Christ:

> So, when the Lord was addressing the apostles, and confirming them in holy humility, after setting the example of the child before them he said, *Whoever wishes to be the greater among you will be your servant* (Mk 10:44). There you are, that's why I didn't do my brother, your future bishop, any wrong when I desired and admonished him to be your servant. Well, if I did do him wrong, I did it to myself first; I mean, I'm not just anyone talking about being a bishop, I'm a bishop talking about it; and the advice and warning I'm giving him I am also afraid of myself, and I call to mind what the holy apostle said about himself.[16]

The great preacher artfully crafts the manner of his exhortation for the hearers. Augustine takes for his admonition to Antoninus, the soon-to-be bishop, a command from Christ in Matthew. If you want to be great, you must be a servant. Then, in a self-conscious aside, he applies this verse to himself. "Well, if I did do him wrong, I did it to myself first." He knows that whatever he preaches, if it comes from scripture, is also a command for him. He demonstrates his humility by subjecting himself to the command of God first. He takes the command seriously enough to name his own fear of what that command entails.[17]

Since this sin of pride is to be avoided at all costs, the rhetor-turned-preacher must look elsewhere for an exemplar of humility. For Augustine, the answer is first and foremost the Word made flesh, so, in his speech, he imitates Christ who shows the humility that he commands. Quoting the Gospel of Mark, Augustine shows how Christ did what he also commanded, saying, "There you have how the Lord served; there you have the sort of servants he commanded us to be. He gave his life as a redemption for many."[18] Drawing

---

16 *s.* 340A.2 ([= Guelferbytanus 32] MiAg 1: 563; WSA III/9, 298).

17 The fear of the preacher's own failing becomes something of a preoccupation for the African bishop, *ss.* 224.3 (RB 79.200), 232 (SChr 116.260), and 335 (PL 38.1470).

18 *s.* 340A.2 ([= Guelferbytanus 32] MiAg 1: 563; WSA III/9, 298)

from the scriptural text, Augustine offers to Antoninus and the community at Fussala the example of Christ who not only commanded his disciples to serve but served them himself. There is his example at work in the scriptures. The preacher brings it to life for the people in the spectacle of the liturgy.

Just as Christ does not give a command he is not willing to follow himself, Augustine also demonstrates his own willingness to obey what he commands. He puts himself under the command, which is after all from Christ himself, by saying:

> So in order for him to be what he's called, let him listen, not to me, but with me. Let us both listen together, as fellow pupils in the same school let us learn from the one master, Christ, whose professorial chair (*cathedra*) is in heaven, precisely because his cross was first of all on earth. He it was who taught us the way of humility (*humilitatis ille viam docuit*); coming down from heaven to go up again later.[19]

In his clever way, Augustine does not set himself over Antoninus or the congregation but levels the playing field by calling them all disciples of one and the same teacher. They are all *condiscipuli unius magistri cuius cathedra in caelo est* "fellow student of one teacher whose seat is in heaven." This phrase has particular pertinence when one considers Augustine's former profession, a *magister* "teacher" or "master."[20] While the *magister* might not have had the prestige of a conquering general, in the realm of education which supplied the ranks of government officials, the *magister* did hold an honored place. The location within the setting of the classroom of the honored position was the *cathedra* (seat) from which he recited the lessons to the students. Augustine lowers himself down to the position of *discipulus* after ascending to the heights of the imperial *cathedra* of rhetoric in Milan.[21] As Christ comes down from heaven, so Augustine comes down from his high *cathedra* placing himself as one with all those gathered at the small rural town of Fussala.

---

19 *s.* 340A.2 ([= Guelferbytanus 32] MiAg 1: 566): "Ut ergo sit quod vocatur, audiat, non me, sed mecum; simul audiamus, simul in una schola condiscipuli ab uno magistro Christo discamus, cuius cathedra ideo est in caelo, quia prius crux fuit in terra. Humilitatis ille viam docuit: descendens ascensurus, visitans eos qui in imo iacebant, et elevans eos qui sibi cohaerere volebant."

20 This theme will be explored further in chapter 5.

21 *conf.* 5.13.23.

Even at that time, the preacher would sit, somewhat like the teacher in a standard rhetorical schoolroom.[22] Augustine follows the kenotic emptying he sees in the humble Christ from Philippians 2, as Christ takes on the *forma servi* (form of the servant). Just as Christ pours himself out for humanity, Augustine pours himself out for his people.

Every single person gathered to hear the bishop speak now take on one title together, *condiscipulus* (fellow student). No one is above the other before the *cathedra caelestia* (heavenly seat) of the one teacher Christ. This is Augustine showing the way of humility through his speech. We see Augustine opening himself up to the love of Christ and bringing the congregation together as one through sharing a mindset as one who also learns from Christ. Antoninus and his congregation have an example first in Christ and then in Augustine following Christ.

Returning to what Christ teaches his Church, Augustine reiterates the necessity of combining word and deed. He says Christ was "a teacher of humility by both word and deed.... He also deigned to teach it by his own example. Our creator came humbly, to be created among us; the one who made us, who was himself made for our sakes."[23] The creator becomes part of his very creation by not merely commanding humility but acting it out. Augustine goes further, "but if you were not to be given a demonstration of humility, of patience, then you should not be given a command about them; if however, you were to be given a command about them in words, then they were also to be demonstrated and commanded to you by example."[24] Christ is the perfect example which the preacher must offer to the congregation because the position of preacher is perilous. That is to say, the preacher cannot be the sole example because he is a fallen human. He will at some point fail in his efforts to mimic Christ.

Should the preacher receive too many compliments himself, he runs the risk of failing to live up to the command he issues in the place of Christ.

---

22 In *s.* 355.2 (SPM 1.125), Augustine apologizes to the crowd for the long sermon to come and indicates that he sits while they stand.

23 *s.* 340A.2 [= Guelferbytanus 32] (MiAg 1: 567; WSA III/9, 300): "Doctor humilitatis sermone et opere: sermone enim semper ab initio creaturae numquam tacuit, per angelos, per prophetas, docere hominem humilitatem; docere dignatus est etiam exemplo suo. Venit humilis creator noster, creatus inter nos: qui fecit nos, qui factus est propter nos."

24 *s.* 340A.2.

The great preacher might receive too many accolades which cause pride to swell. Augustine warns, "Many people fawn on us, many speak ill of us and revile us. The ones who fawn on us put us in greater danger than the ones who revile us."[25] Why would this be the case? "The bowing and scraping of people, after all, tickles our pride."[26] The swelling of pride is the primordial sin, as Augustine has already stated. Furthermore, the punishment for a bishop is greater than that of the average worshipper. As Augustine notes, "but if we are [bad bishops] and have sought our dignity and honor for our own sakes, and neglected God's commandments, and have never cared tuppence for your salvation, greater punishments await us than the rewards which have been promised."[27] The bishop takes a tremendous risk. By climbing onto the *cathedra*, he runs the risk of a greater pride which brings a greater punishment. The punishment is only necessary if his actions do not match the actions he commands as preacher from scripture. There would be a disconnect between word and deed.

The use of word *cathedra* in Augustine's time and writings, as we have hinted at above, is rather complex. In one way, the seat signified an honored place in the rhetorical schools where Augustine previously taught. The pride he took in this position clouded his vision so that he could not see his own sinfulness, nor see Christ as humble. In this very sermon, Augustine draws on another recurring image, the *cathedra Christi*, which was both the place from which preachers taught and symbolized their authority.[28] The seat of Christ relied on the tradition of the *cathedra moysi* as the seat of authority for the Israelites and God's people. A preacher could betray this seat of authority if one sinned and acted wrongly and incur punishment.[29] The language of *cathedra* had resonances both with his days in the rhetorical schools, and then also with the New Testament and the teachings of Christ. It is no surprise that Augustine frequently draws on schoolroom language to explain the Church as a *schola Christi*.[30]

---

25 *s.* 340A.8 [= Guelferbytanus 32] (MiAg 1: 569; WSA III/9, 302).

26 *s.* 340A.8.

27 *s.* 340A.8.

28 *s.* 340A [= Guelferbytanus 32] (MiAg 1: 573). Cf. *in. Io. Ev.* 46.6.13; *en. Psalm.* 36.3.20.

29 *doctr. chr.* 4.27.59 (CCSL 32:163).

30 *s.* 33A (CCSL 41:22); *s.* 98 (PL 38.592); *s.* 122 (PL 38.681); *s.* 177 (CCSL 41Bb:568).

If the bishop's manner of life does not match the bishop's word, he invites scrutiny. While this is certainly true for any person, it is a much greater risk for the bishop who has the authority of speaking in the *cathedra Christi*. The bishop is tasked with presenting to the people the commands of God in scripture and acting that out, in imitation of Christ. When the bishop follows the first part, and issues the commands of God, but does not do the latter, the congregation will rightly call him out for hypocrisy. Thus, the people would feel justified in ignoring the bishop's commands. This is why he deserves a double punishment. He has not only injured himself by failing to live up to God's commands, but he has become a σκάνδαλον "a stone on which one falls" to the congregation to ignore the scripture as well (Rom 14:13). This seems to be what Augustine is afraid of in his own life and sermon. He does what he can to use his words themselves as an action to demonstrate the humility for the people, *via humilitatis agendo*. He wants the praise to go to Christ and encourage people to follow Christ's command, all the while looking himself towards Christ.

In short, this sermon shows one significant feature of Augustine's theology of preaching in microcosm. He uses his speech as means to demonstrate the virtue to which he calls the Church. He goes to the scriptural text to find the command from God by which the Church should live. In this case, it is the call for the bishop to serve the people in humility. One might call this the locution, the very command or word the preacher speaks gathered from scripture. After finding his command and word, he shows it in action in his very words. One might call this the illocution. On this occasion, it is the fact that they are all students in the same school with Christ as their teacher. Finally, he warns Antoninus that if his words and actions do not match, the ability of the people to receive the command is threatened. That is, the perlocution suffers. This means potential punishment in the end for the bishop because of the amount of damage done to the congregation who are now less willing to do what God asks. These terms offered here come from the contemporary philosophical ideas of Speech Act Theory (SAT).

Philosophers of Speech Act Theory:
Searle and Austin

The remainder of this chapter will be on the connection between SAT and the preaching of Augustine. I want to consider the special kind of communication which occurs in the form of the sermon as Augustine understands it. It will be argued here that when the pastor preaches from the text of Scripture, the kind of communication which happens is of a different sort than simply a standard conversation between two people. The sermon has a third participant such that Augustine can say, quoting Paul, "So neither the one who plants nor the one who waters is anything, but only God, who makes things grow" (1 Cor 3:6). Much has been made of Augustine's semiotics and to what extent they are indebted to Plato and to what extent they can be used as an early anticipation of contemporary Wittgenstinian accounts of language.[31] What I will argue for here, however, will be restricted to the interactions between preacher, congregation, and God.

Our account will draw on broader explanations of Augustine's theory of language. Rowan Williams writes in his treatment of *On Christian Teaching* book 2 and Augustine's explanation of *signa et res*, "As so often happens with Augustine, he is most philosophically interesting when he is not being self-consciously philosophical."[32] In that vein, this chapter will find ways

31 Wittgenstein begins his posthumously published treatise on language—which for some signals the departure of Wittgenstein from his earlier accounts of language—with a quotation from *Confessions* 1.8 about how Augustine learned language from adults by watching them speak of an object and grab it, showing the connection between a sign and the thing. He explains Augustine as viewing language as reference, "Augustine does not mention any difference between kinds of word. Someone who describes the learning of language in this way is, I believe, thinking primarily of nouns like "table," "chair," "bread," and of people's names and only secondarily of the names of certain actions and properties," *Philosophical Investigations: the German text, with a revised English translation*, trans. G.E.M. Anscombe (Malden, MA: Blackwell, 2001) 5e. What Wittgensetein famously goes on to explain is that language is something which is understood within the context of a community of use, rather than simple reference.

32 R. Williams, "Language Reality and Desire," *Literature and Theology* 3.2 (July 1989) 138–50, 140. J. Rist in his chapter on this phenomenon in Augustine's semiotics talks about Augustine "opening up gaps" in the explanations of the various philosophical schools for the phenomena of language. He writes, "Thus another sort of gap is opened up: not, this time, between the proposition and the situation it purports to represent, where the underlying problem is that of the relationship between validity and truth, but the relationship between what we should like to convey and what we manage to convey. Man cannot express what he is incapable of experiencing or imagining, but he can experience what he is incapable of putting into words," *Augustine: Ancient Thought Baptized* (New York: Cambridge University Press, 1994), 29. The Stoics sought a theory which can avoid any ambiguity between the language inside (*logos endiathetos*) and the language outside (*logos prophorikos*). The Platonist school seemed unconcerned with

to expand Augustine's understanding of how language works beyond what is cogently and restrictively written about in *On the Teacher* and *Confessions* 1, which views *signa* as reminders of the *res* which one already knows in a Platonic epistemology.[33] We will proceed from statements—in *On Christian Teaching* 4 and throughout the *Sermons* themselves—which indicate that in fact the speech of the sermon can act in a way that is not reducible to merely a sign of a thing which a person already knows. Instead, we will look at the ways in which Augustine anticipates the theories of J. L. Austin and John Searle who argue that speech is a species of action.[34] First we will trace the accounts of Austin and his student Searle which establish a theory of a language considering what words can *do*. Then, we will see how Augustine's notion of the preacher's sermon in *On Christian Teaching* 4 can be understood to have a similar effect on the people gathered but expanded to include the action of God in the sermon.[35]

---

any learning occurring outside the individual communion between soul and the One. Augustine "opens up the gaps" in part by his focus on scripture which tells a different story about the need for communication and the fact that the Word of God becomes incarnate in Jesus Christ.

33 For the view that Augustine was simply mimicking Plato's suggestion that what we know is merely a recollection of what the soul knew in the forms, see Philip Cary, *Outward Signs* (Oxford University Press, 2008), 65–116. Much of the extended treatment found in Cary can be found first in the standard treatment of Augustine's view of the *signa et res* is Markus, R. A. "St. Augustine on Signs" *Phronesis* 2.1 (1957): 60–83. Contra Cary, Williams follows Markus treatment, but as the quote above suggests, he wants to move the conversation forwards into areas of Augustine's thought in *On Christian Teaching* 2 which might demonstrate Augustine recognized language to do more than sign and signify a res. James K.A Smith proposes that when considered from the angle of human creatureliness, language should be expected to be relative to a community. Smith takes Augustine's lead on the relativity of signs to a community as a reason to believe that he is not so far from Wittgenstein, when understood from the creature's point of view. Smith, *Who's Afraid of Relativism* (Grand Rapids, MI: Baker Academic Press, 2014), 64–72.

34 A French phenomenologist, Jean-Louis Chretien, explains his understanding of the speech in action of Augustine this way, "What is this book about? It is about describing as rigorously and as precisely as possible what are, for Saint Augustine, the acts of the voice and the word, how they make an event, how our life or death is at stake in them," *Saint Augustin et les actes de parole* (Paris: Presses Universitaires de France, 2002), 8.

35 To my knowledge, no full-length studies that compare the works of a theologian and the insights of SAT exist. Two shorter articles have analyzed the preaching

In 1955, J. L. Austin introduced to Western philosophy a new paradigm changing the way philosophers think about how human language works. From the title alone, *How To Do Things with Words,* one can begin to see why his work created such a stir.[36] As the title implies, words and language do not merely convey information but are instruments that can serve a great many functions. People *use* language to accomplish acts in the world. The philosophy inspired by Austin has come to be known as Speech Act Theory (SAT). In one sense, as we have been talking about the words and deeds of Augustine, SAT blurs the lines between these two concepts. We find that more than discrete concepts words are deeds and vice versa. For our purposes, we will see that words contain a record of deeds with respect to Augustine who left only his words as a record of his actions.

SAT views language as an action which one performs in order to create an effect on the hearers.[37] When humans use language in a certain way, they perform an action with their speech. These kinds of actions considered under the term "performative utterances" vary widely. That said, if one merely reflects on the sentence, "I now pronounce you man and wife," one begins to see the ways in which language can be used to perform an

---

of Karl Barth and to some extent Martin Luther with respect to SAT, see Markus Thane, "Speech-act theory to enhance Karl Barth's homiletical postulation of a sermon's 'revelatory compliance,'" *Scottish Journal of Theology* no. 2 (2015): 187–200; and Jacob Randolph, "Salvation and Speech Act." Reading Luther with the Aid of Searle's Analysis of Declarations," *Perichoresis* 15, no. 1 (Spring 2017) 101–17. This will be the first study of SAT as applied extensively to one theologian-preacher St. Augustine of Hippo. Kevin Van Hoozer has used the insights of SAT in his magnum opus, *The Drama of Doctrine* (Louisville, KY: Westminster John Knox Press, 2005), as well in his work *Is There a Meaning in This Text?* (Grand Rapids, MI: Zondervan, 1998), both of which seek to employ SAT in a broader systematic treatment.

36 J. L. Austin, *How to Do Things with Words* (Cambridge, MA: Harvard University Press, 1975).

37 Searle contends, "All linguistic communication involves linguistic acts. The unit of linguistic communication is not, as has generally been supposed, the symbol, word or sentence, or even the token of the symbol, word or sentence, but rather the production or issuance of the symbol or word or sentence in the performance of the speech act. To take the token as a message is to take it as a produced or issued token. More precisely, the production or issuance of a sentence token under certain conditions is the speech act, and speech acts (of certain kinds to be explained later) are the basic or minimal units of linguistic communication," *Expression and Meaning: Studies in the Theory of Speech Acts* (London: Cambridge University Press, 1969), 16.

action.[38] Two people become married through the pronouncement of the phrase itself under certain conditions.[39] Similarly, in another sacrament of the church, the words of institution demonstrate the performative power of words.

Broadly speaking in the modern history of the philosophy of language, SAT moves the conversation about language forward from an overly restrictive explanation which limits what language can be explained to do. These kind of simplistic notions about language, restricted to notions of conveying information, though common in preaching and other forms of communication, do not do justice to the myriad ways that speech functions. This is where the SAT of Austin, and John Searle his student, can help expand our ability to understand language and in turn, how Augustine acts in his words through preaching.

The example of how speech can affect the world as in the case of the marriage pronouncement is but one of the many ways SAT categorizes speech acts.[40] Let us return to the wedding vows. In the standard liturgy, a priest says something like, "Now that John and Jane have given themselves to each other by solemn vows, I pronounce that they are husband and wife, in the Name of the Father, and of the Son, and of the Holy Spirit." A locution, like "I pronounce that they are husband and wife," is performed by the speaker in a manner, which in SAT is termed the illocution. Expanding on the notion locution, Austin saw that the phrase, "I pronounce," could be performed in various ways to do something in the world, but it could not merely be said by anyone and have the intended effect. Austin called this the illocution; namely, how the speaker meant to use the phrase to act in the world to, in essence, create a marriage.[41]

38 As Austin says at the beginning of his work, "It was for too long the assumption of philosophers that the business of a 'statement' can only be to 'describe' some state of affairs, or to 'state some fact,' which it must do either truly or falsely," *How To Do Things with Words*, 1.

39 These conditions will be expounded upon below.

40 At any point in which a locution is uttered by a speaker, the speaker intends for someone to understand the utterance. Thus, Searle thinks that the most philosophically important aspect of Austin's tripartite account is the illocution. The locution is only useful for explanation. Any time that the sentence is uttered it becomes an illocution. Searle, *Foundations of Illocutionary Logic* (Cambridge University Press, 1985), 11.

41 It should be noted that Searle has argued that there is no proper distinction

Beyond simply the phrase itself, the locution, and the way it is performed, the illocution, is the perlocution.[42] The phrase "I pronounce you man and wife" is performed by a speaker with a perlocutionary intent to hearers of the speaker to recognize the new reality of a marriage bond.[43] The perlocution is the final aim of the speech act as it is received by those who hear it. The preacher pronounces the statement of marriage with the intention that those who witness the illocution will affirm it. In sum, every speech act for heuristic purposes can be considered under the tripartite form of a locution, an illocution, and a perlocution.

To this point, we have established that a speech act is used to categorize the ways in which speech moves beyond simply referring to something or reducing language to a proposition. Austin thought speech was performed and could be broken up into locutions, illocution, and perlocutions. Searle recognized that certain institutional factors had to be present in order for certain speech acts to be felicitous.[44] These factors include things like location, time, speaker, and hearer. These explanations can help us consider what it means for the preacher to speak before the congregation and what makes his or her words felicitous. The preacher must be ordained and speaking in a church before the congregation. Not just anyone can be said to "preach." The setting may be correct, but the person might not be an ordained preacher, or deputized by a bishop.[45] If a preacher speaks in a bank

---

between locution and illocution. One cannot employ a locution without illocuting. Cf. J. R. Searle, "Austin on Locutionary and Illocutionary Acts," *Philosophical Review* 77 (Oct. 1968), 405–24. Austin defines illocution in his landmark work, *How to Do*, 98.

42 Austin, *How to* Do, 101.

43 Austin explains this by saying, "I cannot be said to have warned an audience unless it hears what I say and takes what I say in a certain sense," *How to Do*, 115. In current debates on SAT, there is a discussion as to whether the perlocution involves the action of the listener or merely a kind of understanding of the listener. For simplicity sake, we will follow Searle and apply the minimal condition of understanding of the listener to the illocution. Searle means to restrict slightly this definition of perlocution to take account for certain illocutions which do not seem to have an "intended effect" other than simply understanding, Searle, *Speech Acts: An Essay in the Philosophy of Language* (Cambridge: Cambridge University Press, 1970), 42–50.

44 Searle, *Taxonomy of Illocutionary Acts* (Minneapolis: University of Minnesota Press, 1975), 15–16.

45 It should be noted that taking "holy orders" or "ordination" is a contested topic in the literature of early Christianity. Augustine himself performed the duties

to non-Christians, this is not a sermon. The person may be ordained, but the setting is incorrect.

These things largely held true in the ancient world as well. The preacher held a special position to offer the words of scripture to the people because of their authority and position. They spoke before Christians on the *cathedra christi*, and only they had the proper role to preach. The words took on a special significance because of all these factors which Searle and Austin delineated. Although they of course did not think of this as an explanation of the sermon, their ideas help us think about preaching in a different way. Would Augustine have agreed that speech is a species of action only possible under the right conditions? Some have said that he was merely a Platonist who thought language just reminded us of what we already knew.

Augustine's Philosophy of Language for Preaching

In an early and longer treatment of how one learns through speech, Augustine argues to his son Adeodatus, "Anyone who speaks gives an external sign of his will by means of an articulated sound."[46] In the second half of *On*

---

of a bishop and preached for the congregation at Hippo, despite the fact that Valerius was then the sitting bishop. See: Peter Brown, *Augustine of Hippo* (Berkeley: University of California Press, 2000) 132–33, and Fr. Jan Michael Joncas, "Ordination, Orders" *Augustine through the Ages* (Grand Rapids, MI: Eerdmans Press, 1999), 599–602. While it is difficult to state conclusively how holy orders worked in every part of the Mediterranean, it is clear that not just anyone could preach without the proper backing by the congregation and the Church hierarchy.

46 *mag.* 1.2 (CCSL 29.158); English: *Against the Academics and the Teacher,* trans. Peter King (Indianapolis, IN: Hackett, 1995), 95: "Qui enim loquitur, suae voluntatis signum foras dat per articulatum sonum." Cary says this is the first part of a simple two-part movement in how Augustine understands speech (*Outward Signs,* 92). He contends that this is an extension of a purely Platonic notion of how speech functions, saying, "The lesson, to put it precisely, is that we use signs to teach, yet we learn nothing from signs. The first half of the lesson gives us the point of Augustine's semiotics, while the second half, startling though it is, is a fundamental semiotic principle that Augustine never goes back on." See, Cary, *Outward Signs,* 92. Peter Ochs cautions of the limits of a study like Cary's, "Here, knowledge tends to ocular knowing, and Cary shows how inadequate that model is to account for performative knowing in the church, of which sacramental life is one instance. But performative knowing would apply, as well, to the study of Augustine's writings. Read "outwardly," Augustine's corpus generates several possible vectors of theological practice. The stronger vectors may point "inward,"

the Teacher Augustine says, "Well, if we should consider this more carefully, perhaps you'll discover that nothing is learned through its signs. When a sign is given to me, it can teach me nothing if it finds me ignorant of the thing of which it is the sign; but if I'm not ignorant, what do I learn through the sign?"[47] This matches perfectly what Augustine says in *Confessions* 1.7–8, as Wittgenstein knew. If we follow the clues in Augustine which suggest a more complete notion of how language works, following Williams, we can see that Augustine's practice conforms with what was later stated in SAT. It might be that although Augustine in some instances seems to lean on a "semiotic-experiential framework"—as Cary terms it—in practice, he does recognize that his speech is a species of action.

Expanding on the philosophical character of speech, Augustine recognized that the speech in a sermon required more than simply a speaker and hearer in *On the Teacher* and in *On Christian Teaching* book 4.[48] Although this

---

but readers should also attend to those (weak or strong) which point to that which is inward, outward, both, and neither." Outward Signs: The Powerlessness of External Things in Augustine's Thought" *Modern Theology* 27, no. 1 (January 2011): 206–8. This study follows that caution by focusing on the so called "performative knowledge" which occurs outwards. Carol Harrison suggests that words do more than we realize, "In their preaching and teaching they became part of this saving economy. Words not only possessed an almost magical power in ancient culture; as we shall see they could create a culture, and, in doing so, convert, reform, and save those who heard them," *The Art of Listening in the Early Church* (Oxford: Oxford University Press, 2013), 11.

47 *mag.* 10.33 (CCSL 29:192; King, 135). Cary interprets this phrase saying, "The second half of On the Teacher thesis that 'we learn nothing from signs,' tries to teach us that the success of teaching does not depend on anything the teacher says but on something more inward, which Augustine depicts as a teaching by Truth itself, a vision beyond all external words and signification," Cary, *Outward Signs,* 92. In contrast to Cary's view which is but an updating of G. C. Stead's view, see John Rist, 'Augustine's "'De Magistro': A Philosopher's View," *SP*, 63–73, Rist contends, "[Stead] commits himself to the view that Augustine holds (or seems to hold) that 'nothing is learnt by means of signs,' but that is to oversimplify Augustine's attitude: Nor need Augustine be saddled with the view that all sentences are statements, even though he is mostly concerned with statements in the *De Magistro, Ancient Thought Baptized,* 32. n. 25.

48 Against a simplistic reading of *De Magistro,* Augustine clearly thinks that humans do learn things from another, as he says in *doc. chr* proemium 6 (CCSL 32:4; WSA I/11, 104): "Then again charity itself, which binds people together with the knot of unity, would have no scope for pouring minds and hearts in together, as it were, and

work has certainly become an overworked soil—trod and re-trod by many different scholar-tillers—no one to this point has considered the connection between SAT and Augustine's account of the preachers action.[49] As is well known, Augustine began this work at the end of the fourth century and returned to it as a seasoned preacher with nearly three decades of experience.[50] He had lived much of his early life captive to the pagan rhetorical education he had received. The ends of this education were to sway the educated public and prove his muster in the well-honed art.[51]

Rhetors were not concerned with making themselves understood by as broad of an audience as possible. The purpose of the education was to demonstrate the learning one had achieved, and at times doing the opposite of making clear communication.[52] Carol Harrison has shown that Augustine had multiple and quite different audiences in mind—both pagans who would want to see some evidence of rhetorical ornamentation and others who merely wanted to understand the text—in *On Christian Teaching,* a work

---

blending them with one another, if human beings were never to learn anything from each other."

49 This chapter will lean heavy on Carol Harrison's "The Rhetoric of Scripture and Preaching," *Augustine and His Critics: Essays in Honour of Gerald Bonner,* ed. by Robert Dodaro and George Lawless (London; New York: Routledge, 2000): 213–30. For different angles on the intent, context, and purpose of *doct. chris.* see the individual chapters by various authors in W.H. Arnold and P. Bright, *De Doctrina Christiana: A Classic of Western Culture* (Notre Dame, IN: Notre Dame University Press, 1995).

50 C. Kannengiesser, "The Interrupted *De Doctrina Christiana,*" in W. H. Arnold and P. Bright (eds), *De Doctrina Christiana,* 4–14.

51 Quintilian's *Instituto Oratoria* and Cicero's *De Inventione, De Oratore,* and *Brutus* are all good places to begin to think about the Latin version of what the rhetor's education was for.

52 See Peter Brown, *Paidea and Peruasion,* and Averil Cameron, *Christian Discourse.* After we explore the ways in which Augustine's should be read to be consonant with the insights of SAT, we will go back through his education and see the ways in which who educated in antiquity desired to make their students to be a different class of people from those to whom Augustine would later preach. This creates problems for Augustine and so later in life he downplays the importance of grammar and rhetoric in interesting ways as a result of his encounter with the humble Christ. The final chapters will trace the ways in which Augustine used his speech as action to demonstrate to people the virtue of humility. In a sense, his whole life, emphasized in his speech, was a testament to the profound impact that the humility of Christ had on him as an individual person.

concerned with the delivery of scripture in preaching.[53] In some ways, he still wanted to appear respectable to his classical counterparts. Yet, Augustine shows an awareness that his sermons targeted a lower class of people, the majority uneducated, whom he hoped would understand and act out the truth of scripture.[54]

This is where Augustine's focus on the action involved in speech, which anticipated SAT, helps us understand what he thought the preacher could do from the pulpit by his words.[55]

He defines an eloquent Christian preacher in this way according to Hill's translation, "so this eloquent speaker of ours is at pains, when he has just and good and holy things to say—he ought not, after all, to be saying anything else; so he is at pains to ensure as far as he can, when he says these things, that his listeners understand them, enjoy them, obey them."[56] Augustine recognizes that the preacher does not merely offer up theological truths to the listeners when he ascends into the *cathedra*. His words do things, like other

53 Harrison basically proceeds on the assumption that the work is concerned with preaching and scripture interpretation, "Rhetoric," 213. Christoph Shaublin has criticized the position that one can even be certain what Augustine was intending with this work but severely disagrees with the idea that it is a preacher's education manual. See "*De Doctrina Christiana*: A Classic of Western Culture?" in Arnold and Bright (eds), *De Doctrina Christiana*, 47–67.

54 Chapter 3 will address fully the question of the audience.

55 Although I want to convey how Augustine understood his speech to perform and act in a certain way for his audience, I risk ignoring the fact that this treatise is a great work on rhetoric more broadly. As W. R. Johnson has noted, "It is hard, I think, for a rhetorician and a Latinist to be very objective about this book: it seems to me not merely the most influential but perhaps the most precious book in the tradition of humanist rhetoric." Johnson, "Isocrates Flowering: The Rhetoric of Augustine," *Philosophy & Rhetoric* vol. 9 no. 4 (1976): 217–31, 220. Later in the same article, Johnson writes, "The more one reads the *Confessions* and the *Civitas* the harder it becomes to distinguish the philosophy from the theology, the theology from the Isocratean rhetoric, the rhetoric from the Ciceronian humanism, and the humanism from the mysticism that informs all of Augustine's thinking and writing, suffering and doing. And when it becomes so hard to make these distinctions that we begin to feel that it is impossible to make them, then perhaps we come to see that it is unnecessary to make them" (228).

56 *doctr. chr.* 4.15.32 (CCSL 32:138; WSA I/11, 219): "Agit itaque noster iste eloquens, cum et iusta et sancta et bona dicit, neque enim alia debet dicere, agit ergo quantum potest cum ista dicit, ut intellegenter, ut libenter, ut oboedienter audiatur." Augustine, *De Doctrina Christiana* (Oxford: Oxford University Press, 1995), 235.

physical actions. A more woodenly literal translation of the Latin matches the words of speech act theory: "He labors, as far as he is able, when he speaks that he is heard understandingly, delightfully, and obediently." (*Agit ergo quantum potest cum ista dicit, ut intellegenter, ut libenter, ut oboedienter audiatur*).[57] His speech is part of his action.[58]

If we look at the sentence closely, we see how intimately tied up speaking is with action for Augustine as he thinks through preaching. The first word in this sentence comes from *agere*.[59] Though certainly a word with a host of possible renderings in English (42 in the OLD), nearly all of them convey a sense of action. In this case, OLD has this entry, "to do, perform, achieve, accomplish; (w. *ut*) to bring it about that."[60] Returning to Augustine, we could

57 *doctr. chr.* 4.15.32 (CCSL 32:138) This phrase is used in similar ways four times in the remainder of the treatise, 4.17.34 (CCSL 32:140): "oret atque agat ut, quemadmodum supra diximus, intellegenter, libenter, oboedienterque audiatur." 4.26.56 (CCSL 32:161): "Illa itaque tria, quae supra posuimus, eum qui sapienter dicit, si etiam eloquenter vult dicere, id agere debere ut intellegenter, ut libenter, ut oboedienter audiatur."

58 Hannah Arendt commented on how one can be said to act through speech, *agere*, "With word and deed we insert ourselves into the human world, and this insertion is like a second birth, in which we confirm and take upon ourselves the naked fact of our original physical appearance. This insertion is not forced upon us by necessity, like labor, and it is not prompted by utility, like work. It may be stimulated by the presence of others whose company we may wish to join, but it is never conditioned by them; its impulse springs from the beginning which came into the world when we were born and to which we respond by beginning something new on our own initiative. To act, in its most general sense, means to take an initiative, to begin (as the Greek word *archein*, "to begin," "to lead," and eventually "to rule," indicates), to set something into motion (which is the original meaning of the Latin agere)" *Human Condition* (Garden City, NY: Doubleday, 1959): 176.

59 The noun form of the word *agere, actio,* has a very specific use in rhetorical theory. They are the physical actions which accompany the words of an orator. One scholar has traced the physical actions which should accompany the verbal displays of the Augustinian rhetor, Anne-Isabelle Bouton-Touboulic, "Body Language in Augustine's *Confessiones* and *De doctrina christiana,*" *Augustinian Studies* 49:1 (2018) 1–23. This is an important contribution to the conversation. That said, in our study, we are primarily concerned with the way in which the words are themselves a species of action. Nowhere in this study does the author discuss the central passage at issue, *doctr. chr.* 4.15.32, and the phrase, *agit cum dicit.* This phrase lends credence to the contention that Augustine recognizes that his speech itself acts on the hearer.

60 *Oxford Latin Dictionary* (OLD) 2 Vols., ed. P. G. Glare (Oxford: Oxford University Press, 2012) *v.*1, 98.

say that the eloquent speaker performs, achieves, or *acts* so that "when he speaks, he is heard obediently, freely, and understandably." His acting in his speaking must bring about certain means of being heard by his congregation, *as far as he is able*. This phrase indicates what Augustine has acknowledged elsewhere as the difficult truth that words do not perfectly convey their meaning, despite the best efforts of the preacher.[61] Using the language of SAT the perlocutionary effects of his illocution are to be heard, "understandingly, delightfully, and obediently." Of the final usages of the word in the OLD, it states that *agere* means "To speak about, discuss, reason about, argue, debate finally, (of an orator or actor), To deliver (a speech). To institute legal proceedings, go to law; plead."[62] What this demonstrates is that the distinction between speech and act—which SAT contends brings together—might be more of a modern problem than an ancient one.[63] Augustine, Cicero, Seneca, and others appear to know that action and speech are connected by a single word.[64]

61 Augustine is always acutely aware of the fact that he cannot make people understand him perfectly. In *cat. Rud.* 2.3 he says, "And when I find that my actual address fails to express what I have before my mind, I am depressed by the fact that my tongue has been unable to keep up with my intellect. For all the insight that I have I want to pass on to my hearer (*Totum enim quod intelligo, volo ut qui me audit intelligat*), and I become aware that, speaking as I am, this is not going to happen," (CCSL 46:122 WSA V, 56). Notice the similarity between what he says a preacher should try to do in *doctr. chr.* 4, but what he recognizes can never happen perfectly in this quote. This clearly indicates he knows his speech cannot replace the work of God in the lives of his hearers and will always fail to communicate perfectly what he knows.

62 *OLD* v.1, 100. In just one example of this usage, Cicero writes in the person of Brutus, the Orator, "But that our conversation may proceed more comfortably, let us sit down if you like and take up our subject," (*Brutus* 1.24; LCL 342: 34–35).

63 Owen Barfield suggests that ancient languages preserve an older undivided meaning of the language that is not chopped up in typical modern lexica: "We must, therefore, imagine a time when 'spiritus' or older words from which these had descended, meant neither breath, nor wind, nor spirit, nor yet all three of these things, but when they simply had their own old peculiar meaning, which has since, in the course of the evolution of consciousness, crystallized into the three meanings specified and no doubt into others also, for which separate words had already been found by Greek and Roman times." Barfield, *Poetic Diction* (Middletown, CT: Wesleyan University Press, 1987), 79.

64 In a line which suggests this strong connection between *agere* and *dicere*, Seneca the Elder says plainly, "cum in foro dico, aliquid ago." *Controversiae* 3.12 [LCL 463:

The shortened form the phrase above, *agit cum dicit,* does not just come up once. It forms a kind of controlling idea for how Augustine conceives Christian rhetoric to work in addition to the one laid out by Cicero. Each time it appears to expand on the threefold account of Cicero by taking it one step further. Not only should the speaker teach, delight, and persuade, but his speaking must act on the hearer so that the speech is understood in producing understanding, pleasantness, and obedience. The final sentence of the phrase is *audiatur* (he is heard). He must take into account how he is heard, the perlocution of his speech.[65] This matches how Augustine understands what the objective is for an orator.

Before Augustine lays out how the eloquent speaker should act when he speaks—*agit cum dicit*—he lays out a threefold typology of oration which matches the content of a speech with its appropriate level of ornamentation. This way of understanding how to approach oration is an adaptation of Cicero. In one of his many treatises on oratory, Cicero outlines in his work *Orator*:

> The man of eloquence whom we seek, following the suggestion of Antonius, will be one who is able to speak in court or in deliberative bodies so as to prove, to please and to sway or persuade. To prove is the first necessity, to please is charm, to sway is victory; for it is the one thing of all that vails most in winning verdicts. For these three functions of the orator there are three styles, the plain style for proof, the middle style for pleasure, the vigorous style for persuasion; and in this last is summed up the entire virtue of the orator.[66]

386–387]. Cicero questions in an oration, "Quid agimus, Hortensi? quid de hac condicione dicimus?" *Pro P. Quinctio oratio* (Teubner, M. D. Reeve, 1992), 45.

65 Another scholar, Therese Fuhrer, argues similarly that Augustine acts as an *Orator Humilis,* "However, I wish to demonstrate in the following that, in Augustine, the preacher repeatedly *slips* into the role of the *orator humilis.* I therefore wish to ask which linguistic resources and which gestures are used to achieve this, and which rhetorical intention he is pursuing by acting this way. I will propose the following thesis: by adopting a pose that is unusual for both a classically trained rhetor and an ecclesiastical dignitary, Augustine the preacher is able to deploy the effects of the unexpected and hence, as a tactic, to unsettle his listeners, thus making them more receptive to his rhetorical aim." Fuhrer, "Orator Humilis," in *Paul as Homo Novus: Authorial Strategies of Self-Fashioning in Light of a Ciceronian Term* (Gottingen: Vandenhoeck and Ruprecht, 2018), 251–66, 256.

66 *Orator* 21.69, (LCL 342, 356–57): "Erit igitur eloquens—hunc enim auctore

For Cicero, the goal of oratory is to persuade which he names the *vis omnis oratoris*, "the power of each orator." When one learns to orate well, he will match the content, be it high, low, or in between, with a corresponding level of ornamentation, extravagant, middling, or simple. This will turn the jury to the side of the speaker which constitutes the highest ability of the orator.

To a large extent, Augustine seems to primarily rehash Cicero in his work on rhetoric. He discusses three levels of content and three levels of ornamentation.[67] Augustine follows Cicero's advice in the next several paragraphs of book 4 (*On Christian Teaching* 4.12.27–14.31). That said, one significant departure in his explanation of Cicero's categories, Augustine does use the term *movere* "to move" rather than *flectere* "to bend." He does not merely want to overturn the canons of rhetoric he has taught and been taught. Rather, he would like to modify their ends for the different community to which he is trying to communicate.

That distinction between *movere* and *flectere*, however, is not nearly as significant for Augustine as what the purpose of all this oration is. Cicero was not a preacher, but simply an orator, as such his goal was to persuade. Augustine was a preacher who offered the Word of God for his people to encounter. His understanding of persuasion worked differently. As he writes,

> But neither is delighting an audience a matter of necessity, seeing that when things that are true are being pointed out in a speech, which is what the function of teaching is about, it is not the concern of the speaker, nor is it expected of him, that either his matter or his speech should give delight; but his matter by itself, being true, delights simply by being shown to be so.[68]

Antonio quaerimus—is qui in foro causisque civilibus ita dicet, ut probet, ut delectet, ut flectat. Probare necessitatis est, delectare suavitatis, flectere victoriae: nam id unum ex omnibus ad obtinendas causas potest plurimum. Sed quot officia oratoris, tot sunt genera dicendi: subtile in probando, modicum in delectando, vehemens in flectendo; in quo uno vis omnis oratoris est."

67 Joost Van Neer, "From Pride to Humility, from Impasse to Resolution, from Day to Day: Structure and Argument in Augustine's Nativity Sermons 195 and 196 with a Division into Five Parts," *Sacris Erudiri* 53 (2014): 69–98.

68 *doctr. chr.* 4.12.28 (CCSL 32:136; WSA I/11, 217): "Sed neque delectare necessitatis est, quandoquidem cum dicendo vera monstrantur (quod ad officium docendi

Cicero systematizes his categories around the high point of persuasion because the ends he imagines for the orator are different than the ends of a preacher: namely, to get a jury to side with the orator. As Augustine shows in the early sections of *On Christian Teaching* 2, the end of scriptural interpretation and the Christian life is the *beata vita* "blessed/happy life." He does not outright condemn persuasion as if it has no purpose, he just shows that the preacher must be concerned first and foremost with the truth. This is likely why the work is called *De Doctrina Christiana*. He is concerned with teaching the truth of the Christian faith as he knows it. He is not, like Cicero, trying to prepare orators for declamations in the senatorial halls.[69]

After Augustine lays out his slightly adapted form of the Ciceronian framework, he comes to the quotation laid out above. He pairs the tripartite structure of oratory with a tripartite structure of action. The *eloquens ecclesiasticus* (eloquent churchman) must act when he speaks so that he is heard in an understandable, enjoyable, and obedient way. This whole focus on *agere* in conjunction with the kind of language is unique to Augustine. The section he works from in Cicero's *Orator* makes no mention at all of any of these latter categories. To some degree, the reason for this is that Augustine is less concerned with persuasion and more with understanding, enjoyment, and obeying. Furthermore, the people he is trying to get to understand him do not have the education or possibly even the desire to hear an orator like Cicero. This is a point which will need to be sketched out further, but, to quote Augustine from an earlier section of *On Teaching Christianity* 4, the *eloquens ecclesiasticus* will speak, *"non sic dicatur ut a doctis, sed potius ut ab indoctis dici solet"* (it is to be spoken of not like the learned, but rather how the unlearned are accustomed to speak).[70] The preacher must speak so that he is understood in a manner closer to the *indocti* (the unschooled), rather than following the rules of the *docti* (the learned). This is something which Cicero as a rhetorician for the elite, could never countenance. We will see the extent to which Augustine does this in chapter 4 and who is audience was in chapter 3.

---

pertinet), non eloquio agitur neque hoc attenditur, ut vel ipsa vel ipsum delectet eloquium, sed per seipsa, quoniam vera sunt, manifestata delectant."

69 We will offer further comment on the way persuasion works differently for these two in chapter 6.

70 *doctr. chr.* 4.10.24 (CCSL 32:132).

The strongest connection to SAT in the remainder of *On Teaching Christianity* 4 is Augustine's discussion of the context of the Christian sermon. Augustine suggests that the *cathedra Christi* carries with it a profound authority. The authority assumed by the one in the *cathedra Christi* comes not by the occupant's excellent rhetoric but from the authority of the Word which he preaches. Augustine offers these words as a description of the office of the preacher, which in a certain sense guarantee the effectiveness of his words:

> They are indeed bent on seeking what is their own, but they dare not teach what is their own, from the higher place, that is to say, of the chair of ecclesiastical authority, which has been established by sound doctrine. So it was that chair, not their own but the one of Moses, that was constraining them to say good things, even while not doing good things. So they were doing their own thing in their lives, but were not permitted to teach their own thing by the chair that belonged to someone else.[71]

The *cathedra* in which the *eloquens ecclesiasticus* sits is not his own *cathedra*. When he takes his seat there to preach, he does not teach his peculiar doctrine but must follow what was once taught by Christ.

Returning to SAT for a moment, Searle argued that for a felicitous illocution of a declaration certain conditions must obtain. The speaker had to be in the right place, with the right authority, and that the speaker intends those declarations as declaration from that position.[72] Augustine has similar notions in mind for the preacher. The right place is the *cathedra christi*. The right authority would be that the person has been ordained. As to the declaration, Augustine argues that the preacher should seek not his own statements or teachings, but rather that which is required for the liturgy of the Church. For "they dare not teach what is their own." The fact that one speaks from this position in the Church means that way even rhetoric should

71 *doctr. chr.* 4.27.59 (CCSL 32:163, WSA I/11, 239): "Sua enim quaerere student, sed sua docere non audent, de loco scilicet superiore sedis ecclesiasticae quam sana doctrina constituit. Propter quod ipse Dominus priusquam de talibus quod commemoravi diceret, praemisit: Super cathedram Moysi sederunt. Illa ergo cathedra, non eorum sed Moysi, cogebat eos bona dicere, etiam non bona facientes. Agebant ergo sua in vita sua; docere autem sua cathedra illos non permittebat aliena."

72 Searle "How Performatives Work" *Linguistics and Philosophy* 12(5): 535–58, esp. 548.

be used is different from the other kinds of *cathedrae* or *rostrae* in which an orator might speak.

So, Augustine has various kinds of admonitions which seek to place this new kind of eloquence in its context.[73] In the context of his conversation with the principles laid down by Cicero, Augustine reminds his reader:

> But in our sphere we have to refer everything we say, above all what we say from our higher position to our congregations, to the welfare of persons, to their eternal, not merely temporal, welfare what's more, which also means warning them to beware of eternal perdition. So here everything we say is a great matter, to the extent that not even what the ecclesiastical teacher has to say about money and acquiring or losing it should be regarded as a minor matter, whether it's a minor or major sum of money involved.[74]

That is to say, nothing is of small importance such that the ornamentation of the language should be minimal. On the contrary, everything which is discussed from the *cathedra christi* is of maximal importance. That would seem to imply for Augustine that all of speech contained therein should be of the most ornate. Nevertheless, this is not the conclusion Augustine draws. He states, "And yet, while this teacher ought always to be setting forth great matters, he does not always have to say them in the grand manner."[75] The rules must be subject always in the *cathedra christi* to the truth which needs to be conveyed.[76] The truth is of paramount

73 Harrison's warning about the sometimes-contradictory nature of Augustine's analysis should be kept in mind, "Augustine moves rapidly between acceptance, rejection and modification of classical eloquence," Harrison, "Rhetoric of Scripture," 216.

74 *doctr. chr.* 4.18.35 (CCSL 32:142; WSA I/11, 222): "In istis autem nostris, quandoquidem omnia, maxime quae de loco superiore populis dicimus, ad hominum salutem nec temporariam sed aeternam referre debemus, ubi etiam cavendus est aeternus interitus, omnia sunt magna quae dicimus, usque adeo ut nec de ipsis pecuniariis rebus vel adquirendis vel amittendis parva videri debeant quae doctor ecclesiasticus dicit, sive sit illa magna sive parva pecunia."

75 *doctr. chr.* 4.19.38 (CCSL 32:145; WSA I/11, 229): "Et tamen cum doctor iste debeat rerum dictor esse magnarum, non semper eas debet granditer dicere."

76 Harrison comments, "However, in his relative evaluation of them Augustine has introduced a radically new note that overturns classical practice—while still, as is often the case, using its terminology—and has more in common, once again, with the philosophical critics of rhetoric. The unadorned, unarmed, naked truth (albeit with a

importance because the declaration of that truth is the purpose of Christian eloquence.

This leads Augustine down the path to a final admonition such that the aim is for the most amount of people to understand what is being said by the *ecclesiasticus orator* "the ecclesiastical orator." Augustine writes:

> What is the point, after all, of correctness of speech which the hearers are unable to follow and understand, seeing that there is absolutely no point in speaking at all, if the people do not understand, whom we are speaking to precisely in order that they may understand? So the person who is teaching will avoid all words that do not in fact teach; and if instead of them he can correctly use others that are understood, he will prefer to choose them.[77]

This is the aim for Augustine. The orator must cede his hard-won command of the rules of polished grammar to the more divine end of helping the uneducated understand.[78] In another of his sermons, Augustine writes, *melius est reprehendent nos grammatici quam non intelligunt populi*: "It is better that the grammarians chastise us than the people not understand."[79] Augustine hones the preaching art to the intention of the people's grasp of the message, in the sermon above, towards humility. Harrison describes this aesthetic well, "It is in this sense, I think, that we can speak of a Christian aesthetic, a new Christian literary culture; one in which rhetoric holds as central a place as

certain uncontrived beauty, and a few unostentatious rhythmic closings, not, of course, deliberately sought, but, rather, in some way natural) comes forth to 'crush the sinews and muscles of its adversary and overcomes and destroys resisting falsehood with its most powerful members' (4.26.56)." Harrison, "Rhetoric of Scripture," 220.

77 *doctr. chr.* 4.10.24 (CCSL 32:133; WSA I/11): "Quid enim prodest locutionis integritas quam non sequitur intellectus audientis, cum loquendi omnino nulla sit causa si quod loquimur non intellegunt, propter quos ut intellegant loquimur? Qui ergo docet, vitabit verba omnia quae non docent, et si pro eis alia integra, quae intellegantur, potest dicere, id magis eliget."

78 This will be further explored below, but suffice it to say for now that I am aware that being less educated in the ancient world did not mean unable or unwilling to follow a complex oral argument. We will look at one of Augustine's sermons on the Trinity which delves deeply into complex trinitarian theology, no easy matter to preach. If Augustine's audience is of the mixed educational sort, one might be surprised to see Augustine go into such an arcane subject.

79 *en. Ps.* 138.20 (CCSL 40: 2004; English, mine).

it did in classical culture, but where it is transformed from a practice that primarily aims to please and persuade, to one which aims to inspire love of, and the practice of, the truth."[80] There is a modification of rhetorical theory because the truth which Christianity proclaims outweighs the love of the language itself.

All of this leads to the ultimate purpose of what is the truth or what is this speech that the *ecclesiasticus eloquens* brings when he sits on the *cathedra christi*. To this point we have established that he acts when he speaks. We have noticed that the context is different from the schoolroom, senatorial halls, or courthouse. Even the rules of eloquence must be held in check for the purposes of guaranteeing the reception of the words by the people. All of this was in service of Christian truth, *doctrina christiana*. Yet, to this point, the argument has only concerned the preacher and the congregation. Theologically, God also is involved in the moment of preaching because Christ has established the *cathedra christi*.

Having summarized SAT and Augustine's similar thoughts on the act of communication between preacher and congregation, it is worth considering how Augustine diverges from SAT. Certainly, SAT does not typically have the sermon in mind as the kind of communication, though it is clearly not antithetical to it. Augustine contends that God works through the sermon to speak both through the preacher and to the congregation.

For Augustine, this begins with prayer. Augustine enjoins his reader to pray before he speaks, advising:

> And he should not be in the slightest doubt that if he can ensure this, and to the extent that he can, it is more the piety of prayer than the ready facility of orators that enables him to do so; by praying then both for himself and for those he is about to address, let him be a prayer before being a speaker.[81]

More important than rhetorical giftedness, as Augustine certainly was, is that the preacher must pray before he preaches. This quotation immediately follows the discussion of how the preacher acts when he preaches. In order

---

80 Harrison, "Rhetoric of Scripture and Preaching," 221.

81 *doctr. chr.* 4.15.32 (CCSL 32:138; WSA I/11, 219): "Et haec se posse, si potuerit et in quantum potuerit, pietate magis orationum quam oratorum facultate non dubitet, ut orando pro se ac pro illis quos est allocuturus, sit orator antequam dictor.orat."

that the preacher be heard understandingly, pleasantly, and obediently, he must begin his sermon with prayer. In this exhortation to pray, Augustine seeks to offset his emphasis on the abilities of the preacher with the recognition that none of it can ensure that he is understood completely. Simply put, he must rest content that he has done his part and let God be the final force which speaks to the congregation.

Using the language of SAT, the analysis of the delivery of the sermon from the preacher to the congregation goes something like this. The preacher takes his locution from scripture and from prayer. Augustine says at the beginning of book 4, "For the man, therefore, who has the duty of saying wisely even what he cannot say eloquently, it is supremely necessary that he should have the words of the scriptures at his fingertips."[82] Wisdom comes from the scriptures which provide the source of the proclamation from the *cathedra christi*. Why the scriptures alone? Williams writes, "if we are not careful [the scriptures'] written character can be misused by working with the text as if it were passive ... a written text requires re-reading; it is never read for the last time, and it continuously generates new events of interpretation. It is fruitful of renewed communication in a way that the spoken word alone cannot be. [The goal] is a continuous openness to the intention of God to communicate."[83] The preacher generates the new event of interpretation by elaborating on what is read from the scripture. That said, the preacher, as well as the congregation—as we shall see—must be open to the God who is communicating from the scriptural text through the preacher to the congregation. God is at work in each part of the locution, the illocution, and the perlocution.

The illocution highlights the person and character of the preacher. In some sense, how the preacher chooses to *mean* the explanation of the text can add or detract from its character. Augustine explains this by saying, "let him so conduct himself that he not only earns a reward for himself, but also gives an example to others, and so his manner of life can itself be a kind of eloquent sermon."[84] The actions of the preacher, even down to their words, give an example for the congregation. The actions and the manner of his life speak in ways that make up for the failure to always say the exact right thing.

---

82 *doctr. chr.* 4.5.8 (CCSL 32:121; WSA I/11, 205).

83 Rowan Williams, *Holy Living* (London: Bloomsbury Publishing, 2018), 42.

84 *doctr. chr.* 4. 29.61 (CCSL 32:165; WSA I/11, 240): "ita conversetur ut non solum sibi praemium comparet, sed etiam praebeat aliis exemplum et sit eius quasi copia dicendi forma vivendi."

The quintessential example of the form of someone's life becoming an eloquent speech is Jesus Christ who came to teach humility. This will be explored in later chapters, but the very fact that Jesus' life is told by fisherman, *piscatores* rather than *oratores,* shows the humility of the one narrated in their words. This means that for a *praedicator* who is no longer simply an *orator,* he must follow the lead of an untrained *piscator.* The new paradigm for an eloquent speaker is not simply Cicero, but a fisherman like John the Evangelist.

Finally, the perlocutionary effect of the preacher must be left to the divine movement in his speech. Augustine ends his introduction to the plan of preaching by saying, "So if the Holy Spirit is speaking in those who are handed over to the persecutors on Christ's account, why not also in those who are handing Christ over to the learners?"[85] The goal of "handing Christ over," *tradere Christum,* is a theme we will return to throughout. The Holy Spirit speaks through the preacher for the benefit of those who are listening. The preacher must rely on the Holy Spirit to work because there are things which the Holy Spirit must teach through the words of the preacher, which are not up to him. In the end, the goal is the presence of Christ in the hearts of the hearer and that perlocutionary effect cannot be guaranteed by the preacher.

All of this establishes the bedrock of the Augustinian theology of preaching. The preacher reads the scriptural text to listen for an understanding of God speaking. He then speaks an interpretation of those words but following the trajectory of the text which he has read. He must do this in a manner that is consonant with the text, so that even his speech becomes part of the sermon and message for the hearer. As Augustine says in *de Fide et Symbolo,* "When we speak truly, we act with our words.... What other objective do we have but to introduce our very mind into the mind of our hearer."[86] Finally, he must allow God to work in the hearts of the congregation to speak using the words of the preacher.

85 *doctr. chr.* 4.15.32 (CCSL 32.139; WSA I/11, 220): "Si ergo loquitur in eis Spiritus Sanctus, qui persequentibus traduntur pro Christo, cur non et in eis qui tradunt discentibus Christum?"

86 *On Faith and the Creed* 3.3–4.4 (CSEL 41.7); English, William Harmless, *Augustine in His Own Words* (Washington, DC: The Catholic University of America Press, 2010), 282: "Sicut ergo verbis nostris id agimus, cum verum loquimur, ut noster animus innotescat audienti, et quidquid secretum in corde gerimus, per signa huiusmodi ad cognitionem alterius proferatur sic illa Sapientia, quam Deus Pater genuit, quoniam per ipsam innotescit dignis animis secretissimus Pater, Verbum eius convenientissime nominatur." Note again the connection between action and speaking, *agere* and *loqui.*

Augustine's Critique of Speech Act Theory

I would like to conclude this chapter by examining one pertinent difference between SAT and Augustine's theology of speech in preaching. The majority of this chapter has been focused on demonstrating the consistency of insights from SAT with Augustine's theology of preaching. The preacher takes the locutions, typically commands or declaratives, from the scriptural text. He then illocutes them before the gathered congregation in his sermon. For this illocution to be heard as a proper command, the preacher must be speaking within a set of contextual constraints. That is, he must have the proper authority given through the Church. He must preach within the liturgy of the Church for the commands issued to be recognized as coming from God. These conditions were outlined as part of Searle's explanation for how certain speech acts created realities in the world, rather than merely describing what was already known. Yet, Searle did not have an analytic category for the lying speech act. If all the proper institutional factors were in place making the locution true and if the perlocution was possible, then what happens when someone does not *mean* their illocution? What should we call someone who promises something they do not intend to fulfill? What if someone commands something they do not wish to be followed?[87]

Augustine had to consider this because this very thing occurred within his sphere of influence in North Africa. There was one egregious instance of a preacher who seemed to preach the right things but did not follow them with his own life. Antoninus of Fussala, the last-minute, stand-in as bishop apparently used his position to amass a great deal of wealth at the expense of his community.[88] In a very delicate situation, at a recently converted community from

87 "A lie is, in a certain sense, a specific kind of speech act that was made up on purpose, and whose goal is not "to have someone know," "to have someone believe what I believe," but "to have someone believe different from what I believe." This speech act, in order to be effective, puts on the camouflage of a truthful speech act of information; nonetheless, it is in fact an autonomous, self-motivated typical speech act, not one invented after the truthful speech act, or secondary with respect to it.... It requires, for strategic reason, a complex structure of different deceptive acts [and] a number of different acts of deception about the speaker's mind: about her goals, her beliefs, her cooperative attitude." Cristiano Castelfranchi and Isaeblla Poggi, "Lying as Pretending to Give Information," in *Pretending to Communicate*, ed. Herman Parret (Berlin: Walter de Gruyter, 1994), 288.

88 J.E. Merdinger, *Rome and the African Church in the Time of Augustine* (New Haven, CT: Yale University Press, 1997), 154–81. W.H.C. Frend, "Fussala: Augustine's Crisis

Donatism, Antoninus abused his authority as a Catholic bishop potentially wreaking havoc on the faith of so many Catholic Christians in his congregation. The sermon which was outlined above was preached at his ordination. It is impossible not to read the sermon with an overwhelming sense of sadness at Antoninus' inability to follow the pleadings of his former mentor. More to the point, it is difficult to read knowing that this congregation will suffer for the poor choice of bishop by Augustine and Antoninus' rejection of the scriptural command.

In order to establish exactly what Antoninus did, it will be necessary to look at two different letters between Augustine and a wealthy woman at Fussala to reconstruct the story. No sermons from Antoninus himself still exist. We must reconstruct the situation from the details provided in letters from Augustine to Pope Celestina and a letter to Fabiola, a well-regarded woman at Fussala. In his letter to Fabiola, Augustine describes what went wrong with the young bishop:

> Not having merited anything by previous service, the soul of the young man was seized with awe and suddenly swept away by the honor of the episcopacy. Then, seeing that the clergy and people were subject to him, as the affair itself reveals, he was puffed up with the arrogance of power, and, teaching nothing verbally but compelling people to everything by his power, he was happy to be feared when he saw that he was not loved.[89]

Consonant with the theme of this chapter, Augustine characterizes Antoninus' sin as being "puffed up with the arrogance of power." This "arrogance of power" matches to some degree what Augustine warned Antoninus against in the ordination service of the young bishop. Antoninus did use his position as bishop as a means to gain acclaim in this world and use that for monetary gain.

Why was he so afraid of this occurring with Antoninus? By his own admission, Antoninus was likely too young and inexperienced for this post. He describes his family's arrival at Hippo, "As a child he came to Hippo with his mother and stepfather; they were so poor that they lacked what they

---

of Credibility (Ep. 20*)", in *Les lettres de saint Augustin* (Paris: Etudes Augustiniennes, 1983), 251–65.

89 *ep.* *20.4 ad Fabiolam (CSEL 88:96).

needed for daily sustenance."[90] In his time with Augustine at the monastery, he had learned to read and speak publicly. Augustine continues to describe the young lad, "Among his comrades he performed the office of lector and soon began to be viewed as a man of such qualities that Brother Urbanus (who at that time was a priest among us and superior of the monastery but is now bishop of the church of Sicca) wanted him, in my absence, to become a priest in a certain large estate situated in our diocese."[91] We learn that other bishops in the area saw much promise in him, but Augustine was hesitant. It is important to remember that this letter was written in retrospect, about the year 423, and Augustine is looking back at the life of Antoninus trying to ascertain what went wrong.

As an arrogant leader, Antoninus used his position to make money from his congregation. It appears that Antoninus stole from many different people in the congregation, down to even helpless widows. He used his position to gain a group of conspirators, including a deacon and a former military man, to protect his scheme of theft from the people of Fussala.[92] For further proof of his criminal pride, when questions were raised about his conduct, he tried an end run around the African authorities and appealed directly to Pope Boniface.[93] This indicates the difficulty of administrating such a broad network of churches in the ancient world at the time.[94] It was possible for a rogue bishop to appeal directly to Rome feeling that it was possible to avoid censure from his own region.

This begs the question why Augustine ever chose Antoninus in the first place. From his correspondence, it would appear that Augustine was in a bit of a bind. The Primate of North Africa had already scheduled and made the trip to Fussala to ordain a bishop.[95] The town had recently converted to the Catholic Church from Donatism and needed a leader. The first candidate pulled out at the last minute and Augustine had to find a quick replacement.

90 *ep.* *20.2.

91 *ep.* *20.2.

92 *ep.* *20.6.

93 *ep.* *20.11.

94 Allen, Pauline, and Bronwen Neil, *Crisis Management in Late Antiquity (410–590 CE): A Survey of the Evidence from Episcopal Letters* in Supplements to Vigiliae Christianae (Leiden: Brill, 2013), 184–85.

95 *ep.* *20.4 ad Fabiolam (CCEL 88.96).

Augustine reached for an up-and-coming monk from his monastery who had some training and acclaim and spoke Punic.[96] Augustine's fateful decision to ordain this inexperienced young man ultimately proved calamitous.

As indication of his guilt and willingness to atone for his failure, Augustine boldly and selflessly bargains with Pope Celestina, who succeed Boniface after his death. Augustine's anxiety over the problems he has caused come out clearly. He pleads,

> Amid this danger to both of them so great a fear and sorrow torments me, as I must confess to Your Goodness, that I would consider withdrawing from the office of administering the episcopacy and devoting myself to lamentations suited to my mistake if I saw that the Church was being ravaged by that man whose episcopacy I supported through imprudence and that it was even perishing—may God prevent this!—along with the destruction of the one who was ravaging it.[97]

He recognizes his complicity in this decision and so offers his resignation. At this point in his career, around 423, Augustine had been bishop for 26 years. He is putting his reputation and career on the line if only Celestine will find in favor of the bishops of Africa who want to censure Antoninus.

All of this merely demonstrates what can go awry in a preacher who has many of the institutional factors in place as indicated in SAT but only uses the locutions from scripture cynically for personal gain. Antoninus has been ordained and so has the right authority to preach. He preaches to his congregation from the *cathedra* at Fussala. When he speaks, because of his position, the people must listen to him. But, even if he preached the commands from the scriptural text, he does not follow through with them. This is what caused Augustine to think differently about how speech functions in the sermon. Augustine had to find a way to explain the difficulty of true Christian teaching coming from someone whose actions countered that truth. Can the proclamation of the Church still be declared as true and received as true by those gathered to hear if the person's life runs counter to the message he proclaims?

96 *ep.* *20.4.
97 *ep.* 209.10 (WSA II/3, 298).

Augustine warns his readers at the end of *On Christian Teaching* 4 that their manner of life can damage their effectiveness as a preacher. As a summary of his advice about a preacher's lifestyle, he writes, "let him so conduct himself that he not only earns a reward for himself, but also gives an example to others, and so his manner of life can itself be a kind of eloquent sermon."[98] The preached word has a more profound effect on the hearers if the preacher carries out what he commands. It is a further means to ensure what Augustine says at the beginning, as discussed above, that a preacher be heard obediently. The preacher through his words and actions provides a living example, as Christ has in the scripture.

It might be argued that if the preacher does not follow through on carrying out the commands of scripture, then his preached commands can be ignored. This is the move you would expect according to SAT. The perlocution suffers and communication does not occur. The promise and the commands are void. The preacher might proclaim that they are under the command of scripture, but willingly flaunt what they command. This appears to be the case of Antoninus of Fussala. He did not heed the command of scripture to protect the widow and the orphan. So, does this mean for Augustine that a congregation should ignore the proclamation of the preacher, which is the preached word of God?

To the contrary, Augustine relies on the fact that because the sermon is preached within the authority of the Church following the scripture, the commands are valid regardless of the life of the preacher. To this point, Augustine writes,

> But since good people who are believers listen obediently, not to any mere human being, but to the Lord himself as he says, Do what they say; what they do, however, do not do, for they say and do not do (Mt 23:3), that is why even those who do not act in a profitable way can be listened to with profit. For they are indeed bent on seeking what is their own, but they dare not teach what is their own, from the higher place, that is to say, of the chair of ecclesiastical authority, which has been established by sound doctrine.[99]

---

98 *doctr. chr.* 4.28.62 (CCSL 32:165; WSA I/11, 76).

99 *doctr. chr.* 4.27.59 (CCSL 32:164; WSA I/11, 239): "Sed quoniam boni fideles non

When the congregation listens to the preacher who sits on the chair of ecclesiastical authority, they are listening to Christ speaking. It has been established by sound teaching. Even if the manner of life of the preacher does not match the manner of life proclaimed in the text, since the chair is established by sound doctrine, they can be listened to with profit. Furthermore, it is worth noting that in Latin Augustine says that the *cathedra ecclesiastica* is established by *sana doctrina* (healthy doctrine). This is resonant of the title of the whole work, *de doctrina christiana*. Augustine does not write this treatise as a treatise on grammar. He is not concerned with whether or not the preacher uses the canons of rhetoric that he has learned. The intention of the work is that the truth of Christian teaching be taught. If what is said is true, it does not matter who says it, or how they say it to the extent that they preach the truth from the *cathedra christi*.

The chair, the *cathedra christi*, is critical for all of this to work for Augustine. Augustine goes on to say that when the holy orator ascends to the *cathedra*, they are not speaking from any normal orator's *cathedra*. It is the *cathedra* Christ has established. To that point, he continues:

> That is why the Lord himself, before speaking about such people as I have mentioned, first said, They sit on the chair of Moses (Mt 23:2). So it was that chair, not their own but the one of Moses, that was constraining them to say good things, even while not doing good things. So they were doing their own thing in their lives, but were not permitted to teach their own thing by the chair that belonged to someone else.[100]

The chair and the teaching are established by Christ who is the head of the Church, and he is heard through his preachers in the Church.[101]

---

quemlibet hominum, sed ipsum Dominum oboedienter audiunt, qui ait: Quae dicunt, facite; quae autem faciunt, facere nolite; dicunt enim et non faciunt, ideo audiuntur utiliter, etiam qui utiliter non agunt. Sua enim quaerere student, sed sua docere non audent, de loco scilicet superiore sedis ecclesiasticae quam sana doctrina constituit."

100 *doct. chrs.* 4.27.59 (CCSL 32:163, WSA I/11, 239).

101 *ep.* 208.5 (CSEL 57.34; WSA II/3, 392): "Christ hear his voice even through the bad teachers and do not abandon his unity, because the good that they hear them speak does not come from them but from him."

Augustine likely has in mind events like those in Fussala in this treatise written in 427, just a couple of years after the Antoninus affair. He was likely thinking of those people of Fussala saying they must not despair that they were being taught lies, even if their pastor was taking advantage of them. Augustine went to great lengths to have him removed but did not want to invalidate all of the teaching of the Church issued from the ecclesiastical seat.

Conclusion

The ordination sermon and the fall of Bishop Antoninus of Fussala provide a significant test case for the claims of the theology of preaching in Augustine. A preacher who draws true promises and commands from scripture offers the promises and commands to a congregation in a way so that they would be followed. The locution, the actual commands, come from scripture, and by extension from God. In the context of the liturgy of the Church, the preacher illocutes those commands, declaring them before the people as still valid and binding. The perlocution, how they are received, depends in part on the ability of the preacher to make them clear through his speech and his manner of life. That does not, however, mean that the congregation can ignore his words if his manner of life does not match his proclamation, as in the case of Antoninus. Ultimately God is the one who works in the perlocution. If the words he speaks are true, sound Christian doctrine, their truth is dependent on Christ and his Church, rather than on the individual proclaiming them. That said, Augustine provides in his own speech the kind of imitable action of humility that evinces a man so thoroughly changed by an encounter with the humble Christ, that even his language itself has changed. In the following chapter, we will look at who Augustine imitated before in his life as an imperial *rhetor* and how his education leads him into the pride that position carried. This pride made it initially difficult for Augustine to see the virtue of humility taught by Christ, which Augustine argues is the ground of virtue.

We will continue to use the insights of SAT to see speech as a species of action. The kind of action which orations were used for in the classical world writ large, was an action which sought to garner praise for the speaker. The orators as lawyers also used their speech to influence judges towards verdicts which the orators may not have even believed to be true.

CHAPTER 2

AUGUSTINE'S THEOLOGY OF CULTURE
The Power of Imitation

Introduction

CONTINUING IN OUR STUDY OF THE CONTEXT of his preaching, we will consider Augustine's Theology of Culture and how his culture shaped him. It will be helpful to consider the influence of a typical Roman education on the young Augustine and his later critiques of it. Additionally, we will explore how Augustine learned the humility of listening. Although Augustine acquired the skill of listening later, to be educated in late antiquity meant knowing the authoritative texts and how to speak well about them for the purposes of influencing society with one's speech. This practice had its roots in ancient Greece and continued in a similar manner up until the time of Augustine.[1]

---

1 Henri-Irenée Marrou begins his landmark study on ancient education with Homer and progresses from there to show the development of education to the time of Augustine, *A History of Education in Antiquity*. This study remains important, though Robert Kaster has updated this study by focusing on the role of the grammarian in *Guardians of Language* (Berkeley: University of California Press, 1988). Peter Brown writes about the influence of paideia in Christian society in *Power and Persuasion in Late*

Much can be said about this type of education, but what concerns us in this study is how it influenced the impressionable young student, Augustine. As a young man, Augustine's success in school inflamed him with the desire for his own glory which led him to the heights of worldly success. None of it proved deeply fulfilling, however, so Augustine chose to leave his ambition behind in pursuit of the humble Christ.[2] He would ultimately return to a kind of public speaking as a priest and bishop, but the kind of speech necessary for that setting was noticeably different from what he knew as a pagan orator.

After hearing the song of the child in the garden calling him to *tolle lege, tolle lege*, the chains of concupiscence fell from Augustine's soul which had previously shackled him to his desire for glory in public speaking. Augustine immediately seeks to be baptized and withdraw from his chair of imperial rhetoric that he had worked so hard to achieve.[3] In *Confessions* 9.2.2, Augustine describes his former vocation in his characteristic verbal fireworks. He says he was "determined to withdraw my tongue from its daily work in the marketplace of rhetoric.... This was to stop youths who were concentrating on the madness of deceit (*insanias mendaces*) and battles in the courts of law (*bella forensia*)—rather than your law and your peace—from buying—from my mouth—weapons to assist their violence (*ex ore meo arma furori suo*)."[4] Then, just a little further along, he puts it as succinctly as possible, naming his former position the *cathedra mendaci* (the chair of lies).[5]

This title, the *cathedra mendacii*, highlights an important contrast from the office he eventually assumes, the *cathedra Christi*. Augustine goes from occupying a seat of lies to the chair of Christ.[6] It seems that Augustine cannot escape sitting on a chair of authority.[7] The language, conduct, and comportment

---

Antiquity: Towards a Christian Empire (Madison: University of Wisconsin Press, 1992). Catherine Chin's work is formative for this study, *Grammar and Christianity in the Late Roman World* (Philadelphia: University of Pennsylvania Press, 2008). The most recent study is Blossom Stefaniw, *Christian Reading: Language, Ethics, and the Order of Things* (Oakland: University of California Press, 2019).

2 No episode in Augustine's life better demonstrates the hollowness of this career than when he desired the life of a drunk beggar more than his own profession. See *conf.* 6.6.9 (CCSL 27.79–81).

3 *conf.* 9.6.14. (CCSL 27.141).

4 *conf.* 9.2.2 (CCSL 27.133; WSA I/1, 211).

5 *conf.* 9.2.4 (CCSL 27.135).

6 *doctr. chr.* 4.27.59 (CCSL 32:163) quoting Jesus from Mt. 23:2.

7 He spends four years at Cassiciacum after his conversion and tries to avoid

of these two *cathedrae*, could not be more different. As we discussed above, the occupant of the *cathedra Christi* must proclaim the truth as found in scripture. He must teach in such a way that his life becomes an example for those who hear him speak in the liturgy of the Church. The language which he uses must be suited for the new audience which will be listening to him. Not only must the language be suited for the people, but it must be true Christian teaching, *doctrina christiana*. Most importantly, the occupant of the *cathedra Christi*, must learn to humbly listen and consider himself in some ways just like the people gathered to hear him speak. He ought not use his position to gain acclaim and wealth, as Antoninus of Fussala did. The occupant worthy of the name of bishop recognizes that all praise which comes from the people hearing his words must be directed first and foremost to the God who inspired the scriptures which instruct all those who will listen first to them.

Contrary to each point listed above, the characteristics of the occupant of the "seat of lies" look starkly different. First, those who occupy this "seat of authority" base their examples and inspiration from classical wisdom, be it Cicero or the great poets of the Greco-Roman tradition.[8] Second, the occupant's manner of life has no impact on his speaking because it is of no consequence if he is lying. Third, the language he deploys must be as elevated as possible to win the favor of those gathered around based on human genius. This favor, which the speaker who occupies the seat of lies seeks, ultimately redounds to his own glory and has the potential to make him proud, and narcissistic.[9]

To contrast these two very different *cathedrae*, this chapter will proceed in three sections, corresponding to important aspects of Augustine's relationship

---

becoming priest, as he states in *s.* 355.2 (WSA III/10, 167): "I had in fact left behind all worldly hopes, and I did not wish to be what I could have been [orator and statesman]; nor, however, was I seeking to be what I am now [priest]."

8 Henri Marrou writes, "But it was only in the time of Augustus that Latin secondary teaching took on its final form and emerged as a serious rival to Greek— when, not long after the year 26 B.C., a freedman of Atticus, whose name Q. Caecilius Eprota, had the hardihood to chose Virgil and the other new poets," *History of Education*, 252. For Cicero's place in the education see Marrou, *History of Education*, 253.

9 Mark Clavier draws out the ancient view of rhetors by saying, "[Rhetors] could become the ancient word's equivalent to celebrities." Mark Clavier, *Eloquent Wisdom: Rhetoric, Cosmology and Delight in the Theology of Augustine of Hippo* (Turnhout: Brepols, 2014), 43.

with the broader cultural milieu: both his pagan classical influences and a humble Christian one. The chapter will begin by laying out how the education of Augustine led him on the path to becoming a rhetorician. He learned at this stage of education in the *artes liberals* the ways to draw on common *topoi* for his speeches of battle (*bella forensia*) in the law courts. Any success in this kind of education, also encouraged an overinflated sense of self and one's own abilities. Augustine will later criticize this, but it was all he knew during his education and early career.

Imitation and one's natural, and sometimes unconscious, desire to imitate are a critical element to Augustine's mature Theology of Culture. As Augustine says in *City of God* "Why should you worship in religion one whom you have no desire to imitate, when the supreme height of religion is to imitate the one whom you worship"[10] The second section will look at the primary example of what this kind of late antique education in the *artes liberales* produced, namely Cicero. Imitation and example were critical to the *artes liberales* which sought to produce a *bonus vir, dicendi peritus* (a good man, experienced in speech).[11] No better example was Cicero, who was studied extensively in Augustine's education.[12] We will analyze one episode in the life of Cicero which demonstrates the extent to which a teacher of rhetoric ought to be called a seller of lies. In this section, we will draw heavily on SAT, to show how language was used to gain fame and glory for the great lawyer-rhetor. Thus, this goal of becoming *bonus vir, dicendi peritus* eventually churns out men who are merely *dicendi periti*, and for that reason are also proud.

Finally, we will move back into the story of Augustine when he meets a great exemplar of the *humilis praedicator*, Ambrose. This Christian preacher will

---

10 *ciu.* 8.17 (WSA I/6, 263).

11 Christine Mohrman also uses the term *vir eloquentissimus* which underscores that these men trained in this way thought of themselves primarily as eloquent speakers, rather than as virtuous men. Christine Mohrman, "St. Augustine and the Eloquentia," *Etudes sur le latin des chrétiens* Tome 1 (Rome, 1958): 351–70.

12 The forefather of all Roman orators was Cato the Elder who wrote to his son defining an orator as a *bonus vir, dicendi peritus,* M. Porcius Cato, *Libri ad Marcum filium* 14.1. This term was used by all great writers on oratory including Cicero in *de oratore* 2.20.85, followed in succession by Quintilian *instituto oratoria* xii.1.1; L. Seneca, *Controuersiae* 1.9.3; Apuleius, *Apologia* 94.104. The term makes its way into the patristic corpus as most early Christian writers were trained in these same arts: Ambrose, *De Abraham* 2.10.76; Augustine *ep.* 2.12. Jerome, *ep.* 69. For a modern study on the term *vir Bonus,* see: Prentice A. Meador Jr, "Quintilian's 'vir bonus,'" *Western Speech* 34.3 (1970): 162–69.

teach Augustine how to humbly listen for the truth in the scriptures before preaching. Ambrose thus becomes a guide for Augustine as he considers his own position later in life at Hippo Regius, in his own telling, thrust upon him against his will.

Augustine's Education

Unlike any person known from the ancient world, in Augustine we have a first-hand account of his education. In his *Confessions,* Augustine provides a detailed description of what the experience of education was like.[13] He famously hated the study of Greek and loved to read about the tears of Dido.[14] These stories provided *topoi* which an experienced orator would draw from in their public speeches to persuade a judge and jury to decide in favor of one's client. Indeed, even in the *Confessions* themselves, they continue to serve as *topoi,* if only to highlight in relief that very thing from which he was attempting to extricate himself. In our assessment of Augustine's education, we will draw on what Augustine tells of his own education in *Confessions* book 1, as well as what can be gleaned from late ancient rhetorical manuals like those composed by Cicero and Quintilian's in order to round out what that education would have been like for Augustine.

At a young age, probably seven, the young Augustine went to a grammarian in Thagaste to begin the long journey of the orator's education.[15] Despite what we might think given our distance in time, North Africa produced some of the best speakers of Latin in the late ancient world.[16] The broad outlines of this education, however, were consistent throughout the empire. It would have been a narrow education; the main purpose of which was to learn to read the standard authors (Vergil, Cicero, Terrence, and Sallust) and learn to speak like them and to use those sources to produce persuasive orations.[17] Augustine summarizes the point of his education:

13 *conf.* 1.9.14–1.10.16; 1.13.20–1.18.29.

14 *conf.* 1.13.20.

15 Marrou, *History*, 265.

16 Ausonius is one major example besides Augustine. See also Juvenal's description of African education as *nutricula causidicorum africa* Satires 7.147–48. Peter Brown, *Augustine of Hippo*, 23–28.

17 Brown, *Augustine of Hippo*, 24.

The program for right living presented to me as a boy was that I must obey my mentors, so that I might get on in this world and excel in the skills of the tongue (*artibus linguis*), skills which lead to high repute (*ad honorem hominum*) and deceitful riches (*falsas divitias*). To this end, I was sent to school to learn my letters, though I, poor wretch, could see no point in them.[18]

As is evident, the later Augustine disdained the intended objectives as they led to *falsas divitias* and *honorem hominum*. These "deceitful riches" recalls the quote from above which describes the teacher of rhetoric as sitting on a chair of lies. He deceitfully sells the use of the tongue to gain not only money, but also *honorem hominum,* lit. (honor among humans). This end of honor would prove seductive for Augustine up until his late twenties.

Honor among humans was as great of a lure for Augustine, as was the wealth and praise that it might also bring. Although disdaining this practice later in his life, as when he was writing *conf.* 1 around 397, Augustine learns to love the honor and praise he receives as he progresses through his education.[19] One of his favorite parts of his learning as a child was the contest of speaking in the guise of a character from the ancient author he was learning. He writes:

I hankered to win myself glory (*amans in certaminibus superbas victorias*) in our contests, and to have my ears tickled by tall stories which only made them itch more hotly; and all the while that same curiosity more and more inflamed my eyes with lust for the public shows which are the games of grown-ups. The people who provide these entertainments enjoy such celebrity and public esteem that nearly all of them hope their children will follow their example; and yet they are quite prepared to see those children beaten for watching similar shows to the detriment of their study, study which, as their parents hope, will bring them to a position in which they in turn will provide the shows![20]

Pride will become the chief sin which would haunt Augustine throughout his life. The very education his parents paid for only seemed to hasten his demise

---

18 *conf.* 1.9.14 (CCSL 27.8; WSA I/1, 49).
19 Brown, *Augustine*, 178.
20 *conf.* 1.10.16 (CCSL 27:9; WSA I/1, 50).

in the chief sin of man.[21] The young Augustine had become so twisted through his education that he learned to love pride more than anything else. His parents had sent him to school to learn to use his words to win contests and "public esteem." The ability to be successful in this education required the right kinds of words and classical allusions as sources and examples.

Augustine goes into depth about only one of these contests which illustrate the kinds of entertainments he described above. As a means to spur the students on to learn to declaim, Augustine's *magister* organized a competition of impersonating a god. The ancient rhetorical manuals called the practice of impersonating a god *prosopopeia* or *ethopoia*, "impersonation," which are rooted in the Progymnasmata. The Progymnasmata was a guide for how a student progressed in his formation to become proficient in the art of speaking. This was essentially the outline of the curriculum of ancient education.[22] Quintilian, a great orator and writer of the most comprehensive guides to ancient education, wrote about *prosopopeia,* "We are even allowed in this form of speech to bring down the gods from heaven or raise the dead; cities and nations even acquire a voice."[23] So the goal of this exercise within the Progymnasmata was to give voice to a pagan god or character drawn from an important classical source.

In this particular case, Augustine chose to embellish on the anger and pain of Juno when this goddess could not prevent Aeneas from going to Italy. Augustine's magister had organized this into a competition where, "That boy was adjudged (*dicebat laudabilius*) the best speaker who most convincingly suggested emotions of anger and grief and clothed them in apt words, as befitted the dignity of the person represented."[24] The young student was described as *laudabilius* (praiseworthy), not the goddess about whom he was

21 See chapter 1.

22 Marrou, *History of Education,* 172–75. Cf. Quintilian, *Institutio Oratoria* 1.9.2 (LCL 124: 208–209): "Let them learn then to tell Aesop's fables, which follow on directly from their nurses' stories, in pure and unpretentious language; then let them achieve the same slender elegance in a written version." For a contemporary study on the place of the Progymnasmata in Augustine's education, see: M. C. McCarthy, "Augustine's Mixed Feelings: Vergil's 'Aeneid' and the Psalms of David in the 'Confessions,'" *Harvard Theological Review* 4, (2009): 465.

23 Quintillian, *Institutio Oratoria* 9.2. ed. and trans. D. A. Russell, *The Orator's Education* (Cambridge: Loeb, 2001), 51.

24 *conf.* 1.17.27 (CCSL 27:15; WSA I/1, 58). Cf. Virgil's *Aenead* 1.37–49.

speaking. The contrast between the *praedicator* and the *orator* is critical. Once Augustine assumes the *cathedra Christi* he will be speaking on behalf of the God for whom he hopes to garner praise. In the *Confessions*, he begins the book by calling God *laudabilis*, rather than seeking to be called that himself.[25]

The voice which the oratorical student used for their god or character had to be clothed in the proper speech. The orator's education provided the time and discipline to acquire these habits of speech. Throughout their education, ancient students were taught to avoid certain solecisms and barbarisms, which their exemplars avoided.[26] Augustine describes it this way:

> Men were set up as example (*imitandi proponebantur*) for me to imitate who would have been mortified if, when they were recounting some acts of theirs (acts not wrong in themselves), they had been criticized for mispronunciation or making a grammatical error (*cum barbarismo aut soloecismo*). But if they gave full and elaborate descriptions of their immoral behavior in rounded and well-constructed phraseology, they boasted of the praise they won for it (*laudati gloriabantur*).[27]

If the education centered on language, the greatest error a student could commit was transgressing the grammatical code. Their models would have thus been "mortified" if they did not follow their rules for imitation found in the proper *auctores* (authorities).[28] Of course, the subject matter held no importance, merely the fact that the person describing it spoke without an error of speech. If this were done well, as it was in the case of Augustine, the use of proper speech led to praise in which the speaker could take pride. Augustine learned the speech proper to an orator through the imitation of proper authors, like Cicero.[29]

This notion of imitation is still formative for the later Augustine in his preaching. He still considers the *praedicator* to be a model for those gathered

---

25 Contrast this with the first line of the *conf.* 1.1.1, "magnus es domine et laudabilis valde."

26 Barbarism and Solecism will be covered more in depth in chapter 4.

27 *conf.* 1.18.28 (CCSL 27:15–16; WSA I/1, 58–59). cf. Suetonius, *frg.* 176, "soloecismus in sensu fit, barbarismus in voce"; Augustine's *doctr. chr.* 2.13.19. We will return to this in chapter 4.

28 Cf. Catherine Chin, *Grammar and Christianity*, 16–17.

29 He describes his first encounter at *conf.* 3.4.7.

to hear him. As a preacher, his efforts of speaking are intended to convince people to follow him as he follows Christ. He does not want them to imitate him to gain acclaim either for himself, or for those who would imitate him. The point is not that Augustine tried to unwind his rhetorical education, but that it must be reimagined in light of the truth that God became humble in the Word made flesh.

Later in his life as bishop, Augustine will be criticized for being too much like a sophist in his engagement with the Donatists. In the *Contra Cresconium*, Cresconius contends that Augustine practices *ars mala,* drawing on Plato's critique of the Sophists in the mouth of Socrates in the Apology.[30] At the end of the first book of the treatise, Augustine summarizes how he understands eloquence properly understood. He writes, "Thus, I have proved from the holy scriptures also, and from lucid reason that any eloquence and dialectic need not be feared by those who contend for the truth."[31] From this, it is evident that Augustine does not outright disdain rhetoric and clever speech, provided that it is used in defense of the truth, much like Plato argues in the Apology.[32]

Returning to the standard Greco-Roman education, the process of learning to become a *vir bonus, dicendi peritus* led to what later writers would characterize as a different class of human. Diomedes Grammaticus (late 4th century), known only by his oratorical manual the *Ars Diomedis*, wrote this in his *proemium* to his work:

> It still remains that individual things are steadfastly committed to memory (by thinking again) so that this work does not vanish in vain with time. By this work, we are recognized to stand above the unskilled, as much as they seem to differ from cattle. The unskilled harm by the syntax of their speech through the greatness of their rusticity. Indeed, they darken and pollute the polished light which comes forward through art.[33]

30 *Cresc.* 1.2.3 CSEL 52 (M. Petschenig, 1909), 327.

31 *Cresc.* 1.34.40 (CSEL 52. 358), translation my own.

32 Marina McCoy, *Plato on the Rhetoric of Philosophers and Sophists* (Cambridge: Cambridge University Press, 2008).

33 *Ars Grammatica,* "praefatio" (*Grammatici Latini* 1.299.1, translation mine), "superest ut singula recolendo memoriae tenaci mandentur, ne frustra cum tempore euanescat labor, quo tanto maxime rudibus praestare cognoscimur, qui rusticitatis enormitate incultique sermonis ordine sauciant, immo deformant examussim normatam

Those people who go through the rhetorical education learn through severe punishments how to speak in a form of Latin that required tremendous work. The grammarian labored to produce people who spoke the highest caliber of Latin, hammered into the minds of young students through painful lessons of forced memory. The speech of the unpolished rustics, although similar in some respects to the Latin which the grammarian taught the wealthy students, harmed (*saucient*) the pure speech of the grammarians. Diomedes' *proemium* establishes a three-tiered ordering of living creatures: 1) the beasts of the field who cannot speak at all, 2) the field laborers who worked with them in a degraded form of Latin, and 3) the men who learned polished Latin in grammar and speech. He says that the difference between the ones who could speak correctly, differed from the *rudes, incoliti* (unpolished, uncultivated) as far as they differed from cattle. The only way one could learn what the grammarian taught was through great hardship and toil. It was *labor*. And this labor produced men who could lead society with their beautiful words. Through such efforts, Augustine was being inaugurated into a different class of humans.

Cicero aimed at this same end when he says in one of his last works to his son about the intent of his education:

> But it is essential to every inquiry about duty that we keep before our eyes how far superior man is by nature to cattle and other beasts: they have no thought except for sensual pleasure and this they are impelled by every instinct to seek; but man's mind is nurtured by study and meditation; he is always either investigating or doing, and he is captivated by the pleasure of seeing and hearing. Nay, even if a man is more than ordinarily inclined to sensual pleasures, provided, of course that he be not quite on a level with the beasts of the field (*for some people are men only in name, not in fact*).[34]

---

orationis integritatem politumque lumen eius infuscant ex arte prolatum, quanto ipsi a pecudibus differre uideantur."

34 Cicero *de officiis* 1.30.105 (LCL 30: 106–7): "Sed pertinet ad omnem officii quaestionem semper in promptu habere, quantum natura hominis pecudibus reliquisque beluis antecedat; illae nihil sentiunt nisi voluptatem ad eamque feruntur omni impetu, hominis autem mens discendo alitur et cogitando, semper aliquid aut anquirit aut agit videndique et audiendi delectatione ducitur. Quin etiam, si quis est paulo ad voluptates propensior, modo ne sit ex pecudum genere (*sunt enim quidam homines non re, sed nomine*)." Italics mine.

In this passage, Cicero develops a similar three-tiered hierarchy, though not as firm as that of Diomedes.

Cicero of course wrote several centuries before the time of Augustine, but the result of education was still often the cultivation of honor and pride in those so educated as we will see in the case of Cicero.[35] In *de Officiis*, Cicero says in his introduction that nature and reason have given occasion for humans to learn to live honorably. To wit:

> And it is no mean manifestation of Nature and Reason that man is the only animal that has a feeling for order, for propriety, for moderation in word and deed; It is from these elements that is forged and fashioned that moral goodness which is the subject of this inquiry— something that, even though it be not generally ennobled, is still worthy of all honour (*honestum, quod etiamsi nobilitatum non sit*); and by its own nature, we correctly maintain, it merits praise, even though it be praised by none.[36]

Roman law appears to have favored the *honestiores* over the *humiliores*.[37] Whether Cicero meant it in precisely this fashion is hard to say. Contrasting an *honestior* and *humilior* provides some helpful depth to how the distinction will be used by Augustine who, as an orator, would shun anything associated with *humilis* as a man legitimately pursuing a career as an *honestior*. Recall above that Augustine craved "*honor hominum*" as well, the same root word as Cicero uses here.[38]

In contrast to Diomedes, Cicero certainly includes the import of learning Latin and Greek well, but he does not say that it is the language itself which

---

35 Cicero, *de officiis* 2.14.51 (LCL 30:221): "Then, too, briefs for the defense are most likely to bring glory and popularity to the pleader, and all the more so, if ever it falls to him to lend his aid to one who seems to be oppressed and persecuted by the influence of someone in power."

36 Cicero, *de officiis* 1.4.14 (LCL 30: 16–17).

37 G. Cardascia, "L'apparition dans le Droit des Classes D'"Honestiores" et d'"Humiliroes" *Revue historique de droit français et* étranger V. 27 (1950), 461–85. By one account, Augustine would have been born an *honestior*. Lee Yun Too, "Education, Grammar, and Rhetoric," *Augustine in Context* (Cambridge: Cambridge University Press: 2017), 80.

38 *conf.* 1.9.14 (CCSL 27.8; WSA I/1, 49).

transforms the human into a better kind of person.[39] Cicero still encourages his son in *de Officiis* to pursue virtue. Diomedes, on the other hand, refers to the "*incolti sermonis*" and "*rusticatas*" of those who are above the beasts, but lower than the educated.[40] It is only the speech, not the virtue, which makes the difference. The goal of late ancient education had ignored and subsumed the *vir bonus,* into the *dicendi peritus*. It was no longer important to have a virtuous character, merely the right kind of speech. The milieu in which Augustine was educated retained its emphasis on the *dicendi peritus*. Such an emphasis persisted among educated Christians well after the time of Augustine.[41]

This education led to the kind of pride that Augustine speaks of so frequently in the first eight books of the *Confessions*. As Augustine recounts:

> I began in the company of these people to study treatises on eloquence (*eloquentiae*). This was a discipline in which I longed to excel, though my motive was the damnably proud desire to gratify my human vanity. In the customary course of study I had discovered a book by an author called Cicero, whose language is almost universally admired, though not its inner spring (*pectus*).[42]

In his first encounter with Cicero, Augustine thinks that he will learn from the great orator how to speak well (*eloquentia*). That was how he had been taught to read him by his magister. They ignored the heart of his works; its *pectus*.[43]

---

39 Cicero, *de officiis* 1.1.2

40 By the time Augustine learns rhetoric from these late antique grammarians, the style has become so obtuse that it is difficult for many learned men to even understand. Marrou notes, "Il ne suffit pas pour les [late ancient orators] caracteriser de dire que l'eloquence était devenue plus vide, plus artificielle, plus scolaire, plus fleurie. Il faut prendre conscience du degré que chacun de ses défauts pouvait avoir atteint," Marrou, *Saint Augustin et la Fin de la Culture Antique* (Paris: Editions E. De Broccard, 1958), 526. He goes on to characterize the style of his period "l'extrême décadence." Augustine's education was characterized by this same extreme decadence, which has departed from even the intent of the style of the authors they claimed to love, like Cicero.

41 Sidonius, a later Gallic bishop, continues to follow the thinking of Diomedes when he writes, *Epistulae* 4.17.2 (LCL 420: 128–29): "the educated are no less superior to the unlettered than men are to beasts" *Quanto antecellunt beluis homines, tanto anteferri rusticis institutos.*

42 *conf.* 3.4.7 (CCSL 27:30; WSA I/1, 80).

43 James O'Donnell makes the bewildering claim that Augustine was "belittling"

Despite the efforts of his *magister*, Augustine learns something which will ultimately lead him away from the vain pursuits of rhetoric. He writes:

> My interest in the book was not aroused by its usefulness in the honing of my verbal skills (which was supposed to be the object of the studies I was now pursuing …); no, it was not merely as an instrument for sharpening my tongue that I used that book, for it had won me over not by its style but by what it had to say.[44]

He became persuaded to seek wisdom from the *Hortensius*. He did not immediately find the wisdom of God but was set on a path which ultimately led to that. No longer was his only aim verbal skill, but the wisdom contained in those words. Seeking wisdom was in its own way a rejection of the teaching he had received from his teachers.[45] The ability to penetrate deeper into the meaning of the text will serve Augustine well in his role as *praedicator*.

In his education, from ages seven to roughly nineteen, Augustine learned the great works of Latin and Greek, how to speak well in using them, and who to imitate in order to become the most successful orator. At one point, while reading Cicero from his work the *Tusculan Disputations,* Augustine describes the importance of imitation:

> Who among our hooded masters of oratory give sober consideration to the cry of one who was of the same clay as themselves, "Homer invented these stories and attributed human actions to the gods, but I wish he had rather provided us with examples of divine behavior"? It would be truer to say that Homer did indeed make up these tales, and thereby seemed to invest the disgraceful deeds of human beings with an aura of divinity, so that depraved actions should be reckoned

---

Cicero with the quote mentioned above. Although it seems quite evident from context that Augustine is saying his teachers only read him for his words, not for the deeper truths they conveyed. This seems to be what he means by *pectus*. See: O'Donnell, *Augustine: A New Biography* (New York: Ecco, 2005), 189.

44 *conf.* 3.4.7 (CCSL 27:30; WSA I/1, 80).

45 Clavier comes to a similar conclusion, "He does not criticize so much the actual eloquence taught as the failure to unite that eloquence with truth" Clavier, *Eloquent Wisdom*, 60.

depraved no longer, since anyone who behaved so could pretend to be imitating not abandoned humans but the gods above (*non homines perditos sed caelestes deos videretur imitatus*).[46]

What Augustine learned from these stories and from those authors he read in early life, he desired to imitate. In this case, the fabricated gods of Homer provided quite negative models for imitation.[47] This suggests the centrality of imitation in the thought of Augustine throughout the *Confessions*, and even in his theology of preaching. The preeminent classicist and historian, James O'Donnell, writes in his multi-volume work on the *Confessions*, "Mimesis is a recognized path to behavior acquisition (22x in *conf.*), but how models are treated determines whether the behavior is good or bad."[48] Moving into the next section of the argument, it will be important to keep in mind the crucial category of imitation as we will described the examples of Cicero as the prototypical orator and Ambrose as the prototypical preacher for Augustine.

Cicero, "A Good Man Experienced in Speech"

This section explores how the orator uses his words to gain the acclaim that the orators in training, like Augustine, so earnestly desired. The language and sources learned through education provided the weapons which the mad orators deployed in their *bella forensia*, as Augustine had called them. We will turn to one particular legal case in the long corpus of Cicero's legal work, the *Pro Sexto Roscio Amerino*.[49] This case, read in the proper way, showcases how an orator used their words to gain fame.

Before wading into the text of the *Pro Sexto Roscio Amerino*, it will be important to note that although we will be using Cicero as the kind of orator which provided a sort of negative type, Augustine's relationship to him is

46 *conf.* 1.16.25 (CCSL 27.14; WSA I/1, 57).

47 Quintilian, *Instituto Oratoria* 2.2.8 (LCL 124: 272) "Licet enim satis exemplorum ad imitandum ex lectione suppeditet, tamen viva illa, ut dicitur, vox alit plenius, praecipueque praeceptoris quem discipuli, si modo recte sunt instituti, et amant et verentur. Vix autem dici potest quanto libentius imitemur eos quibus vavemus."

48 O' Donnell, *Augustine: Confessions II, Commentary on Book 1–7* (Oxford: Oxford University Press, 1992), 87.

49 Most of the historical information surrounding this particular speech are found in Ann Vasaly, "Cicero's Early Speeches," *Brill's Companion to Cicero*, ed. James M. May (Leiden: Brill, 2002), 77–111.

complicated. As noted in *Confessions* 3, Augustine began reading Cicero in a manner quite a bit different from the way he was taught. Cicero was first and foremost read in the oratorical schools of the late antique period as the example of the finest manner of speaking. This would persist throughout the history of Latin, especially in the Renaissance and even contemporary studies of Latin. When Augustine, however, reads Cicero's *Hortensius*, he realizes that Cicero himself did not think that mere purity of language constituted a truly wise and good person.[50] The *bonus vir* of course knew how to speak Latin and Greek, but it was ultimately wisdom which he was pursuing.[51] Augustine thinks that this is right, even after his conversion. He does not think that Cicero understood the humility of Christ, which is the one thing that the philosophers lack.[52] Augustine can thus mine Cicero for a great many insights, excepting of course his teaching of humility.[53] We will now turn to Cicero's first great public oration to see what those who read him would have learned to imitate.

In the year 81 BCE, the son of a relatively poor young nobleman, Sextus Roscius, was accused of murdering his father, the elder Sextus Roscius. Marcus Tullius Cicero, a young *novus homo* with no public litigating experience, took up his case. Almost all the evidence about the particulars of the case comes from Cicero's own written record of his speech.[54] The young orator seizes on the opportunity to defend someone and make a name for himself. Cicero convincingly advocates that the younger Sextus Roscius does not in fact kill his father. Rather, he argues it was the work of two relatives, Titus Roscius Magnus and Titus Roscius Capito, with the help of a powerful freedman named Lucius Cornelius Chrysogonus. Chrysogonus wanted the

50 Cicero writes in *De Inventione*, "For my own part, after long thought, I have been led by reason itself to hold this opinion first and foremost, that wisdom without eloquence does little for the good of states, but that eloquence without wisdom is generally highly disadvantageous and is never helpful" (*De inv.* 1,1 [LCL 386: 2–3]).

51 *conf.* 3.4.7 (CCSL 27:30; WSA I/1, 80).

52 *ep.* 118.3.17, (WSA II/2 115), "But the Platonists were not able to become the living example of true reason as those other philosophers were able to become living examples of their errors. For they were all lacking the example of divine humility, which was revealed at the most opportune moment by our Lord Jesus Christ."

53 During his time in Milan, Augustine will meet Marius Victorinus, who models how an orator can read Cicero with philosophical insight. The example of Victorinus is another means for Augustine's conversion because Victorinus submits even his philosophical and rhetorical wisdom to Christ, *conf.* 8.2.4–5.

54 Andrew Dyck, *Pro Sexto Roscio* (Cambridge: Cambridge University Press, 2010), 4–12, 17–19.

property of the elder Sextus Roscius and was able to purchase his land at a reduced price because Chrysogonus added the elder Sextus to the proscription list of Lucius Cornelius Sulla. As the recently named dictator, Sulla created proscription lists to kill all those who opposed him and confiscate their property for little or no remuneration.[55] Sextus Roscius fell prey to this violent political situation in the tumultuous late republican period.

Cicero saw this moment as a great political opportunity and uses the trial to advance his cause. Historian Ann Vasaly describes the speech of the defense of Sextus Roscius in this way, "In this speech, then, we witness the young Cicero addressing both his original as well as his reading audience on crucial political issues, crafting a public image that would transcend the circumstances of Roscius' trial."[56] Cicero knew that words could be used as a species of action which would gain him fame and glory. In the terms of SAT, Cicero knew that the perlocutionary effect of his words would be greater than what they say at the locutionary level.

The insights of SAT can aid our understanding of how Cicero was able to use the case for an end greater than the case itself. First, at the locutionary level, Cicero lays out the case like this, "It is argued that Sextus Rosicus killed his father."[57] This accusation, analyzed as a locution, could be simply true or false. Either Sextus did kill his father, which would be parricide and one of the greatest Roman crimes, or he did not. The end of Cicero's words, the proximate goal of the illocution, is to persuade the judges that Sextus did not kill his father. He takes a position for the immediate purpose of the speech that it is true. He proceeds to make his case about why this is so, the illocutionary level of the defense.

In another place in the same speech, Cicero's words can be tied closer to the insights of SAT in so far as we can see the intended action of Cicero's speech. Cicero argues:

> In the first place, I request Chrysogonus to be satisfied with our wealth and property, and not to ask for our life-blood; secondly, I ask you, gentlemen, to resist the villainy of audacious rascals, to alleviate

---

55 J. H. Freese, "Introduction," *Cicero* VI, LCL 240 (Cambridge: Harvard University Press, 1930) 113.

56 Vasaly, "Cicero's Early Speeches," 81–82.

57 Cicero, *Pro Sexto Roscio* 1.13 (LCL 240: 154–55): *"Occidisse patrem Sex. Roscius arguitur"* (Translation mine).

the misfortunes of the innocent, and in the cause of Sextus Roscius
to avert a danger which threatens us all. But if any ground for the
accusation, any suspicion of guilt or even the slightest thing can be
discovered, which would make them appear to have had at least some
reason for bringing the charge, and lastly if you find any other explanation of it than the booty of which I have spoken, we make no
objection to the life of Roscius being abandoned to their passion.[58]

The sentence takes the form of a request to the jury that they "alleviate the
misfortunes of the innocent" by exonerating Sextus for the crime of killing
his father. His illocution is a request, a form of a directive, in the language
outlined above. Finally, the illocution and the stating of the sentence in this
specific way aim for the result of persuading the judges to so act. In this
case, Cicero, and by extension Sextus, desire that the judges acquit him and
find him not guilty of killing his father. Whether the judges decide to so act
is still outside the control of Cicero. The best he can do is to arrange his
arguments in such a way that the judges can understand and follow his line of
reasoning to have the chance of being persuaded to acquit Sextus. This being
so persuaded is the most immediate perlocution of the speech.

Cicero does not care about the truth or falsity of the locution: Sextus
Roscius killed his father. On the surface, the whole point of this case would
have been to get to the bottom of whether this was true. If it were, the
younger Sextus Roscius should be put to death. If it was not, then he should
be acquitted. But Cicero knows that the trial can do more for him if he wins.
So, he does not particularly care whether Sextus Roscius killed his father. The
ability to ignore the truth or falsity of the claim for the sake of gaining fame
troubles the wizened Augustine, as we described from *On Christian Teaching* 4.
It is this ambivalence about the truth which leads Augustine to conclude that
oratory is too often only used for *bella forensia*. The words could be used to
fight battles, irrespective of their veracity or the content of the words. Indeed,
he finds that his own teachers seem to be reading Cicero just for his ability to
speak, reading against the stated aims of Cicero's own account of rhetoric.

On a higher level, which demonstrates the power of rhetoric and its
broader aims, Cicero and rhetoricians could use their speech to do more than
merely persuade juries. They also performed speeches to advance in their
political careers. Cicero knew that he could not achieve much on the battlefield

---

58 *pro sexto roscio* 1.17 (LCL 240, 126–27).

like Caesar, nor did he have the wealth to buy an army and gain political influence like Pompey, but he could use his oratory in front of nobleman, *honestiores*, to gain an influence in Roman politics. And so, he did. We know the name of Cicero because he was successful in using his words and oratory to achieve not only influence and power in Rome but a legacy.

Vasaly is once again helpful in providing context for some of the defense speeches of Cicero. She argues that Cicero used this speech to gain authority:

> From the time of the *Pro Roscio Amerino*, Cicero had begun to be a public man, and for him the Roman public man every public event was to some extent 'definitional'—a moment in which his persona was further elucidated and his *auctoritas* enlarged or diminished. Therefore, even if we resist the temptation to use the speeches to determine Cicero's 'real' sentiments, a rhetorical analysis of the orations demands consideration of their attempted manipulation of the multiple audiences to which they were addressed.... As Laurand has written, "[they] were the pamphlets of their time ... functioning not simply as models for young people [studying rhetoric] but also acting upon public opinion."[59]

Cicero manipulated his audiences through the perlocution of his speeches. As we already know from his place in the canons of rhetoric, he was quite successful. From a historical standpoint, we cannot say whether or not Cicero believed his own locution that Sextus Roscius did not kill his father. This would have been part of the trouble the later Christian Augustine had with the kind of work that a lawyer was required to do with his words.[60] They become empty if they are used only to gain a lawyer fame.

This case was but the beginning of Cicero making a name for himself towards the goal of completing the *cursus honorum*. This case is about Cicero

59 Vasaly, "Cicero's Early Speeches," 106.

60 *doctr. chr* 4.2.3 (CCSL 32:117; WSA I/11, 202): "Rhetoric, after all, being the art of persuading people to accept something, whether it is true or false, would anyone dare to maintain that truth should stand there without any weapons in the hands of its defenders against falsehood; that those speakers, that is to say, who are trying to convince their hearers of what is untrue, should know how to get them on their side, to gain their attention and have them eating out of their hands by their opening remarks, while these who are defending the truth should not?"

showing off his oratorical ability to gain supporters for his rise through the ranks of the *coursus honorum*, which he eventually completes.[61] The first sentence of the case demonstrates that really this whole episode centers on Cicero himself:

> Gentlemen of the jury, you probably wonder why, when so many eminent orators and illustrious citizens remain seated, it is I, rather than any of them, who have risen to speak, though neither in age, nor ability, nor authority, can I be compared with them. All those whom you see here supporting the accused are of opinion that in this case an unjust charge, concocted by an unexampled act of villainy, should be repelled, but dare not undertake the task themselves owing to the unfavourable conditions of the times.[62]

No one else will defend Sextus Roscius because the dictator Sulla lurks behind the scenes. If Cicero can just get this jury to acquit through his ornamented speech, he can shock the noble Senatorial classes and Cicero can gain acclaim for himself, the upstart lawyer. Cicero makes this point in a later treatise, *de Officiis*, arguing: "it is always the business of the judge in a trial to find out the truth; it is sometimes the business of the advocate to maintain what is plausible, even if it be not strictly true."[63] The younger Sextus Roscius and the truth of the situation minimally concern Cicero. His defense of Roscius is merely a means to an end.[64]

The ornamented speech, carefully worded, achieves its composer's aim. Cicero becomes central to Roman education because of that very eloquence, which won him this first case among many. His words worked to earn him recognition among the upper classes. Upon reflection, later in his career, Cicero prides himself on how this particular case launched his career, even if he did not consider it one of his finest speeches.[65] The

---

61 Vasaly, "Cicero's Early Speeches," 80.

62 *pro sexto roscio* 1.17 (LCL 240: 126–27).

63 *de officiis* 2.14.51 (LCL 30:221). Cicero goes on to say that he would not say this in an ethical treatise, but clearly this indicates the frame of mind of a trial lawyer.

64 In *de officiis* 2.14.52, Cicero explains that one uses cases to gain popularity and glory if one defends someone of lower status against the influence of someone in power and specifically uses this case as evidence for his own deployment of the tactic.

65 *Brutus* 90.312; *Orator* 30.107.

victory in this case did not come without a price, as Cicero had to flee Athens under the pretense of sickness to avoid the wrath of Sulla.[66] Once Sulla lost his dictatorial power (81 BCE), however, Cicero returns and quickly find himself competing with Hortensius for fame as the greatest lawyer and defense attorney.[67] His calculated move to defend Roscius worked to gain him fame, catapulting his career.

Later in his life, Cicero mentions this case in his words on oratory, which suggest how he understood these defense speeches to work. In one of his three works on rhetoric, *Brutus*, he writes:

> Thus my first criminal case, spoken in behalf of Sextus Roscius, won such favourable comment (*tantum commenationis*) that I was esteemed not incompetent to handle any litigation whatsoever. There followed then in quick succession many other cases which I brought into court, carefully worked out, and, as the saying is, smelling somewhat of the midnight oil.[68]

He won such great approval (*tantum commenationis*) that he received a great number of further trials. The perlocution of his speech on the jury and the larger Roman world was exceedingly successful. His words and his ability to compose arguments garnered him great fame.

Many years later, Cicero would plead a case on defense of Sulla, his erstwhile opponent. This case pits Cicero against one of his long-time friends Torquatus.[69] In short, Cicero defends his former antagonist by arguing a case against one of Sulla's freedmen, Chrysogonus. Although the reasons for Cicero's choosing to defend Sulla are somewhat murky, it appears that Cicero wanted a wealthy nobleman to oppose an otherwise

66 *De officiis*, 2.14.51.

67 Vasaly, "Cicero's Early Speeches," 88. This same Hortensius becomes the namesake for the famous work which inspired Augustine 400 years later.

68 Cicero, *Brutus* 90.312 (LCL 342: 271–72).

69 C. Macdonald, "Introduction," *Pro Sulla* (LCL 324: 307): "It is surprising at first sight that he was ready to take the part of a man whom he clearly did not like against so close a friend as Torquatus, but we have to realize what deep personal differences could be overridden in the interests of *amicitia*. Nonetheless Torquatus was deeply offended by Cicero's unexpected defense of Sulla—after all the story was that his father was to have been murdered by Sulla."

strong political faction, the *Populares* under Pompey.[70] The historical details only serve to demonstrate that orations—and what an orator says while defending someone in a law court—create a difficult situation for the person concerned with truth.

What these cases, first the *Pro Sexto Roscio Amerino* and then the *Pro Sulla,* showcase is the extent to which Cicero uses trials for his own personal advancement. In the language of SAT, the lawyer Cicero does not care about the truth of the locution, he merely illocutes in his defense of his clients to get the jury to acquit, his perlocution. When speech is detached from the truth it becomes a weapon in the hands of someone who does not care about the costs of how they use their words. This is unacceptable to Augustine who begins to realize the power of words through a humble preacher Ambrose. Ambrose models in his words and deeds for Augustine the truth contained in the scriptures which detail how God came to earth to teach humans humility.

Ambrose, "The Humble Preacher"

To this point, we have seen how Roman education instilled the desire for ambition in a young orator through learning how to speak well in contests and encouraged the orator to see himself as a different class of human. This language he learned through the reading and imitating of previous great orators like Cicero, the emblematic *vir bonus dicendi peritus*. The famed Cicero used his ability in language and speaking to gain for himself a wide sphere of influence in the greater Roman world. All with the power of his language, a man well versed in the classics could gain the praise of the influential people to propel himself forward in worldly achievements. Augustine was able to work his way up to one of the highest positions in the Empire using his oratorical abilities, selling his own giftedness at rhetoric to aspiring students and capitalizing on his role as an imperial propagandist.

In the mold of an *honestus vir*, Augustine spent his energy speaking as much as possible. Reading had only been a practice to gather words and ideas for how to speak with a certain sort of decadent eloquence. He learned this from teachers as he read Cicero's *Hortensius*. The goal of the reading for the teachers was that the students learn the right kind of speech. Augustine's

---

70 C. MacDonald, "Introduction," (LCL 324: 208): "If he had Sulla tied to him by the debt of a successful defense, his own situation would be greatly strengthened."

penetrating mind realized that the beauty of the language only served to underline the more noble pursuit of wisdom.

Augustine far outclassed his contemporaries in the art of public speech but found it wanting. It was not until Augustine met Ambrose that he learned the importance of listening. While this seems like a simple point, we will show that it had a profound effect on Augustine and became the source of his transformation. The humble preacher listens first. When the preacher prepares to speak on the scriptural text, one is not listening merely to a human author, but a divine author. This practice set Augustine on a different trajectory from his upbringing in the *artes liberals* centered on pride and ambition.

This ambition, fostered in the education and culture of Augustine, was not healthy in Augustine's more mature evaluation. In a concise summary of Augustine's former state of mind as ambitious orator, he laments:

> The prestigious (*honesta*) course of studies I was following looked as its goal to the law-courts, in which I was destined to excel and where I would earn a reputation (*laudibilior*) all the higher in the measure that my performance was the more unscrupulous. So blind can people be that they glory even in their blindness! Already I was the ablest student in the school of rhetoric. At this I was elated and vain and swollen with pride (*tumebam typho*).[71]

O'Donnell notes that throughout the *Confessions*, Augustine uses the Greek term *typho* as a "leit-motif for ambitious pride."[72] The pride which comes with public acclamation and the designation *laudabilis* so inflates the recipient that he blinds himself to those around him. We have seen that this began for Augustine as a young schoolboy and continues throughout his career as a rhetorician.

This blind ambition led Augustine along to Milan, the center of the empire, where Ambrose happened to be a bishop. The young imperial rhetor Augustine wanted to get to know his cultural surroundings and went to listen to Ambrose orate. He describes his frame of mind thusly:

71 *conf.* 3.3.6 (CCSL 27.29; WSA I/1, 79).

72 The full quote with additional references "typho: A leit-motif for ambitious pride; see on 7.9.13 ('typho turgidum'); often associated with 'swollenness'; with tumidus or tumesco at *ciu.* 11.33, c. Iul. 4.3.28, en. Ps. 149.10, *s.* 4.30.33." (*Augustine: Confessions II*, 161).

I was taking no trouble to learn from what Ambrose was saying, but interested only in listening to how he said it, for that futile concern had remained with me, despairing as I did that any way to you could be open to humankind. Nonetheless as his words, which I enjoyed, penetrated my mind, the substance, which I overlooked, seeped in with them, for I could not separate the two. As I opened my heart to appreciate how skillfully he spoke, the recognition that he was speaking the truth crept in at the same time, though only by slow degrees.[73]

Apparently forgetting the lesson he learned from reading Cicero's *Hortensius,* Augustine intends to hear Ambrose only for the quality of his language. He thinks that he can hear and listen without paying attention to the content, like his teachers in the rhetorical schools. As he listened, some of what Ambrose preached pierced the tumor of pride of Augustine. He relearned the lesson from Cicero and found the *pectus* of Ambrose's preaching.

Thanks to the painstaking work of several scholars, we have some idea of what some of those sermons which Augustine heard from Ambrose might have been.[74] Writing about his time listening to Ambrose, Augustine describes the transformative power of the phrase from 2 Corinthians 3:6, "The letter kills but the spirit gives life." In *Confessions* 6.4.6, Augustine discusses the realization that he can read the scriptures at a deeper level by looking at the spirit, rather than merely the letter.[75] Ascertaining this difference provides the mental framework for seeing that more was to be gleaned from scripture than met his oratorically skewed mind.

73 *conf.* 5.14.24 (CCSL 27:71; WSA I/1, 131–32).

74 Wilbrand, "Zur Chronologie einiger Schriften des hl. Ambrosius," *Historiches Jahrbuch*, *XLI* (1921), 1–19, Palanque *S. Ambrose et l'Empire Romain* (Paris: 1933) Appendix III, and Pierre Courcelle, *Recherches sur les "Confessions" de saint Augustin*, (Paris: Boccard, 1950) 98.

75 Michael Cameron's study on this point in Augustine's life rightly calls attention to the import of the common rhetorical training of Ambrose and Augustine. He argues that Augustine does not accept Ambrose's teaching on purely philosophical grounds, as many scholars do, but rather roots it in his rhetorical presentation, Michael Cameron, *Christ Meets Me Everywhere* (Oxford University Press: Oxford, 2012), 23–42. Our study follows Cameron's lead to look at the rhetorical backgrounds, but still looks to a different point within the preaching of Ambrose which might have been more formative on Augustine's learning the virtue of humility.

The earliest likely sermon preached in 386 by Ambrose when Augustine arrived in Milan comes from a work titled *De Jacob*.[76] Scholars have pinpointed several sermons which discuss the phrase, "The letter kills, but the spirit gives life." For the purpose of this study, we will focus on the section of the earliest sermon to coincide with the time of Augustine's listening to Ambrose' preaching which mentions humility. Several paragraphs below the point where Ambrose discusses the profound truth of the spirit in the scriptural text, he also discusses the importance of humility. Ambrose preaches:

> Learn humility, O man, and recognize the power of the apostolic teaching. Should you say that you are a slave, you are a freedman; should you boast that you are free, you are a slave. For the man who has been redeemed as a slave has his freedom, and as for the man who has been called as a free man, it is good for him to know that he is a slave of Christ, under whom servitude is safe and freedom secure.[77]

Without going into a full explication of the whole sermon, Ambrose suggests to his audience the importance of a virtue Augustine had to this point in his life resisted. Nothing about what Augustine had learned from school, or imitated in previous great rhetoricians, celebrated the virtue of humility. Now, in this sermon from a well-regarded preacher and orator, Augustine is commanded to learn a new virtue, humility. As an example of this kind of humility, Ambrose continues preaching on the scriptural teaching that there is neither slave nor free in Christ.[78] Those people Augustine would have

76 Courcelle et al. have determined that several sermons likely were preached during 386 or 387: *De Interpellatione Iob et David, in Lucam,* and *De Jacob.* Only the *de Jacob* appears to have been preached early in 386. This would have therefore been heard before Augustine decides to leave his imperial chair of rhetoric. Brown, *Augustine,* 64, suggests that Augustine was converted in late August 386. Ambrose left Milan for Trier in the summer or Autumn of 386.

77 *De Jacob* 3.12 in *Seven Exegetical Works,* trans. Michael McHugh (Washington, DC: The Catholic University of America Press, 1977), 127.

78 In *De Jacob* 3.11, Ambrose preaches from Romans 6:16 on the nature of slavery and freedom, saying, "Therefore, let our will not put us up for sale. The Apostle cries out, 'Don't you know that if you offer yourselves to anyone as obedient slaves, you are the slaves of him whom you obey, either slaves of sin to death or of obedience to justice?' If, then, we are slaves either to sin or to justice, let us consider on which side the servitude is more endurable and the fruit richer." *Seven Exegetical Works,* 126.

spurned as less than human because of their lack of ability to speak well are being set on par with freedmen, the *honestiores* with the *humiliores*. All divisions previously necessary for the kind of world Augustine was entering have been overturned by humility.

As evidence that this sermon permeated the thought of Augustine, we find him discussing scripture in a totally different fashion than he had before in *conf. 6*. In one of his prayerful asides as he tells his story, Augustine described his changed attitude toward the world and scripture after hearing Ambrose. Just one section beyond his descriptions of Ambrose's preaching he writes:

> The authority of the sacred writings seemed to me all the more deserving of reverence and divine faith in that scripture was easily accessible to every reader, while yet guarding a mysterious dignity in its deeper sense. In plain words and very humble modes of speech (*verbis apertissimis et humillimo genere loquendi*) it offered itself to everyone, yet stretched the understanding of those who were not shallow-minded. It welcomed all comers to its hospitable embrace, yet through narrow openings attracted a few to you—a few, perhaps, but far more than it would have done had it not spoken with such noble authority and drawn the crowds to its embrace by its holy humility (*sanctae humilitatis*).[79]

The words of scripture demonstrate something new for the arrogant *vir bonus, dicendi peritus*. God can be found, indeed must be found, *in humillimo genere loquendi* (the humblest kind of speaking).[80] The contrast between what Augustine had anchored his life on, i.e., elevated speech, and the God he finds in the simplest words could not be greater. He had previously thought that everything which was worth pursuing should be found in the words of those who spoke the most eloquently. This was why he wanted to become the imperial rhetor of Milan and teach rhetoric from the *cathedra*. But in fact, the

---

79 *conf.* 6.5.8 (CCSL 27:78–79; WSA I/1, 142).

80 It is worth noting that of course, this *humillimo genere loquendi* would have seemed humiliating to God to the young Augustine. He was taught to see simple speech as undignified for God. We will explore this further in chapter 4. Suffice it to say, if God chooses to use this kind of simple speech himself, it is no longer humiliating, merely humbling.

words with the most authority are in humble speech because the scriptures and the God who spoke in them was the God of all, the *inculti* and *rudes* included. Now Augustine has a reason to call this *cathedra* on which he sits as rhetor the *cathedra mendacii*. He begins to see the importance of truth versus the lies of a rhetorical education which taught that the only thing which mattered was the quality of one's language.

Just as Augustine begins to ruminate on the scriptures as preached from Ambrose, he must go before the emperor and a crowd to give a speech in the most elevated language possible for the benefit of the empire. On the day when he should have been happier than any other, when he gave his great panegyric for Valentinian II, he hated himself. Thinking of this moment in his life, he writes:

> I recall how miserable I was, and how one day you brought me to a realization of my miserable state. I was preparing to deliver a eulogy upon the emperor in which I would tell plenty of lies with the object of winning favor with the well-informed by my lying; so my heart was panting with anxiety and seething with feverish, corruptive thoughts.[81]

He knew that his words were lies praising an emperor whom he did not find praiseworthy. He was merely bought off by the fame and money he would receive as a result of this lavish public speech.[82]

With his whole life pursuits called into question, Augustine goes in search of advice from the bishop. Ambrose seemed to have great fame which

81 *conf.* 6.6.9 (CCSL 27:79; WSA I/1, 143).

82 This speech no longer exists. The form is typically called a "panegyric," a type of public address given to celebrate the accomplishments of an emperor. John Cavadini remarks on the absence of this style in Augustine, following the studies of Christine Mohrmann, "Apart from the very early sermons from the period of Augustine's presbyterate, a reading of the *Sermones ad populum* betrays not the slightest hint that there ever was a 'second sophistic'; Augustine has nothing to offer comparable to the funeral orations of Ambrose or the Eastern homilists," John Cavadini, "Simplifying Augustine," in *Educating People of Faith: Exploring the History of Jewish and Christian,* ed. John H. Van Engen (Grand Rapids, MI: Wm. B. Eerdmans, 2004), 69. For a description of how one learned to create such a piece of rhetoric, see Marrou, *Education,* 198–199. For a history of the "Second Sophistic," see George A. Kennedy, *Classical Rhetoric and Its Christian and Secular Tradition from Ancient to Modern Times* (Chapel Hill: University of North Carolina Press, 1999), 47–50.

impressed Augustine, though of course Ambrose preached the humble scriptures Augustine scorned.[83] He came to him to learn and found something which he did not expect:

> Now I regarded Ambrose as a fortunate man as far as worldly standing went (*felicem quendam hominem secundum saeculum*), since he enjoyed the respect of powerful people (*sic tantate potestates honorarent*); it was only his celibacy which seemed to me a burdensome undertaking. I had not begun to guess, still less experience in my own case, what hope he bore within him, or what a struggle he waged against the temptations to which his eminent position exposed him, or the encouragement he received in times of difficulty, or what exquisite delights he savored in his secret mouth, the mouth of his heart, as he chewed the bread of your word.

This memory of Augustine is likely written about the time he ascends into the *cathedra christi* himself. The young presbyter of Hippo recalls the great example of Ambrose and sees how he balances the honors he has from the people around him with a practice of reading and listening to the holy scriptures.[84] These same holy scriptures which had at one point seemed so poorly written to the young Ciceronian Augustine, now mediate to Augustine the humble God and so become saving words.

If the newly minted Bishop of Hippo is going to be able to succeed in this new role, he will have to continue to pray and listen to scripture to fight against temptations like Ambrose. He spent most of his life seeking the praise of men. After he is baptized, he gives up his position as a magister because the temptation would be too great to continue to seek honor. How

83 Our analysis has focused on Cicero and Ambrose, though Clavier highlights the intermediary role of the philosophical rhetoric of Marcus Victorinus. He writes, "If Augustine wished to reorient Cicero's rhetoric to the demands of Christian theology, then much of that work of adaption had been already completed by the likes of Victorinus. Although the gulf between Cicero's civic-minded orator and Augustine's preacher may have been a large one, the gulf between Victorinus's and Augustine's was much less so" (*Eloquent Wisdom*, 50).

84 Carol Harrison notices that Augustine also listens to the word in *conf.* 8 at his conversion, possibly learned from Ambrose himself. Carol Harrison, *Art of Listening in the Early Church* (Oxford: Oxford University Press, 2013), 6.

can he fight against that deep desire fostered over the course of 20 or so impressionable years?[85]

Ambrose fights it through listening to the scriptures, "chew[ing] the bread of the word" and learning from the teacher contained therein. Later in his preaching career, Augustine will come to an understanding of the place of listening and praying that he could not have known the first time he finds Ambrose in this practice. He will later say, "Your prayer is a conversation with God: when you read, God is speaking to you; when you pray, you are speaking to God."[86] The very act of reading the scriptures without speaking is listening to God. It is part of the prayer and conversation one has with the divine before the sermon. Harrison describes several aspects of listening, "In this sense, the practice of listening was just as influential on how Scripture was read and interpreted as on how it was presented and heard. Listening implies attentiveness, receptivity, openness—what Augustine describes as prayer."[87] This had never occurred to Augustine before seeing Ambrose engaged in the practice. Augustine has modeled before him a preacher who is attentive, receptive, and open to the Word of God.

Although Augustine could not speak much one-on-one with Ambrose, Ambrose does not refuse to let him see what he does with his time.[88] Augustine writes,

> He was habitually available to serve [his congregation] in their needs, and in the very scant time that he was not with them he would be refreshing either his body with necessary food or his mind with reading. When he read his eyes would travel across the pages and his mind would explore the sense, but his voice and tongue were silent.... We watched him reading silently. It was never otherwise, and so we too would sit for a long time in silence, for who would have the heart to interrupt a man so engrossed?[89]

---

85 *conf.* 9.2.2.

86 *en. Ps.* 85.7 (CCSL 39.1182; WSA III/18, 228): "oratio tua locutio est ad deum; quando legis, deus tibi loquitur; quando oras, deo loqueris."

87 Harrison, *Art of Listening*, 164.

88 For a full study of the various explanations for why Ambrose might have refused him, see: O'Donnell, *Augustine: Confessions II*, 339–43.

89 *conf.* 6.3.3 (CCSL 27:75; WSA I/1, 138–39).

Augustine finds the great preacher listening to a teacher within.[90] Before Ambrose ascended onto the *cathedra christi*, he would listen to the teacher who taught through the scriptural text.[91] The scriptures written in the *humillimo genere loquendi* were his source. He did not speak first but listened to humble speech. He was still a student listening silently to another teacher. He did not refuse others who needed his care either. Although much of his time was spent caring for his congregation in Milan, he would still steal away for some precious time to listen to the scriptures first. This man teaches Augustine lifelong lessons which impact Augustine's own theology of preaching.

Towards the end of his life, Augustine corresponds with a father, Firmus, who has sent his son through a rhetorical education to become a *vir bonus, dicendi peritus*. The father wants Augustine to be impressed by the boy's speeches. The wizened old erstwhile rhetor writes,

> The ancients thought that they should define not the man of eloquence—for eloquence can exist without wisdom—but an orator in such a way as to say that he was "a good man skilled in speaking (*eum esse dicerent uirum bonum dicendi peritum*)." If we remove from that definition what is put in the first place [i.e. *vir bonus*], what we are left with does much harm. On this account they thought and said that, when the principles of speaking are taught to fools (*cum insipientibus dantur*

90 J.A. Mazzeo contends that Augustine imitates Ambrose's silent listening in his conversion in the garden. Thus, it would have been impossible for the conversion to take place without Ambrose as an example first. He writes, "I think, therefore, that it is safe to say that we are to understand that St. Augustine had finally learned the meaning of silence and that St. Ambrose's "good reason" for silence was nothing else than listening to the instruction of the inner teacher," Joseph Anthony Mazzeo, "St. Augustine's Rhetoric of Silence," *Journal of the History of Ideas* vol. 23, No. 2 (1962): 175–96.

91 Although Augustine would not have been able to articulate such a point at this time, he would eventually come to see the sacramental import of the scriptures. Augustine says in *en. Ps* 103.4.1 (CCSL 40.1521; WSA III/19, 168), "There is but a single utterance of God [unus sermo dei] amplified through all the scriptures, dearly beloved. Through the mouths of many holy persons a single Word makes itself heard. That Word, being God-with-God in the beginning, has no syllables, because he is not confined by time. Yet we should not find it surprising that to meet our weakness he descended to the discrete sounds we use, for he also descended to take to himself the weakness of our human body."

praecepta dicendi), they are not made into orators, but weapons are put into the hands of madmen (*non eos oratores effici sed arma quaedam furentibus dari*).[92]

Eloquence can become a weapon in the hands of a madman. Who is Augustine describing but his younger self? Throughout his life, Augustine knew what harm he caused through his words, though they were the right kind of words. Contrary to Diomedes who thought that incorrect speech harmed the noble, Augustine learned that the content of the speech harmed far worse than an incorrect case after a preposition might. He learned it ultimately through the preaching of Ambrose who offered to him the *humilis Deus* as mediated in the Gospel written by *piscatores* ("fishermen").

Conclusion

Throughout this chapter, we have traced Augustine through his success in education to become an orator, a *vir bonus dicendi peritus*. The *magistri* from whom he learned to speak Latin thought that the most important thing was using the right kind of language learned from the right kind of sources. Going against the grain of his teachers, Augustine learned from Cicero that the *pectus*, the heart, of what was being said counted as much as the words themselves, although this was a lesson that took him a great deal of time to learn. When he first encountered Ambrose, he was still only listening for the quality of language. It would have been difficult not to for the aspiring orator who imitated great speakers like Cicero. The young Cicero used his speech well to gain *potestas* (power) among the *honestiores*. Augustine sought to do the same. It was not until he encountered another kind of speaker, Ambrose, who chose to listen first.

In a sermon on Psalm 139, Augustine contrasts the man who loves to talk versus the man who listens first. He writes,

The talkative man (*vir linguosus*) will not be guided on earth. A talkative man loves lies. What gives him pleasure? Only talking. He does not even listen to what he is saying; all that matters is to keep talking. It is not possible for a person like that to be guided aright. Let us

92 *ep.* *2.10 (CSEL 88.20; WSA II/4, 241).

enjoy interior realities and engage in external affairs out of necessity, not by choice (*Non ergo amemus magis exteriora, sed interiora: de interioribus gaudeamus; in exterioribus autem necessitatem habeamus, non voluntatem*).[93]

Augustine was this talkative vain man. Cicero was the kind of person who spent more time loving his words than listening. Ambrose modeled for Augustine how to listen not to the external speakers only, but inside to another.

This chapter has established how the education in the *artes liberales* instilled a love of pride in the young Augustine. It was a culture of pride. He followed the example set before him of the great lawyer Cicero, as Augustine knew well the power of imitation. Cicero's own speeches, when viewed through the lens of SAT, show how words can be used to gain acclaim and fame for the speaker. In a manner just like the preacher, the orator acts in his speech. That said, the orator cannot depend on God to provide the increase, *incrementum dat Deus* (1 Cor 3:17). For Augustine, this encounter with God made the speech of the preacher fundamentally different from that of the orator.

93 *en. Ps.* 139.15 (CCSL 40.2023; WSA III/20, 297).

CHAPTER 3

AUGUSTINE'S THEOLOGY OF EVANGELISM

Speaking to an Audience in Hippo

Introduction

WE ARGUE IN THIS CHAPTER THAT AUGUSTINE'S language and manner become humble, not only because Christ himself was humble, but also out of circumstantial necessity. He needed his audience to understand him if they too were going to encounter the one Mediator between God and humanity, Jesus Christ. As classicist W. R. Johnson compellingly argued, "Where Augustine transforms the traditional [rhetorical] doctrine radically is in his definition of what the audiences now are, of whom they are now composed. For a Quintilian no less than for an Isocrates, the audience consisted of the happy few who had the money and the leisure to pursue happiness and who therefore needed and had a right to the freedom that literacy helps to ensure." Quintilian, Cicero, and the earlier orators could assume their audiences enjoyed a certain education and respite to consider the speech. Augustine could not. Johnson continues, "In his time, everyone, not merely in theory but also in fact, had a right to pursue happiness because the concept of happiness had been completely transformed. Happiness now meant understanding that

God loves us and that we can come to love God."[1] The focus of this chapter is establishing who these people were and how Augustine could speak to them, and indeed prepare them, to pursue happiness in God.

This indicates how Augustine understood the nature of evangelism, that is, Augustine needed to be able to connect and communicate with his people where they lived and worked. The great preacher was not deaf to the concerns of people who might not understand his more sophisticated cultural allusions. Augustine's sermons record that he engaged with the people as he spoke extemporaneously. This indicates that Augustine's approach to evangelism and communicating the good news of the advent of Christ relied on a careful attention to the world of his audience.

Much of the research in the succeeding part of this study will be predicated on knowing the kind of audience Augustine spoke to in North Africa. I argue that the Bishop of Hippo needed to learn humility in order to teach humility to those who gathered in the basilica to hear him preach in his own diocese as well as in Carthage, the most frequent locations for his sermons. The role of the orator required the wordsmith to flatter the emperor and stir an audience. Typically, this appears to have been done with excessive ornamentation and a show of skill in word choice and reference to the proper authorities.[2] To be sure, not all orators gave panegyrics as Augustine did; some used their skill in the law courts, as we described from Cicero. That said, the primary audience for Cicero and Augustine as imperial rhetor, likely would have been more literate than the coastal town of North Africa, Hippo Regius.

Across the distance of 1500 years and many different invasions of the area, it is difficult to establish precisely who came to the sermons of a preacher like Augustine. To determine what kinds of people heard Augustine, we will look first at the evidence from studies on North Africa. We will establish the primary trades and education levels of Hippo at large. From this point, we will turn to the evidence in the sermons. As this is a study on the *Sermones ad Populum*, we will restrict our evidence to what is found therein. No single book has ever tried to tackle precisely what the composition of the audience was, but there have been many articles and other studies which offer two alternatives: 1) a primarily educated urban audience (*urbani*); 2) the

---

1 W. R. Johnson, "Isocrates Flowering," *Philosophy & Rhetoric*, v.9.4(1979): 221.

2 Eusebius' *Vita Constantini* is one place to begin to look for an example of this kind of speech.

target audience was mixed of educated and uneducated (*et urbani et rustici*).[3]
We will trace the two arguments of the major camps, offering an assessment
of the evidence in favor of either position. We will also present some counter
evidence which militates against the conclusion that the audience comprised
only wealthy elites. Finally, we will use one complex sermon, *s.* 52 on the
Trinity, to proffer evidence for how Augustine could meaningfully explain the
Trinity to a primarily illiterate, yet still intelligent, audience.

To establish how Augustine communicated with his audience as a
preacher, it will be necessary to consider the social, geographical, and
economic conditions of his potential audience. Of course, this endeavor
requires some filling the gap on the part of the historian to sort through such
a difficult question due to the limited evidence. Specifically, we want to know
the characteristics of the preacher's audience in Hippo and Carthage in North
Africa, as those are the two primary locations where Augustine preached.
Having a sense for his audience will give us a better indication of how he
came to be so influential.

3 The article at the center of the controversy is Ramsay MacMullen's "The Preacher's Audience," *Journal of Theological Studies* (40.2 1989), 503–11. The scholars who
follow MacMullen's judgment without qualification are Peter Brown in *Power and Persuasion* (Madison: University of Wisconsin Press, 1992), 76, n. 26, James J. O'Donnel,
Augustine: A New Biography (New York: Harper Collins, 2005), 31–32 and 345 n.63,
and Leslie Dossey, *Peasant and Empire in Christian North Africa* (Berkeley: University
of California Press, 2010). Gert Partoens in his article, "Augustin Als Praediger,"
Augustin Handbuch (Tübingen,: Mohr Siebeck, 2007), 245, reluctantly cites in favor
of MacMullen. Eric Rebillard says that MacMullen's conclusion should be accepted
with "light qualifications." Rebillard, "Sermons, Audience, Preacher," *Preaching in the
Patristic Era* (Leiden: Brill, 2018), 89. On the other side, many scholars have seen fit to
question the assumption that Augustine spoke to an educated elite, John C. Cavadini,
"Simplifying Augustine," in John Van Engen ed. *Educating People of Faith: Exploring the
History of Jewish and Christian Communities* (Grand Rapids, MI: Eerdmans, 2004), 67. F.
van der Meer, *Augustine the Bishop: The Life and Work of a Father of the Church,* trans. Brian
Battershaw and G.R. Lamb (London: Sheed and Ward, 1961), 412–14. Maurice Pontet,
L'Exegese de S. Augustin Predicateur (Paris: Aubier, 1944), Alexandre Olivar, *La Precicacion
Cristiana Antiqua* (Barecelona: Editorial Herder, 1991), 761–70, Phillip Rousseau, "The
Preacher's Audience: A More Optimistic View," *Ancient History in a Modern University.
Volume 2 Early Christianity, Late Antiquity and Beyond* (Cambridge: Cambridge University
Press, 1998). Some merely cite MacMullen without making judgment like Anthony
Dupont in *Gratia in Augustine's Sermones Ad Populum During the Pelagian Controversy: Do
Different Contexts Furnish Different Insights?* (Leiden: Brill, 2013), 11.

The Town of Hippo Regius,
and North Africa in General

From the archaeological and textual evidence, Hippo Regius was likely the third largest town in Numidia.[4] The town takes it cognomen "Regius" from the fact that Numidian kings lived in the town before the Roman arrival in North Africa.[5] By the time of Augustine, the city of Hippo had three major functions in the life of North Africa. One, it was an extremely fertile area with many farms.[6] Two, Hippo supported a major port with ships coming and going all over the Mediterranean largely exporting agricultural products to Rome and elsewhere.[7] Three, it also served as an important halfway point between two larger cities, Cithra and Carthage.[8] After Augustine returned from Italy, he would never sail again, but took advantage of the busy port by sending letters to colleagues and dignitaries around the Roman Empire.

The town itself was a regional hub with likely 30,000–40,000 people.[9] Before Augustine arrived, most of those people probably worshipped in one of the larger Donatist basilicas. We know of three basilicas and three chapels. The Great Basilica was 20 by 42 meters, not including the largest nave of seven square meters.[10] During the time of Augustine, at least one basilica was either built or converted from a Donatist Church to a Catholic church to make likely three basilicas, in the main part of town.[11] The complex of the *Basilica Pacis* or *Basilica Maiorum*, Augustine's seat, had a monastery, convent, and a library.[12] This basilica alone could likely hold up to 2,000 people.[13] Augustine's sister oversaw the convent, adjacent to the basilica.[14] The monastery itself would produce many bishops and preachers that would go to lead churches across North Africa, some of whom were nearly illiterate

4 Van der Meer, *Augustine the Bishop*, 19.

5 Erwan Marec, *Hippone: Antique Hippo Regius* (Algiers: Dir. de l'Intérieur et des Beaux-Arts [Serv. des antiquités], 1954), 20.

6 Marec, *Hippone*, 26.

7 Brown, *Augustine*, 185.

8 Van der Meer, *Augustine the Bishop*, 19.

9 Van der Meer, *Augustine the Bishop*, 19.

10 Marec, *Hippone le Royale*, 55.

11 Van der Meer, *Augustine the Bishop*, 20.

12 Van der Meer, *Augustine the Bishop*, 20.

13 Van der Meer, *Augustine the Bishop*, 23.

14 Possidius, *Vita Augustinii*, 26.

themselves.[15] Interestingly, it was not required of the bishops that they be as broadly educated as Augustine was, merely that they be able to read.[16] Antoninus was one example of this phenomena, which we saw in chapter 1. The Christian part of town was closer to the shore and just off the main section of the town. In several of Augustine's sermons, he refers to the Donatists making noise, as well as the sound of the revelers on the street which was likely just behind the *exedra* where Augustine would preach from his *cathedra*.[17]

The town certainly had its wealthier *urbani*, but the entire area from which people would come to Hippo was a largely fertile, farming area. The main crop appears to be grain which was grown just outside the town.[18] Even more than simply using biblical references to farming, Augustine mentions that it is harvesting season while explaining a biblical passage about working the fields.[19] More than any other occupation, Augustine discusses agriculture the most frequently across the *Sermones ad Populum*. That said, the kinds of trades mentioned in the sermons span everything from farming and fishing to mercantilism and medicine.[20] The very fact that Augustine makes mention of so many and varied trades exhibits the familiarity he has with the world of his hearers, even if he was not actively engaged in those occupations.

The other occupation not mentioned as frequently but critical for our study is the trade of the fisherman. Augustine mentions fishing and fishermen in 21 sermons in the *Sermones ad Populum*.[21] The proximity of Hippo Regius

15 Brown, *Augustine*, 195.

16 Apostolic Constitutions 2.1.2 "Let him be educated (*pepaideumenos*), if that is possible. But even if he is illiterate (*agrammatos*), let him be experienced in scripture, having the proper age." Quoted from Claudia Rapp, *Holy Bishops in Late Antiquity: The Nature of Christian Leadership in an Age of Transition* (Berkeley: University of California Press, 2013), 179. For a thorough review all the evidence, see: *Holy Bishops*, 173–78.

17 Van der Meer, *Augustine the Bishop*, 20–21.

18 Brown, *Augustine*, 186.

19 *s.* 87 (PL38:530).

20 Marie Getty catalogues every single reference to life in North Africa from the sermons of Augustine in her dissertation published under Roy Deferrari, *The Life of the North Africans as Revealed in the Sermons of Saint Augustine* (Washington, DC: The Catholic University of America Press, 1931). This study is a valuable reference to find what Augustine says about these occupations. It is, however, of a somewhat limited value as she makes no indication of the date or location of the sermons and as it was published in 1931. She also had no knowledge of the recently discovered sermons of Dolbeau, Wilmart, and Mai.

21 *s.* 43 (CCSL 41.51), *s.* 51 (CCSL 41a.15), *s.* 68 [Mai 126] (CCSL 41A.445), *s.* 87

to the Mediterranean also made fishing an important aspect of life in Hippo. On one occasion, *s.* 61, Augustine mentions eating fish as a sign of poverty which appears to be standard in North Africa. The fishmongers mostly sold sturgeons and mullet fish.[22] As was common in the ancient world, fishing was not a hobby but a common trade. Fishing as a trade is attested by mosaics displaying fishermen, semi-nude using various means to make their catch.[23]

Most of those working these trades likely did not have an education and spoke Punic as well as Latin.[24] The previous bishop, Valerius, likely spoke very poor Latin, as a native Greek speaker. This put him at a disadvantage in the struggle with Donatism as the majority of some 35,000 people who lived in the area spoke Punic, like Augustine's mother, Monica.[25] Although Augustine knew some Punic, nothing exists which demonstrates Augustine's fluency in the language.[26] In certain cases, he does show familiarity with the language as both Punic and Hebrew have a shared linguistic lineage.[27]

As for education considered writ large, the town of Hippo does not appear to have had a rhetorical school. Augustine received his rhetorical

---

(PL 38.537), *s.* 198 [Dolbeau 26] (EAA 147 p. 414), *s* 223G [Wilmart] (MiAg 1.690), *s.* 229m [Guelferbytanus 15] (MiAg 1:488), *s.* 248 (PL 38.1158), *s.* 249 (PL 38.1161), *s.* 250 (SC 116. 310), *s.* 252 (PL 38.1172), *s.* 252A [Wilmart 13] (MiAg 1.712), *s.* 272A (RB 84.265), *s.* 298A (PLS 2.1161), *s.* 311 (PL 38.1416), *s.* 335C (PLS 2.753), *s.* 341 [Dolbeau 22] (EAA 147.554), *s.* 350E (WSt 122.199), *s* 360B [Dolbeau 25] (EAA 147.265), *s.* 361 (PL 39.1608), *s.* 381 (PL 39.1683). For some unknown reason, Getty leaves out the occupation of fishing in her study. One explanation might be the number of references which come from studies which were not available to her at the time, the Wilmart sermons and the Dolbeau sermons (5 of the 21 references).

22 Hamman, *La vie quotidienne en Afrique du Nord au temps de Saint Augustin*, 74. Further down the page, Hamman points out that Augustine rarely ate anything but a vegetarian meal with his fellow monks at Hippo. J. J. O'Donnell overlooks this point in trying to portray Augustine as a wealthy upper-class elite who enjoyed lording his status over his North African counterparts. cf. O'Donnell, *Augustine: A New Biography*, 21.

23 Hamman, *La vie quotidienne*, 83–84.

24 Van der Meer, *Augustine the Bishop*, 27.

25 Brown, *Augustine*, 184.

26 In *s.* 167.4 (CCSL 41Bb.358), Augustine translates a Punic proverb into Latin.

27 *Locutionum in heptateuchum Loc.* Genesis, locutio: 24.108 (CCSL 33:384): "quod scriptum est: et extendit manum suam, accepit eam et induxit eam ad semet ipsum in arcam, locutio est, quam propterea hebraeam puto, quia et punicae linguae familiarissima est, in qua multa inuenimus hebraeis uerbis consonantia; nam utique sufficeret: et extendit manum, etsi non adderet 'suam.'"

education in Carthage which would have been from the ages of 12–17.[28] In one of his letters, Augustine mentions that he cannot even procure a copy of one of Cicero's works.[29] Brown describes the town this way, "the truly lettered only formed a small caste in the towns and a tiny fraction in the villas and on the land."[30] It is hard to determine the overall education of North Africa in the fourth century. The most comprehensive study to date suggests a mere 10% of the population could read.[31] On this judgment, Van Der Meer writes, "What the fullness of Augustine's spirit here put into words was clearly intended for quite uneducated people. The impression we gain concerning Augustine's parishioners is that they must have been very simple people, for he explains everything to them in the most elementary manner and with a multitude of repetitions."[32] Many in the town could not even write their own name.[33] In his section on Augustine's preaching, Van der Meer suggests the opposite of MacMullen saying simply, "He spoke not for the educated but for ordinary people."[34]

This quick overview serves to show that North Africa in general, and Hippo Regius in particular, was comprised of people from many differing social locations. Most people were involved in agriculture or farming and were, for the most part, unlettered. Even the educated in Hippo did not have easy access to a great education or libraries of books cultured people would require. North Africans like Augustine had to go to Carthage for these pursuits, which in the case of the wealthier, was indeed possible. This does not settle the question of who among these people attended the services in which Augustine preached but does suggest the kinds of people who could have heard the great preacher in his basilica. MacMullen and others will suggest that in fact only those who had the wealth to own the villas near the Christian quarter of Hippo were present for the sermons.

28 Van Der Meer, *Augustine the Bishop*, 134.

29 *ep.* 118.2,9 (CCSL 31b.118).

30 Brown, *Augustine*, 134.

31 V. Harris, *Ancient Literacy* (Cambridge, MA: Harvard University Press, 1989), 322. Cavadini, "Simplifying Augustine," 66 n. 12 gives a more thorough bibliography for the possibilities.

32 Van der Meer, *Augustine the Bishop*, 132.

33 *ep.* 213.6.

34 Van der Meer, Augustine the Bishop, 417.

MacMullen, *The Educated Urbanites*
 as the Preacher's Audience

The genealogy of the conversation concerning the preacher's audience is fairly simple to trace. The first group of scholars outlined above assume that the Christians who went to hear preachers like Augustine were primarily *urbani* or more wealthy elites. These scholars who draw this conclusion about the "Preacher's Audience" tend to take the study of Ramsay MacMullen as the landmark study. Lesslie Dossey, in her 2010 work *Peasant and Empire in Christian North Africa,* which encompasses the largest amount of evidence on the side of an urban educated audience, begins her investigation with this quote, "Ramsay MacMullen has made this case most vigorously."[35] She ends her study by saying, "This analysis of Augustine's sermons leads to the same conclusion as MacMullen's: Augustine's typical congregation 'was a distinctly upper-class audience, enriched or impoverished, depending on one's point of view, by a less narrow sampling of the population on certain days of special importance.'"[36] Both Dossey and MacMullen conclude from their assessments of the sermons of Augustine that the audience was "upper-class." The only exception from their point of view is that on certain feast days a larger audience might have gathered. Dossey goes on to explain what she means by upper class, "The people whom Augustine personally instructed during Lent were property owners, merchants, lawyers, and a smattering of artisans."[37] If Dossey and MacMullen are correct, Augustine spoke to the same sorts of people he knew in Milan and aspired to be when he left North Africa.[38] They were people with at least some wealth and education like him. Likely they could read and write and were property owning people with more social mobility than the majority of their 90% illiterate peers.

Before attending to the sermons and arguments in favor of this position, it is worth pointing out that MacMullen seems to have modified his position over the course of several years. In 1966, MacMullen made the claim

35 Lesslie Dossey, *Peasant and Empire in Christian North Africa. The Transformation of the Classical Heritage* (Berkeley: University of California Press, 2010), 148.

36 Dossey, *Peasant and Empire*, 152.

37 Dossey, 152.

38 This position was popularly put forward by James O'Donnell in *Augustine a New Biography*, 89.

that "communication between high and low in society was as important as it was increasingly difficult."[39] He goes on to say that the upper-crust educated *urbani* were outright hostile towards their rustic country counterparts, arguing "a people of Augustine's social standing (though not he himself) felt contempt for peasants."[40] This of course changes with the publication of the most cited article on the question of the preacher's audience published in 1989, "The Preacher's Audience." The rest of the article deals precisely with the argument set forth in the later article, but it is worth noting that MacMullen himself seems to have changed his position.[41] In the last decade, MacMullen has made an even more specific case that the "top 5%" of North African society were the only ones who could have possibly even fit inside the basilicas of the Christian churches. This argument is made from the archaeological evidence, which MacMullen details in his work *The Second Church*.[42]

The most well-known social historian of the period, Peter Brown, on the whole shares the opinions of Dossey and MacMullen. His work on the power of the educated elite based on their culture affluence, *Power and Persuasion*, simply states, "Their preaching tended to address the wealthier and more educated members of the congregation."[43] Despite the fact that the celebrated clergy like Augustine tended to be highly educated, Brown thinks, "to have

39 Ramsay MacMullen, "A Note on *Sermo Humilis*," *Journal of Theological Studies* (19.1, 1966) 108–12, 108.

40 MacMullen, "*Sermo Humilis*," 111.

41 Before the publication of MacMullen's second article, Robert Kaster cites MacMullen's earlier article in his own landmark work on the grammarian's role in society, *Guardians of Language*, published in 1987. He characterizes Augustine's work saying, "Augustine wanted such a style to reach a largely uneducated audience and to extend the "franchise of the Latin language" in a mixed population of Punic and Latin speakers by simultaneously pressing Latin's claim as the only point of entry for full participation and making the entryway as wide as possible" (*Guardians of Language*, 84).

42 For a critical, but cordial, response, see: Robert Louis Wilken and Ramsay MacMullen, "The Second Church: Popular Christianity A.D. 200–400; Ramsay MacMullen," *Conversations in Religion & Theology* 8 (2): 120–25. For a thorough investigation of MacMullen's claim on the urban thesis across the Mediterranean, see: Thomas A. Robinson, *Who Were the First Christians?: Dismantling the Urban Thesis* (Oxford: Oxford University Press, 2017). Although this work was cited by Rebillard, "Sermons, Audience, Preacher," 88, no other study we have seen cites the book *The Second Church* at all. Rebillard does not agree with the heavier handed assertions of MacMullen.

43 Brown, *Power and Persuasion*, 74.

presented Christianity in this manner [as simple] was a master stroke of writers who were, themselves, highly educated men.... Master practitioners of Greek and Latin style, men such as Ambrose, Jerome, and Augustine and their innumerable colleagues in the Greek world basked in the limelight that they had brought to bear on the illiterate monks, apostles, and martyrs."[44] As a justification for his position, Brown takes MacMullen's judgment, but he provides little additional textual evidence.[45] To be fair, the majority of *Power and Persuasion* is focused on the Greek East, rather than Augustine and the Latin West.

Despite the citations, MacMullen's case is a feeble one and is built on the citation of only four sermons. The *Sermones ad Populum* collection, with the updated sermons of Dolbeau, make up roughly 550 sermons, 11 books in English translation.[46] In making his case MacMullen writes, "[Preachers] could generally assume they were addressing the most educated audience that the region could supply, meaning, of course, the well-to-do."[47] How does he sustain this judgment? He cites one quote from a sermon of Augustine where he does address the well-educated, "I'm not, after all, speaking to illiterate people (Neque enim rudibus loquor)."[48] In one case, Augustine does say he makes a point specifically for the literate on the meaning of the word "virgin."[49] This hardly bears out the judgment that he only spoke to these kinds of people.

On the contrary, Augustine does in fact address the poor in some specific incidences. MacMullen, however, contends that the poor Augustine seems to have addressed are rather the middle class or the poor with some wealth because they appear to have some kind of home.[50] He bases this on *s*. 85.2–6 and two other sermons which he gestures towards in a footnote.[51] The focus of *s*. 85 seems to be that Augustine address the poor, but does not indicate how wealthy the poor are. In *s*. 107, Augustine says that the poor might have

---

44 Brown, 74.

45 Brown, *Power and Persuasion*, 76, n. 26. Though he updates his view in *Through the Eye of a Needle*, 339–58, which has considerable nuance on the question of the audience. This will be mentioned briefly in the notes where relevant.

46 Cavadini, "Simplifying Augustine," 66 n14.

47 MacMullen, "Preacher's Audience," 509.

48 *s*. 52.10 (CCSL 41Aa.66; WSA III/3, 55).

49 *s*. 52.10.

50 MacMullen, "Preacher's Audience," 509.

51 MacMullen, "Preacher's Audience," 509 n. 16.

a *bonum peculium*, that is a "good savings," and this is what MacMullen cites in his note. The irony for MacMullen is that his primary citation is *s.* 85 where Augustine explicitly states that the poor actually do not have homes or any kind of wealth, "You have the world in common with the rich; you don't have a house in common with the rich, but you do have the sky, you do have the light in common with them."[52] Later in that same section of *s.* 85, Augustine addresses both wealthy and poor in the same sermon demonstrating that both were present before him at the sermon. So, the record of the four sermons which he cites is at least decidedly mixed.

Although the studies of Brown, MacMullen, and the more recent one by Dossey, share the same opinion about the audience, only Dossey goes in depth in her study of the sermons themselves to see if the evidence of the text bears out the argument. Dossey makes her case, based on the sermons which were given to *competentes*, those seeking baptism. As this is the case, the sermons she analyzes are those which come primarily from Hippo Regius, rather than Carthage. Dossey mines these 16 sermons for references to things which indicate a wealthy audience. The audience might have villas, wives, slaves, and should not be embarrassed to act like poor before God as the emperor did. Moreover, there are references to law, trading, and marriage. Dossey states blithely, "The 'poor' were mentioned as beneficiaries of charity or models for penitent Christians, not as the direct second person listeners of Augustine's sermons."[53]

While it is true Augustine makes no address to the poor in this particular sermon, he does make direct address to the poor in other places within the larger corpus of the *Sermones ad Populum*.[54] He uses the phrase "pauper est" 7 times, indicating a direct address of a poor person.[55] Of course, this

---

52 *s.* 85.6 (PL 38.522; WSA III/3, 395).

53 Dossey, *Peasant and Empire,*150.

54 Peter Brown categorizes the crowd during the sermons of Augustine by saying, "Altogether, the *pauper* of Augustine's sermons was not usually a beggar. He was a typical Roman *plebeius*. . . . Augustine preached not only to the *paupers*. The rich were also present in the basilica" (*Through the Eye of a Needle*, 347). He makes use of Dossey briefly in the same chapter though Dossey's *Peseant Empire*, 2010, was written before Brown's *Through the Eye of a Needle*, 2012.

55 *s* 20A [= Lambot 24] (CCSL 41. 273); *s.*106 (PL 38. 627); *s.* 114B [= Dolbeau 5, Moguntinus 12] (EAA 147.443); *s.* 123 (PL 38.686); *s.* 299E [= Guelferbytanus 30] (MiAg 1. 554); *s.* 339 [Maur. 339 + Maur. 40 = Frangipane 2] SPM 1.114; *s.* 359 (PL 39.159).

is just a crude measurement, but it shows that despite the fact that Augustine does not mention a poor person directly in these 16 sermons, he does on other occasions.

The next category of evidence that Augustine addressed *urbani* in the sermons arises from the text of the sermons in which Augustine does somewhat infrequently draws on agricultural metaphors. Dossey finds seven sermons which do make a reference to agricultural metaphors but concludes from those that they do not indicate an agrarian audience. She states breathlessly, "It would be dangerous to conclude much from these agricultural figures of speech: they were firmly grounded in the scriptures being read shortly before Easter, had become almost *topoi* in ecclesiastical authors, and took second seat in terms of both space and originality to Augustine's other metaphors. Moreover, some of Augustine's sermons on the Creed and Lord's Prayer contained no agricultural metaphors at all."[56] While it may be dangerous to conclude too much from the sermons, we do find that Augustine made reference to the seasons of the year in deploying his agricultural metaphors, suggesting that he is quite aware of his surroundings while preaching.[57] She found 12 sermons which display a familiarity with "trade, the law courts, the military, and other features of an administrative center."[58] From these two comparative judgments we are meant to believe that the references to what might relate more to a wealthy audience are far more important than the agricultural metaphors.

Augustine's usage of agricultural references do not always support Dossey's findings. Augustine mentions the word *agricola* "farmer" in 28 different sermons.[59] On one occasion, Augustine preaches explicitly that he speaks to both farmers and city dwellers, admitting that the farmers will already know what he describes from an agricultural metaphor.[60] Dossey cites the word *iurisperitus* (skilled in law) as critical evidence that the people who were meant to have heard these sermons were more likely wealthy people going to court. Any forms of *iurisperitus* occur a mere four times in the rest

56 Dossey, *Peasant and Empire,* 152.

57 *s.* 87 (PL38:530).

58 Dossey, *Peasant and Empire,* 153.

59 This is far from an exhaustive way of capturing how frequently Augustine draws on agricultural metaphors, but it is instructive that he speaks frequently about farmers.

60 *s.* 361.11 (PL 39.1604).

of the *Sermones ad Populum*.[61] The cross section of the entire corpus provides a decidedly mixed picture of the audience.

Dossey and MacMullen's work do not adequately settle the question of whether Augustine's audience came primarily from a wealthy elite. Yet, it should at least raise some doubts as to whether the evidence is as strong as she suggests. All of this at least calls that facile conclusion in doubt. It's hard to assume that MacMullen has really done a thorough presentation to warrant his judgment, "They could generally assume they were addressing the most educated audience that the region could supply, meaning, of course, the well-to-do."[62] This summarizes the position of Dossey and MacMullen which skews the evidence towards those sermons which indicate a wealthier, more educated audience.

The Evidence from More Sermons

My contention is that in fact the audience was far more mixed and even leans towards those who would be at work farming, fishing, or practicing other low skilled trades. One quick point worth making centers on simple numbers. If William Harris is correct that only 10% of the population of North Africa was likely literate, Hippo could only have had 3 to 4,000 people who were literate. Augustine's basilica hosted as many as 2,000 people according to Van der Meer. Current stipulations in the United States dictate that a person needs roughly one third of a square meter for standing room. The dimensions of the Basilica Pacis given in Marec's archaeological account are 20 meters by 42 meters, or 840 square meters, enough for 2,500 people. This makes Van der Meer's account seem small. MacMullen on the other hand argues that every person needed at least a full square meter.[63]

Archaeological evidence tells us that there were at least eight basilicas in Hippo, though smaller than the Basilica Pacis, of which only two have been excavated.[64] Van der Meer suggests that Augustine's church may have been one of the largest in Numidia, with only possibly two larger churches in Carthage.[65]

---

61 *s.* 47 (SL 41.596); *s.* 58 1.1 (CCSL 41Aa.199); *s.*114 (RB 73.27); *s.* 356 (SPM 1.135).

62 MacMullen, "Preacher's Audience," 509.

63 MacMullen, *The Second Church*, 14.

64 MacMullen, *The Second Church*, 129.

65 Van der Meer, *Augustine the Bishop*, 22.

To date, only two basilicas have been excavated in ancient Hippo. For the other basilica, MacMullen gives the dimensions of 23.7 meters by 18.5 meters, for a total area of about 450 meters.[66] That is roughly half the size of Augustine's Basilica Pacis, meaning by modern estimates as many as 1000 people could fit in the building. If only the educated elites came to the basilicas, they could not possibly fill up those eight basilicas, even if we assume that every educated person attended a Catholic Christian church. The simple fact remains that the sheer numbers suggest that if the basilica of Augustine was ever full people would have had to come from outside the class of educated urban elites.

We do not need to rely on a numbers' argument alone. Pontet and Cavadini offer other counter evidence to the position of MacMullen and Dossey. Pontet, in 1944, writes, "the audience is greatly varied. There were patricians and slaves, rich and poor, the poor though, as in all eras, were the greatest number."[67] Cavadini more recently suggests, "Augustine's audience varied with time and place, but generally included both educated and uneducated, literate and illiterate members, and he developed a homiletic style that was intentionally simple, shorn of rhetorical intricacy, plain and vivid, specially created to reach just such a heterogeneous group."[68] Pontet makes his case based on only a couple of sermons which indicate that some of the audience could not read.

In a similar way, Cavadini finds textual evidence that in many cases Augustine states that the audience might only know stories like the Aeneid from the theater. This claim makes sense only if many of the audience could not read. In what follows, I will present the evidence from Pontet and Cavadini. I will end by adding my own study of several places where Augustine indicates that some in the audience were slower to understand than the rest of the audience. This provides more support for the conclusion that the congregation of Augustine's church comprised people from different social stations.

Pontet only discusses the audience very briefly, as if to indicate that it is obvious that the audience was quite mixed. The significant quotations are from two sermons, *ss.* 14 and 51. Coincidentally, scholars have dated both

---

66 MacMullen, *The Second Church*, 129.

67 *L'Exegese de S. Augustin Predicateur* (Paris: Aubier, 1944), 55. "L'auditoire est fort varie. Il y a des patriciens et des esclaves, des riches et des pauvres, les pauvres etant, comme dans la vie, le plus grand nombre" (translation my own).

68 Cavadini, "Simplifying Augustine," 67.

sermons around 418 and one of them has an appended location, Carthage.[69] In *s.* 14, Augustine argues that the people should read the text for themselves first, *Lege Scripturas et invenies quod dico* "Read the scriptures and you will find what I say." Then after making the citation he corrects himself saying, *Lege, aut si legere non potes, audi cum legitur, et vide* ... "read, or if you cannot read, listen when it is read and see,"[70] indicating that some of those gathered on this Sunday could not read.

Similarly, in *s.* 51, Augustine remarks about the probable education of his audience. In order to connect the Old Testament which had not been read that particular day to the lectionary, Augustine states, *Qui Scripturas legunt, recordentur nobiscum: qui non legunt, credant nobis* "those who read the scriptures, they recall them with us: those who do not read, let them believe with us."[71] Again, these two arguments do not sustain an incontestable argument about the nature of the audience, but they offer some indication that many in the audience could not read and would thus not be counted among the wealthy *urbani*.

Cavadini uses another ingenious device to test whether the audience of Augustine's sermons could read. In a sermon preached at Hippo, *s.* 241, Augustine discusses how knowledge of Vergil's Aeneid spread in his town when referring to stories in the epic.[72] In one of three sermons on the nature of resurrection and the transmigration of souls, Augustine preaches:

> One of their authors was horrified at the idea, when it was pointed out to him, or rather when he led onto the stage a father in the underworld pointing it out to his son. Yes, nearly all of you know about this; and I'd much rather only a few of you did. But only a few of you know about it from books, many of you from the theater, that Aeneas went down to the underworld, and his father showed him the souls of the great Romans who were going to come into bodies.[73]

69 Gryson, *Répertoire général des auteurs ecclésiastiques latins de l'Antiquiteé*, 232, 234.

70 *s.* 14.1 (CCSL 41.187).

71 *s.* 51.9 (CCSL 41A.25). In a related phrasing, Augustine mentions the learned and unlearned, likely meaning those who could read and those who could not. Cf. *s.* 150.4 (REAug 45.42): "Breuiter ergo dico: Indocti credant nobis, docti iudicent de nobis."

72 Cf. *s.* 105 (PL 38:623).

73 *s.* 241 (PL 38.1135; WSA III/7, 53). cf. *ss.* 240–242.

Augustine's own estimation of his audience is that it is clearly mixed. This would be one of his more intellectual arguments in a sermon about transmigration of souls, but it shows that many could not in fact read.[74]

I will now examine other evidence from the sermons to further uncover Augustine's audience. So far, the evidence on the side of a mixed audience has been concerned with the ability of the preacher's audience to read. On a number of occasions, however, Augustine chastens the more intellectually gifted in their impatience to move ahead with the rest of the audience. The example of one of the sermons which MacMullen ushers to his defense indicates the opposite point he tries to make. Although Augustine does explicitly state in *s.* 52, "I'm not, after all, speaking to illiterate people," later on he offers a more complete picture of the gathered faithful.[75] He confesses to his audience that he misperceived how much they would understand of his discussion of the Trinity and memory, "I undertook to discuss this matter and put it across with the greatest trepidation; I was afraid, you see, that I might delight the wit of the clever, and bore the less clever to tears."[76] At the very least this demonstrates that Augustine knew he was not speaking to a monolithic audience of high intelligence and education. But the word he uses for "slower," *tardus*, can be used to locate other places where Augustine expects at least half of his audience to not always be so swift in understanding.

This recognition and accommodation to the slower in the congregation occurs seven times in the *Sermones ad Populum*. Of these seven instances, *ss.* 101 and 169 were preached in Carthage, and *ss.* 229 and 250 were preached in Hippo.[77] The location of the other three, *ss.* 76, 352, and 379, is undetermined.[78] In a sermon explaining why all must rely on God's strength, Augustine warns, "Moderate your speed, so that the slow coaches can catch up. I've said it once, and I'll say it again: the only ones who get strength from God

---

74 For an argument about how even those who cannot read might be capable of greater reasoning than many moderns realize, see: Rosenberg.

75 *s.* 52.10 (CCSL 41Aa.66; WSA III/3, 55).

76 *s.* 52.18 (CCSL 41Aa.77; WSA III/3, 61): "Metuebam enim ne forte laetificarem capacium ingenium, et facerem grave tardioribus taedium."

77 *s.* 169 (CCSL 41Bb. 408; WSA III/5, 227).

78 *s.* 352.4 (PL 39.1554; WSA III/10, 143); *s.* 379.3 (RB 59.64; WSA III/10, 356–57).

are those who are aware of having weakness from themselves."[79] Augustine drives home the need for reliance on God by admonishing those who voice their frustration at the slowness of the sermon to slow down and wait for everyone to understand.

Similarly, in a separate sermon from early in his preaching career, Augustine comments on those slower to understand. He engages with his audience by saying, "I see you have caught on quickly. However, I mustn't stop there just for that reason. I mean, you haven't all got the point so quickly. By their exclamations, I see some have understood; by their silence I see rather more of you still looking for the point. But because we are talking about a road, let's go on walking as on a road. Quick walkers, wait for those who are slower, and walk together."[80] After the warning, Augustine proceeds to explain another way of understanding the passage in question. The significance again is that Augustine shows awareness of preaching to a wide ranging audience of varying intellectual capabilities.

In two sermons preached around the time of Easter, which is precisely the time frame considered by Dossey above, Augustine hints at the heterogeneity of his audience. He uses the same words about those who are slow, *tardus,* and fast, *velocis.* He cautions the *velocis,* "Many of you, however, know what I am going to say; those who do must put up with the delay. When two people are walking along the road, one quick and one slow, it's in the power of the quick one for them to walk along together, if he waits for the other. So the one who knows what I am going to say is the quick walker; but he should wait for his slower companion."[81] In *s.* 250, Augustine gives a benefit for the *velocis* if he or she waits for the *tardus,* "You don't lose anything by hearing what you knew already, and because you don't lose anything, you ought to rejoice that the one who didn't know it is being instructed."[82] Not only does Augustine feel the need to consider all who are present, but it is also for the upbuilding of the quicker because they can rejoice in the understanding of all.

79 *s.* 76.6 (IP 24.60; WSA III/3, 315): "Temperetur uelocitas, ut sequatur tarditas. Hoc dixi, et hoc dico: Audite, capite, facite. Nemo a Deo sit firmus nisi qui se a seipso sentit infirmum."

80 s. 101.9 (SPM 1.52; WSA III/4, 70).

81 *s.* 229M [= Guelferbytanus 15] (MiAg 1.491; WSA III/6, 318) preached 412 in Hippo (Gryson, *Repetoire General des Autueurs ecclesiastiques Latins*, 245).

82 *s.* 250 (SChr 116.308; WSA III/7, 125).

s. 52 on the Trinity and Communicating in an Oral Culture

The preceding sections have laid out various arguments about the kind of congregation to which Augustine preached at Hippo and Carthage. If we conclude that the audience included both urban dwellers and rustic farmers, the majority of which were uneducated, we might think that Augustine only preached surface level sermons. That is, Augustine might have resisted the temptation to speak at the level he was capable in such works as *On the Trinity* or in his some of his letters to more cultured interlocutors. It would be of course hard to summarize the intellectual difficulties of all the *Sermones ad Populum*, in two sermons—*ss.* 52 and 71—Augustine expounds on the nature of the Trinity for the kind of congregation so constituted.

While the bulk of this chapter has focused on a simplistic dichotomy between "literate" and "illiterate" when one considers the kinds of sermons Augustine preached, it is important to recall that the Christian people of late antiquity are more complex. Stanley Rosenberg has captured the distinct cultural milieu of Augustine's age well:

> Conflating literacy and rationality risks confusing the Late Antique world with an educational development not seen until a much later period. Interpreting the Roman world in this way applies a social situation identified with a profoundly literate society and a view not found in the West until after the eleventh century. Rather than fixating on literacy, it would be more appropriate to emphasize Late Antiquity as a literary-shaped culture.[83]

Rosenberg highlights the fact that an illiterate audience could still follow a difficult argument given their practice at listening and memorizing in a more oral culture. We also find in the sermons of Augustine evidence of a strong culture of memorization. In one memorable introduction to a sermon, Augustine says, "though we are many we have been singing with one voice, because in Christ we are one," in reference to the practice of singing the Psalms together. It would only have been possible for them to sing together if they had memorized the Psalms.[84] Many may not have had access to the text itself, but they knew it well.

83 Rosenberg, "Beside Books," 428–29.
84 *s.* 16 (b) (WSA III/1, 363; CCSL 41.231).

In his explanation of how one might be thought to learn the scriptures, though illiterate, Rosenberg continues: "The fact of illiteracy offers us in this case relatively little information. It tells us how they learned, not what they learned. Arguments for illiteracy do not necessarily lead to the conclusion that the audience could barely understand their bishop's eloquent words."[85] In thinking about a sermon on a complex topic like the Trinity, one does not assume that only literate listeners would have had the capacity to follow. Augustine understood the sermon and the liturgy to be a kind of school, steeped in the text of scripture for authority, though also not a place where learning to read was taught. Rather, Augustine taught by relying on the memory and intellectual capacities of an audience shaped in an orally literate culture.

Turning to this one fine example, we will see that Augustine prepares his audience for the difficult journey ahead and guides them along the way with critical repetitions. The text for the day is the baptism of Christ, an obvious illustration to Augustine of the Trinity. He explains this doctrine through recap and rhetorical questioning, leading to the following passage:

> So let me call your thoughts back to the difficulty of the question. Someone may say to me, 'You have said that the Father does nothing without the Son, nor the Son without the Father.... Now you tell me, apparently speaking against yourself, that the Son, not the Father, was born of the virgin; the Son, not the Father, suffered; the Son rose again, not the Father.'[86]

This demonstrates how Augustine carefully leads them through the potential contradictions and even anticipates their questions on this difficult matter. Augustine knows that he cannot just say things once and assume that they all have understood. He recognizes that there will be questions on such an arcane subject. As we know, the congregation could at times be quite vocal in their engagement with the extemporaneous preacher, but they appear to appreciate the explanation because Augustine speaks directly to them, "So you like the way the problem is set, do you?"[87]

85 Rosenberg, "Beyond Books," 431.
86 *s.* 52.7 (WSA III/3, 53; CCSL 41Aa:63).
87 *s.* 52.8 (WSA III/3, 54; CCSL 41Aa:64).

As he moves through his explanation of how he understands the Trinity through scripture, Augustine shows that the audience has memorized the passage from John with the following remark, "you are well taught in the school of the heavenly master; like people who listen carefully to the readings and devoutly repeat them, you are not unaware of what follows."[88] The mixed audience of literate and illiterate people can quote the passage from memory.

To end the sermon, Augustine dutifully summarizes it again, but this time also placing himself in the category of those who struggle with this mysterious teaching. He concludes, "Let's reserve these greater matters for those who can grasp them; for the weak, as one of them, I have done what I can."[89] Augustine has diligently and carefully led his congregation through one of the most difficult subjects in Christian teaching. Along the way, the kind of engagement between preacher and orally literate audience becomes visible. Through the audience's verbal responses and Augustine's rhetorical questions, he can lead them through a difficult discussion. It is evident that although they may be technically illiterate, they are by no means unlearned and unable to follow a convoluted argument from a gifted and humble preacher.

Conclusion

In conclusion, the sermons of Augustine when scrutinized show a much wider variance in audience than commonly assumed. Although MacMullen and Dossey have had considerable influence over the literature, when the textual evidence is considered in its wider context, the diversity of the audience becomes apparent. In contrast, scholars, like Pontet and Cavadini, who considered a wider variance of text have found sufficient evidence to show a less educated and less wealthy audience. Finally, Augustine's repeated references to the fast and the slow indicate that Augustine was well aware of those to whom he spoke, which could not possibly have been simply from the city.

Before leaving the question of the Preacher's Audience, it is worth citing two contrasting quotes from opposing scholars on the question of the kind of audience to which Augustine spoke. In describing the *"simpliciores"* "the more simple ones," whom MacMullen thinks were absent from the preaching

88 *s.* 52.13 (WSA III/3, 56; CCSL 41Aa:67).
89 *s.* 52.23 (WSA III/3, 62; CCSL 41Aa:79).

of Augustine, supposes, "it can't have been very pleasant to overhear such talk [terms like *simpliciores*], for those who belonged to the middling or lower classes; nor was it always in just this way that they saw themselves."[90] On the contrary, a textual scholar who focuses on the Latinity of Augustine's preaching corpus suggests a more nuanced approach. Christine Mohrman describes Augustine's language this way, "without descending to the level of the people, he speaks a language which remains accesible."[91] While the language of Augustine may not be called the same as that of the rustics, he did intend to speak in a way to be understood by them. We will consider this claim in greater detail in chapter 4 which explicitly covers the language of Augustine, but suffice it to say that Mohrman's judgment is borne out when considering a large swath of other texts from Augustine where he adapts his language to the understanding of an audience that included a significant number of uneducated farmers and fishermen.

90 MacMullen, *The Second Church*, 109. He cites Augustine's *cat. Rud.*, a text that we will analyze below. Suffice it to say, Augustine does not look down on the rustics in this text contrary to what MacMullen claims. In fact, Augustine calls himself a *"simplicior"* on at least one occasion (*Io. eu. tr.* 6.13).

91 Mohrman, "Saint Augustin prédicateur" in *Etudes Sur les Latin des Chretiennes* V.1 (Rome, Italy: Edizioni di Storia e Letteratura, 1961) 396.

PART 2

AUGUSTINE'S THEOLOGY OF PREACHING AT WORK

In a letter to a young student embarking on the path of rhetorical education, Augustine's guidance included a reworking of one of Demonsthenes' anecdotes. Demonsthenes, when asked what the three keys to rhetoric are, responded: delivery, delivery, and delivery. Following this tripartite pattern, Augustine defined the Christian approach to truth by saying:

> I wish, my Dioscorus, that you would be subject to [God] in complete piety and would not construct another way to reach and to gain the truth than that way which he constructed who, as God, saw the weakness of our steps. That first way, however, is humility; the second way is humility, and the third way is humility, and as often as you ask, I would say this. It is not that there are no other commandments that should be mentioned, but unless humility precedes and accompanies and follows upon all our good actions and is set before us to gaze upon, set alongside for us to cling to, and set over us to crush us down, pride tears the whole benefit from our hand when we rejoice over some good deed.... So too, if you ask and as often

as you ask about the rules of the Christian religion, I would answer only, "Humility," even if necessity would perhaps force me to say something else.[1]

The only way to reach hold of the truth comes by following the mediator on the path in humility. God knew the weakness of humanity and led the way by taking on human flesh. Humility is the ground of virtue and the cornerstone of Christian living. The whole letter is a kind of assessment and even partial rejection of rhetorical learning. To put it simply, the way of rhetoric leads one to pride and the only antidote to pride comes in the embrace of the humble Word. The African bishop in his embrace of the humble Word has been freed to invigorate these rhetorical tools with theological significance. The above quote can only be understood by recognizing the diverse influences on the rhetor-turned-preacher. The sometimes-vain pursuits of rhetoric can still be beneficially employed in the illumination of the Word through preaching.

1 *ep.* 118.22 (CCSL 31B.127; WSA II/2, 117).

CHAPTER 4

AUGUSTINE'S CHRISTOLOGY

The Form of the Servant as Proclaimed by Fishermen

THE SECOND PART OF THIS STUDY WILL proceed to the text of the sermons themselves. The emphasis shifts to an analysis of how Augustine uses his language as a species of action to preach the *via humilitatis*, which is mediated in the Word made Flesh. We will show how Augustine taught humility in word and deed through his preaching of the humble scriptures. In the first chapter, we showed that Augustine's mature thought on the nature of preaching rested on the notion that the preacher *agit cum dicit*, "he acts when he speaks." This gave us occasion to consider SAT, which divides speech into three parts: locution, illocution, and perlocution. This threefold division helped us organize our understanding of Augustine's theology of preaching which takes its locution principally from the authority of the scriptural text, in the humble *sermo piscatorius* "fisherman's speech."[1] The preacher then

---

1 Although Augustine rather frequently employs this contrast, many other patristic authors play with the notion of the teaching and speaking of fishermen. Tertullian makes a comparison between the philosophers Christ could have chosen rather than the *piscatores* he did (*de anima* 3.3). Libanius chides Basil of Caesarea about his Greek to

offers those locutions in his own voice and action through what SAT terms illocution. Finally, Augustine understands preaching as a form of speech which does not rest solely on the persuasion of orators, but on the work of God to give the increase (1 Cor 3:7).

Chapters two and three of the first part of the study provided historical context for the preaching of Augustine and connected them to Augustine's theology of language, culture, and evangelism. This chapter will continue some of the research on Augustine's education by further examining ancient authorities for language, like those Augustine would have learned in his education in the *artes liberales*. Classic works of Greek and Roman authors were read and examined for their authority, *auctoritas*, as what was considered true *latinitas*. Educated men would learn to speak and surpass their uneducated contemporaries in their linguistic abilities. The very process of education formed his desire for fame and celebrity, the bedrock of his pride.

When the people of Hippo chose Augustine as the successor to Valerius, the young preacher had to re-learn how to speak to a different kind of audience then would have heard him in orating before the Emperor in Milan. Augustine had begun to read the scriptures in Milan, but he requested even more time before he became a full-time priest to study the scriptures.[2] As he familiarized himself with these texts, written in a humbler style, Augustine found a new authority for his speech. The great orator abandoned much of his highly ornamented rhetoric for an audience in North Africa, especially Hippo, which included many farmers and fishermen, so that they might understand the Word became flesh.

After Augustine accepts his role as a *praedicator* "preacher," the source of his authority for speech and oration changes. The words of God contained in scripture become the binding locution—or the new *auctores*—which Augustine must follow as a fellow learner and proclaim as preacher. Augustine acts this out before his audience gathered altogether into one body of learners before the *cathedra* of Christ which is in heaven.[3] This humble listening to

---

which Basil replies that he is a disciple of fishermen, referring to the New Testament (*ep.* 356). Gregory Nazianzus preaches about the need for all to be caught by the words of fishermen (*Orat. XVII, Funebris in patrem*). John Chrysostom speaks of the doctrine of the fishermen (*Home. VIII*). Theodoret of Cyrrus has a similar statement about the poor speech of fishermen compared to the writings of Demosthenes and Thucydides (*ep.* 12).

2 *ep.* 21.3.

3 *s.* 261.2 (SPM 1.89): "In hac enim schola omnes sumus condiscipuli: caelum est cathedra magistri nostri."

the locution of Christ displays before the church the Christian virtue of humility. Augustine thus preaches to his people a way to follow by listening to the commands and teachings of Christ.[4] Not only does Augustine hear the command, but he puts it into action by his very words, ignoring his once held title and choosing for himself a lesser one.

Although the linguistic elements will be the focus of this chapter, they will be so, not to obscure the theological elements, but merely highlight them in their context. That is to say, Augustine's way of describing Christology is much like any of his theological treatises, they come out in the rhetorical flair of his words. As Brian Daley notes:

> Augustine tended to express the complex reality of Christ less in the technical language of person, nature, and substance than in sharp, simple phrases that underlined rhetorically the paradox he embodies ... 'a whole human being is with the Word, and the Word with a human being, and the human being and the Word are one human being, and the Word and the human being are one God' (*en. Ps.* 5.56.5).[5]

As a man steeped in words, it is no surprise that Augustine would find many playful expressions to lead hearers into a deeper understanding of a profound subject. It is the lyrical quality of Augustine's language which draws hearers in, not the rigid application of technical theological vocabulary. To listen to Augustine's preaching would be both to be delighted by their artful description as much as their theological sophistication. Augustine drew his hearers into the deep theological truths which undergirded his prosaic language. So, while we will attend to those words, we ought never lose sight of the fact that Augustine composed them for deeply theological reasons about the nature of the Word made flesh, the *Deus Humilis* which buttresses his willingness to upend centuries of conventions of speech.

Moreover, it is Augustine's deep love of scripture as his new authority which influences his love for the dichotomy of *forma servi* and *forma dei* as a means to express, and perhaps anticipate, later Christology.[6] Augustine

---

4 This image of Christ as the Teacher and the preacher as student will be further developed in chapter 5.

5 Brian Daley: "Christology," *Augustine through the Ages*, 165.

6 Anne-Marie La Bonnardière sums up Albert Verwilghen's work on the subject this way,

does not spend much time concerning himself with persons and wills but returns to the Apostle Paul's hymn in Philippians 2 as the load-bearer of his Christology.

As Augustine reflects on how a preacher or teacher in the church instructs newcomers, Augustine modifies the *auctores* of good speech as seen in his change in attitude towards the role of grammar in instruction for the Church. As such, we will begin with the treatise on instructing catechumens *On the Catechism of the Uninstructed*, where Augustine shows a pastoral attentiveness to the broad range of people who attended his sermons. Having established that the low speech has a specific function for the entire Church, we will look at the way Augustine communicates the truths of scriptures, even when they transgress grammatical principles, like barbarism, solecism, and *tapinosis* (humble speech). The speech of the scriptures has been at times mockingly termed the *sermo piscatorius*, as it was composed by fishermen.[7] We see how that plays out in two different literary genres of Augustine, in his sermons and in one instance in the *City of God*. This will show how Augustine deployed the speech of the humble fishermen in different ways for different audiences. Ultimately, this supports the notion that Augustine's locution, his speech, becomes so suffused with scripture that it too becomes humble, evidencing the change of the character of his words.

"It is better for the people to understand than for us to be scolded by Grammarians"

We will turn to the nature of the scriptures themselves, and how those words provided the basis for a change in Augustine's own language. Marrou's masterful and wide-ranging study on education in the ancient world offers

---

That is to say that this hymn does not concern only the theology and the exegesis but all the way of all Christians. The reason for this is clear to Augustine: Christ has given us, in the destruction of the Form of the Servant, the example and the secret of walking in the only way that leads to the Father, the way of humility.... Christians are invited to the contemplation and imitation of the humility and obedience of Christ.

La Bonnardière, *Christologie et Spiritualité selon Saint Augustin* (Paris, France: Beauchesne, 1984), 11.

7 G. J. M. Bartelink. "Sermo piscatorius. De wisserstaal van de apostelen," *Studia Catholica* 35 (1930): 267–73.

this perspective on the authority of texts in shaping what constituted correct speaking in the traditional *artes liberales*:

> "[The grammarian] took stock of the material that had been used by the great classic writers, the language which in their masterpieces had been hallowed for all eternity. A tyrannical classical ideal dominated this teaching.... Latin was—it was there for all time in the great writers; the science of correct speaking—*recte loquendi scientia*—based in the last analysis on *auctoritas*."[8]

As a result of Augustine's encounter with the humble Christ in scripture, Augustine transferred the sense of authority to scripture from the classical texts he knew so well. Catherine Chin summarizes the project of Quintilian and other Latin grammarians this way, "Quintilian's construction of correct Roman linguistic behavior, beginning with proper grammatical instruction in the necessary *auctores*, is clearly engaged in more than the task of promoting literacy—it also uses literacy as a site at which to call into being an ideal Roman person."[9] The ideal Roman person spoke good Latin as known in the great authors like Cicero and Vergil. Augustine finds a new ideal in the Christian scriptures, which for him were the myriad translations known as the *Vetus Latina*.[10] Humility in speech becomes a new paradigm for Augustine and rearranges the status of the classical *auctores*.[11] It is not that he outright ignores Cicero, as we see in *On Christian Teaching*, but in practice he places a new emphasis on clarity of speech. He foregrounds the *sermo humilis*.[12]

Not only does Augustine use titles and metaphors to act in his speech humbly as we have described above, but he is willing to change the character of his language which he has learned and taught for so long. Augustine will do this for several reasons: 1) he must not allow his arrogance to dominate

---

8 Marrou, *Education in Antiquity*, 277.

9 Chin, *Grammar and Christianity*, 4.

10 *doc. Chr.* 2.15.22.

11 Auerbach summarizes Augustine's view of the *sermo humilis* this way, "In Augustine's subsequent remarks, the highest mysteries of the faith may be set forth in the simple words of the lowly style which everyone can understand," in *Literary Language*, 37.

12 *doc. Chr.* 4.17 in contrast with Cicero, *Orator,* 101. See also, Erich Auerbach, "Sermo Humilis."

him as it once did, 2) his new authoritative text does not require him to do
so (and in fact often using the *sermo humilis* of common speech) and 3) the
purpose of all his speech changes to be for the benefit of those gathered to
learn the humility taught from Christ. Moreover, humility in speech becomes
a virtue rather than something tolerated in some cases but known as a vice
in others.[13]

Throughout, we have made a thorough study of Augustine's educational
pursuits and his complaints about them. Trained in the liberal arts, Augustine
was supposed to live up to the ideal of a *vir bonus, dicendi peritus* as learned
in the correct pagan authors. That said, he knew that by this point in late
ancient education, the *magistri* focused more on the latter than the former.
Although this would not have pleased Cicero, he was still required reading
by late ancient *magistri* in Augustine's North African education. Augustine
himself recognized that reading Cicero as an authority for language rather
than as a philosophical authority missed a critical piece of Cicero's intention.
Cicero desired to inculcate wisdom as well as good speech. Although we do
not know precisely what Augustine taught in his position as *magister oratorum*
(teacher of orators), he later mocked his position as a chair of lies.[14] The
influence of Cicero's love of wisdom though stayed with Augustine and sent
him on a path pursuing more than simply good speech, leading Augustine to
find the truth in Christ.

After encountering the humble Christ in the scriptures, Augustine
renounced his position in the liberal schools and unwittingly found himself
in the role of presbyter. As *magister oratorum* he had to teach the highest level
of language ornamentation possible. In the Church, he had to reconsider
how he would communicate with a different audience.[15] The goal in this
case was to be understood by all his hearers and be an example for them of

13 We will consider the oratorical vice known as *tapinosis* further in the chapter.
Seneca says in letter 39.2 of his *Epistulae Morales* to Lucilium "Neminem excelsi ingenii
virum humilia delectant et sordida; magnarum rerum species ad se vocat et extollit"
(LLA 335.PH 118).

14 The closest we come to an Augustinian syllabus so to speak are the Cassiciacum dialogues and one dubiously attributed *Ars Grammatica*. Current scholarly
consensus is that Augustine did not write a complete treatise on grammar in a way like
many other grammarians and rhetoricians of his day. See: G. Madec, *Introduction Aux
'Révisions' et à la Lecture des Oeuvres de Saint Augustin* (Paris: Institut d'Études Augustiniennes, 1996).

15 The audience was described in chapter 3 above.

the right kind of living.[16] Recognizing the failure of his former teachers, he wanted the Church to be different. Augustine deemphasizes the grammatical instruction of his past in favor of being well understood. As discussed in chapter 1, Augustine argues in *On Christian Teaching* 4 "He acts, as far as he is able, when he speaks, that he is heard understandingly, delightfully, and obediently."[17] This educational and grammatical objective also demonstrated his own change of virtue. By this move, he was acting humbly.

One sustained account of what this change looked like comes in Augustine's treatise on how to instruct those who were desiring to become Christians, *On the Catechizing of the Uninstructed*. In this work, Augustine replies to Deogratias' question on how to best offer this kind of teaching. The most significant moment comes when Augustine delineates who the instruction is for and how to handle the differing social classes one might be instructing all at once. Augustine was attentive to the fact that those desiring to become Christians came from all sorts of backgrounds. Some were well educated *magistri*, sticklers for precise language and arrogant, and some were farmers and fishermen, what Diomedes would call *inculti,* and what Augustine will call *rustici.*[18] One might also name them *dicendi imperitus* (unskilled at speaking).

The title of this work from Augustine places *all* those people into one grouping. He teaches Deogratias how to instruct the *rudes.* The Oxford Latin Dictionary defines *rudis* as "not yet refined by civilization, primitive, rude, unsophisticated."[19] In a sense, by the title alone, Augustine categorizes all those who want to become Christians into one large genus of unsophisticated humans. This might not be surprising to the fishermen or farmers in the audience but would be a slap in the face to a *grammaticus* who had spent his life in perfecting the kind of speech which he would make his living from. The *grammaticus* would have been considered polished and sophisticated, or a *peritus* "expert" in *Latinitas* "pure Latin." By the art of speaking well, the grammarian brought the next generation of Roman boys into the class of men they needed to become to rule society. But, in as much as he was *peritus* in the *artes liberales*, he was *rudis* in the *schola christi*. Augustine had made this move in his own life and offered this as a model for all to follow.

---

16 As we emphasized in chapter 1 from *doct. chrs.* 4.

17 *doc. Chr.* 4.15.32 (CCSL 32:138; WSA I/11, 219): "agit ergo quantum potest cum ista dicit, ut intellegenter, ut libenter, ut oboedienter audiatur."

18 We will explore the historical status of such a claim below.

19 *OLD* V.2, 1836.

All who enter the Church do so as *rudes,* regardless of any prior social status or distinction.[20]

At the outset of the treatise, Augustine looks like a typical *urbanus*—an educated elite—by describing an address to different sorts of educated people.[21] His distinction consists in two types of persons trained in the *liberal arts.* The first type already knows much about the Christian faith because their education trained them to read and understand well what they read. So long as they have not read too many heretics and have a generally humble disposition, Augustine says that they can move through explanation of the faith quickly.[22] In sum, Augustine encourages Deogratias, "when we lay claim to teaching authority—so as to put him on his guard against the errors of presumption—we should do so only to the extent that his humility, which has brought him here, now seems ready to allow."[23] We do not know much about the background of Deogratias, but it would not be uncommon for a presbyter in North Africa to potentially be less educated than some in their congregation.[24] Thus, Deogratias should be aware of the kind of humility that it would require for a person desiring to be baptized to go and learn and listen from someone less well educated than themselves. Augustine wants Deogratias to be attentive to this fact, but to not avoid assuming his proper

20   The example of Marcus Victorinus indicates how difficult this was for a person of a higher social status. Cf. *conf.* 8.2.3 (CCSL 27:114–115; WSA I/1,187): "These gods Rome had once vanquished, but now worshiped, and the elderly Victorinus with his terrible thunders had habitually defended their cults; yet he was not ashamed to become a child of your Christ and be born as an infant from your font, bending his neck to the yoke of humility and accepting on his docile brow the sign of the ignominious cross."

21   Early in his young life, Augustine desperately desired to be considered "urbanus" indicating perhaps that he never felt like one. *conf.* 3.1.1 (CCSL 27.27).

22   *cat rud* 8.12 (CCSL 46.134; WSA V, 84).

23   *cat rud* 8.12 (CCSL 46.134; WSA V, 84): "tantum assumta praecipiendi auctoritate (ut caveat praesumptionis errores) quantum eius humilitas quae illum adduxit, iam sentitur admittere."

24   Apostolic Constitutions 2.1.2 "Let him be educated (pepaideumenos), if that is possible. But even if he is illiterate (agrammatos), let him be experienced in scripture, having the proper age." Quoted in Claudia Rapp, *Holy bishops in late antiquity: The nature of Christian leadership in an age of transition. The Transformation of the Classical Heritage,* (Berkeley: University of California Press, 2005), 179. For a thorough review all the evidence, see *Holy Bishops,*173–78.

authority as an ordained presbyter. He has *auctoritas*, which was previously reserved for educated people like Augustine and the texts which taught proper Latin.[25]

The other kind of semi-educated person presents a greater problem for the presbyter to instruct. Augustine describes them as being in between the well-educated and the totally uneducated. He then warns, "when they present themselves to us to become Christians, therefore, we ought to be more emphatic with them than we are with the uneducated in pointing out that they are to clothe themselves in Christian humility."[26] These people seem to have little humility on entering the catechumenate and want to flaunt their more refined habits of speech. Augustine continues thus, "They had been in the habit of actually attaching more value to a trained tongue than to a pure heart, but they should not venture even to make the comparison."[27] This description fits perfectly the "guardians of language" which we will describe further in chapter 5. These kinds of people believed that it was their job to find flaws in other people's speech yet seemed unconcerned with the virtue of themselves or those they were correcting.

The reason for Augustine's emphasis on sifting through the attitudes of those gathered is twofold. One, a group of Christians chastising lesser educated Christians creates unnecessary dissension within the body of Christ. These grammarians might look down on their sisters and brothers for their lack of education. In some cases, as Augustine will argue below, they might even have trouble praying because they will only be focused on the words themselves rather than what they are trying to convey. Augustine thinks that this is of course a detriment to unity and their ability to love their neighbor. They will not have humbly opened themselves up to the love of God and neighbor as Christ taught. Second, the proud attitude of a grammarian also poses a greater problem for these guardians of language to learn from the scriptures, which in some cases was written in the language of the less educated. He goes on, "what these people should be taught in the first place is to listen to the divine scriptures, so that they may put aside their view that the

---

25 Chin describes a pre-Christian *auctoritas* this way, "The idea of *auctoritas* is complex, and the authority of the grammarians was very much bound up in that of the *auctores* whose texts they quoted and taught." Chin, *Grammar and Christianity*, 15.

26 *cat. rud.* 9.13. (CCSL 46.135; WSA V, 84–85).

27 *cat. rud.* 9.13.

solid language of the scriptures is to be despised because it lacks a high-flown quality."[28] If they only consider the quality of language, they risk missing how God speaks in those words, as Ambrose taught Augustine himself.

One recalls Augustine's own critique of his teachers as a youth. The teachers only looked for the quality of language and so missed the truth of what Cicero was trying to convey about pursuing wisdom in the *Hortensius*. The *magistri* only looked at Cicero as an authority on language and so looked for the high ornamentation of his speech, which they found. They missed the underlying truth in the fine speech. The Christians who are somewhat educated in the grammatical and rhetorical arts, whom Augustine chastises in this section of the treatise, only look at the quality of language in the scriptures and write it off as too simple. In this case, they miss the truth because they spend their time criticizing its humbleness. Augustine knows that some of the scriptures come in low speech for the purpose of teaching humility but wants them to look past the quality of speech to see what is being communicated. The form functions in its lower quality to force the proud to humble themselves.

The form here is the humble speech of the scriptures to which God willingly submits. Michael Cameron states Augustine's understanding of this well, "Just as humility is the external teacher's key to the inner teacher's work, Scripture's humble form melts human pride in order to render us fit to hear the inner teacher's voice. Scripture not only portrays his humility; its humble form imitates the teacher's humility in flesh."[29] The kenosis of the incarnation of the Word is not merely the Word being made flesh, but also the Word being spoken of in the *sermo piscatorius*. There is divine humility in the scriptural text itself, and Augustine does not want Deogratias or any other teacher for young Christians to be ashamed of this important aspect of how the scriptures work as a healing ointment for the sickness of pride.

These semi-literate catechumens need to learn humility as Augustine, and those educated who approach with humility, did. Augustine argues these words communicate a deeper truth than simply what appears on the surface.[30]

---

28 *cat. rud.* 9.13. (CCSL 46.135; WSA V, 84–85): "Maxime autem isti docendi sunt Scripturas audire divinas, ne sordeat eis solidum eloquium, quia non est inflatum."

29 Cameron, "Augustine and Scripture," in *Wiley-Blackwell Companion to Augustine*, ed. Mark Vessey (Oxford: Wiley-Blackwell Publishing, 2012): 200–214, 203.

30 Cameron ties Augustine into a great line of speakers who recognize the power of words, "So Augustine participated in a tradition running from Isocrates and Cicero

To wit, "from this it follows that they should listen to the words of the instruction for their truth rather than for the eloquence with which they are spoken."[31] Everyone must learn to accept the fact that they approach the baptismal font with humility. It is faith seeking understanding, *credas ut intelligas*. One must be willing to trust that these words have more to teach than can simply be learned from the liberal arts.

The emphasis on the humility to listen to imperfect perfect speech has relevance for the leaders of the Church who do not always have the best education. Augustine continues:

> Let them also recognize that the only utterance to reach the ears of God is the devotion of the heart. Then they will not scoff if they happen to notice that some bishops and ministers of the Church lapse into barbarisms and grammatical mistakes when calling upon God, or fail to understand the words that they recite, and punctuate them incorrectly.[32]

This is a radical move by a trained rhetorician and well-educated man since he is saying that some barbarisms need not be corrected.[33] The last thing a custodian of correct language wants to hear is that in the service of the church of God, a barbarism or solecism is admissible. This kind of purity of language was required for those who were going to look polished and needed their cultural authority to win arguments at court.[34] This was the whole telos of the *liberales artes*, polished language for the arrogant to prove their worth in the world to gain fame and power.

The liturgy of the Church requires new rules. If the new authoritative cultural texts are the scriptures, which contained barbarisms and solecisms,

all the way to Northrop Frye, Marshall McLuhan, and Barack Obama, that refuses to honor a divorce between linguistic form and meaning. Speech matters because words not only describe things but also do things," Cameron, *Christ Meets Me Everywhere*, 36.

31　*cat. rud.* 9.13. (CCSL 46.135; WSA V, 86).

32　*cat. rud.* 9.13.

33　R. P. H. Green has reservations about how widespread this was for Augustine in "Augustine's De Doctrina Christiana: Some Clarifications," *Respublica Litterarum*, 15 (1992), 101–2. I hope to show that Augustine was willing to make this a regular part of his preaching when necessary. While it may not have been his entire mode of speaking, it is used in certain instances to make himself understood.

34　Peter Brown, *Power and Persuasion*, 35–70.

these must be permissible. Permissible for many reasons. For the educated, the simple language forces them to reject their pride for the humility which God came to teach. For the uneducated, it allows them to understand a language which they would not otherwise be able to without the proper education. In typically Augustinian fashion, the great preacher sums it up precisely:

> language mistakes should be borne with a good heart by people who have learned that, while to be well-spoken in the law courts is a question of oratorical style, in the Church it is a question of prayer. Thus, while the language of the law courts can perhaps on occasion be called good speech, it can never be called benediction.[35]

Augustine plays on the Latin phrases *bona dictio* and *benedictio*. The latter is blessing and is the truly good speech, even when it does not follow the culturally superior styles learned in the grammatical schools. All those who want to come to the baptismal font must come in humility.

As Augustine proceeds through the treatise, helping Deogratias address himself to the widest audience possible, he even includes those who have no education at all.[36] Augustine encourages those teaching catechumens to be aware of the country folk, the *rustici*,[37] writing, "And even when we are speaking under these circumstances, important differences arise depending on whether there are just a few people present or many, whether these are educated or uneducated or a mixture of both groups, whether they are city-dwellers or country-people (*urbani an rustici*)."[38] With the wisdom of a preacher and a teacher of many years, Augustine notes that one cannot speak the same way to all people. Moreover, he explicitly states that those desiring baptism are not just wealthy urban elites, *urbani*, but also include uneducated, country people.

The realities of what this entails for the population are not lost on Augustine. He cautions, "it is indeed inevitable that these different audiences

---

35 *cat. rud.* 9.13. (CCSL 46.135; WSA V, 86).

36 *cat. rud.* 9. 13. (CCSL 46.135). In this passage, Augustine uses both the phrase *idiota* to describe the uneducated, as well as *illiteratti*. Later on in *cat. rud.*16.24, he will talk about how the *genere idiotarum* come to the church wanting to become Christians.

37 E. G. Clark, "Pastoral Care: Town and Country in Late-Antique Preaching," in *Urban Centers and Rural Contexts in Late Antiquity* (East Lansing: Michigan State University Press, 2001), 265–85.

38 *cat. rud.* 15.23 (CCSL 46:147; WSA V, 112).

will in each individual case have a different influence on the state of mind of the one who is about to speak, and that the address given will in a certain fashion mirror the actual state of mind of the one who gives it."[39] Whoever teaches this loose gathering of people must adapt even their mind to the mixed congregation. As Augustine states in his sermons, this gathering of a diverse group is good for the entire body, the *totus Christus*. He ends this quote saying, "even as the listeners themselves also influence one another in various ways by their very presence."[40] While this work is intended for a possibly less educated teacher, Augustine hints at what is learned by being in the presence of a different societal class. Imagine an urbane sophisticated wealthy Carthaginian standing next to a country farmer who has made the long trek into the city center to hear the famous Augustine. They are going to look, smell, speak, and act differently. Augustine says that this influence is part of what makes up the body of Christ. They are all *rudes*. The poorly dressed country farmer and the fisherman coming off the docks, as well as the nobleman and lawyer, all come into one class at the church. This is part of the influence that Augustine thinks is important in the catechumenate for those who want to become *condiscipuli* with Augustine himself in the *schola Christi*. They all come to learn from the scriptures, which as the new authority permits different ways of using Latin, which one might call *Latinitas Christiana*.

Latin Style for the Less Educated

For Augustine, the purpose of the scriptures in less high-flown style has a two-fold importance. On one level, it allows the less educated to understand better. On another, it forces the educated to learn humility. He does not make this case fully in the *On the Catechizing of the Uninstructed*, but he does in many different instances throughout the sermons.[41] As he stated above in *On the Catechizing of the Uninstructed*, Augustine thinks that "barbarisms and solecisms" should not be a hindrance to those who know good Latin style from worshipping in the Christian community. In what follows, I will first establish what barbarisms and solecisms meant to the grammarian and then how Augustine undermines that definition in his preaching.

---

39 *cat. rud.* 15.23 (CCSL 46:147; WSA V, 112).
40 *cat. rud.* 15.23 (CCSL 46:147; WSA V, 112).
41 *cat. rud.*16.24, *s.* 124.3, *s.* 198.60.

Most late ancient Latin manuals of grammar contained a section on defining barbarism and solecism based on the first great treatise of rhetoric, the *Rhetorica ad Herrenium*.[42] Once thought to be written by Cicero, this manual has served as the standard by which most other grammatical manuals were written. In Book IV, the manual makes a simple distinction between two classes of vice:

> Latinitas is that which keeps speech pure and removed from every vice. Vices in speech, which is less than pure Latin, can be named two ways, solecism and barbarism. A solecism is when one uses many words for what can better be described by one higher quality word. A barbarism is when something is said by an error of pronunciation.[43]

In an attempt to preserve the *sermo purus* (pure speech), one must remove all *vitia* (vices) from speech.

The relationship of Augustine with these two forms of linguistic vice changes somewhat throughout his life. As we have already shown earlier, in his youth he learned to fear barbarism more than actual vice. Augustine confesses, "It made me more wary of committing some barbarism in speech than of being jealous of others who did not commit it when I did."[44] Augustine's attitude towards these linguistic vices shows some development over time. Critically, he seems to fear these vices more in the earlier Cassiciacum dialogues, written for a literate audience. In *On Order* (390), composed at Cassiciacum, he states that sometimes poets use something similar to barbarism and solecism though they call them metaplasm and schemata.[45] When one considers what

---

42 Daniel J. Taylor, "Varro and the Teaching of Latin." *The Classical Outlook* 92.1 (2017): 9–14. Cf. Marrou, *Education in Antiquity*, 170 and 252.

43 *Rhet. Her.*, IV, 12, 17 (Calboli, 1993; English, translation mine): "Latinitas est, quae sermonem purum conservat, ab omni vitio remotum. Vitia in sermone, quo minus is Latinus sit, duo possunt esse: soloecismus et barbarismus. Soloecismus est, cum in verbis pluribus consequens verbum superius non adcommodatur. Barbarismus est, cum verbis aliquid vitiose efferatur." We see this same taxonomy of vice in most of the Late Ancient Grammars including Diomedes, Donatus, and Charisius.

44 *conf.* 1.19.30 (CCSL 27.16; WSA I/1, 60).

45 *ord.* 2.4.13 (CCSL 29.114): "Soloecismos et barbarismos quos vocant, poetae adamaverunt; quae schemata et metaplasmos mutatis appellare nominibus quam manifesta vitia fugere maluerunt."

is found in the poets, some things which were formerly known as *barbarismus* or *solecismus* can rightfully be called *metaplasm* or *schematum*. In neither case does he totally reject calling something a barbarism. This demonstrates that after his conversion, Augustine changes his attitude slightly.

As the scripture becomes for Augustine his new authority, he can choose to overlook what would have once been considered poor Latin in the scriptures.[46] On one occasion, Augustine even says that Christ gets to decide what is good Latin. For instance, in 1 Timothy 1:15, Augustine finds the phrase, "*Christus Iesus, Christus Salvator.*"[47] He says to ignore what the grammarians might find unpleasing about this neologism *Salvator*. The word should be *salus*, according to Augustine.[48] *Salvator* was not used in the sense that it is used in scripture until it was recorded there. The ancient authorities would not have permitted this kind of innovation in the language. But for Augustine who has changed his authority from the *Aeneid* to Holy Scripture, he says that these words can now be considered and used as Latin. When Christ came, he made these words Latin.[49]

By the time Augustine has been preaching in Hippo for several years, he shows outright disdain for the quest for purity of language. In a sermon on the Gospel of John likely preached at Hippo in 406, Augustine delights in challenging the *Latinitas* of his day,

> But, these, how are they born to him? In what way not of bloods, as
> of a man and a woman. Bloods is not Latin; but because the Greek

---

46 Philip Burton notes the question of Augustine's *Latinitas* has been labeled the "*Sondersprache*" hypothesis. I share Burton's hesitation to apply this too broadly to the question of whether Christian Latin is really its own language, but it is quite evident that words are used differently in the context of a community based in the scriptures. Burton, "Augustine and Language" *A Companion to Augustine* (Oxford: Blackwell Publishing Ltd, 2012), 124.

47 *s.* 299.6 (AugR 57.475): "Christus, inquit: Iesus, id est Christus Salvator. Hoc est enim latine Iesus. Nec quaerant grammatici quam sit latinum, sed Christiani quam verum. Salus enim latinum nomen est. Salvare et salvator non fuerunt haec latina antequam veniret Salvator: quando ad latinos venit, et haec latina fecit."

48 The word "salvator" does not appear in the OLD. The OLD also supports the judgment of Augustine that the word "salus" would be the expected word for a "savior." OLD V.2 1856–1857.

49 Augustine makes a similar point here: *en. Ps.* 105.10 (CCSL 40.1559–1590).

has it in the plural, the translator preferred to keep it and speak what the grammarians would say is not Latin and still spell out the truth so that it could be heard by the weak and feeble.[50]

Blood, *sanguis*, in Latin only exists in the singular. But Augustine finds a deeper meaning in what would otherwise be a barbarism.[51] Augustine explains why this is bad Latin:

> You see, if he said "blood" in the singular, he would not be spelling out what he wished to; human beings after all are born of the bloods of male and female. So let us say it then and not be afraid of a caning from the grammarians, provided we can get at the sure and solid truth. To find fault with what he understands is to be ungrateful for having understood.[52]

Digging into the incorrect Latin of the Psalm text, Augustine finds that the plural blood offers a more nuanced interpretation. To the extent Augustine does overlook this *barbarism*, he says it is for the truth. Though grammarians would have beat a student who wrote this kind of poor Latin, Augustine thinks that if it expresses a deeper truth, the *sermo purus* should be relinquished. The scriptures here sound more like the speech of *rustici*, the *rudes* than the *honestior* speech Augustine once learned and taught.

For Augustine the preacher, one submits to the truth rather than a particular style of speaking. Theologically, Augustine now understands that the *sermo piscatorius* has a divine agenda. God wants to accommodate some who might not understand a higher register, and, indeed, to teach all the need to rely on Christ as the *via humilitatis*. Augustine's change in style arises out of his own encounter with the humble Christ. He could not go on speaking as he once did. It becomes evident the more one looks at his language in the sermons where he communicates with the *rustici* and *urbani* the *doctrina Christianai* that the *Verbum caro factum est* (John 1:14)!

The transformation of style does not stop here. Augustine prefers using another barbarism in his speech for the benefit of those listening to him.

---

50 *Io. eu. tr.* 2.14 (CCSL 36.18).
51 He makes the same move in his homily on this very verse, *en. Ps.* 50.19.
52 *Io. eu. tr.* 2.14 (CCSL 36.18).

When Augustine preached on Psalm 138, there was a reference to *os*. This word in Latin, depending on the pronunciation—either a long "o" or short "o"—could either mean "mouth" or "bone." In the middle of a sermon, Augustine uses impure speech, saying, "My bone is not hidden from you, he says, for it was you who created it in that secret place. I have a certain *ossum* hidden within me (we prefer to use the word *ossum*; better that linguistic experts should find fault with us than that people should not understand)."[53] In common North African Latin, some speakers chose to make the word for bone end in the more typical ending *ossum*. This movement to make a 2nd declension noun from a 3rd declension noun came into more common use because North African pronunciation did not distinguish between these two ways of saying "o."[54] Augustine boldly chooses to follow local custom.

His reasoning for saying "*ossum*" rather an "*os*" is slightly different than his explanation of "*sanguines*." In the sermon above, he overlooked the improper word use of the scriptures for the sake of truth. In this sermon on Psalm 138, he chooses the improper speech for the sake of understanding of the people. The Latin is a phrase sometimes still used in Italy, *melius est reprehendant nos grammatici, quam non intellegant populi*.[55] The orator turned preacher unashamedly reverses course on his own education and status preferring to use the speech most likely to be understood by the greatest amount of people.[56] For the sake of truth and for understanding, Augustine chooses to transgress grammatical rules in his preaching and commentary on scripture.[57]

Those two reasons more likely suit the less educated part of his congregation. As an explanation for how his preaching could benefit even those

---

53 *en. Ps.* 138.20 (CCSL 40.2004–2005): "habeo in abscondito quoddam ossum. sic enim potius loquamur: melius est reprehendant nos grammatici, quam non intellegant populi."

54 Augustine admits to being ashamed of this fact, *doc. chris.* 2.13.19.

55 "It is better to take the abuse of the grammarians than the people not understand."

56 See also, *en. Ps.* 36.3.6 (CCSL 38.372): "tota die miseretur et feneratur. feneratur quidem latine dicitur et qui dat mutuum et qui accipit; planius hoc autem dicitur, si dicamus fenerat. quid ad nos quid grammatici uelint? melius in barbarismo nostro uos intellegitis, quam in nostra disertitudine uos deserti eritis."

57 This same move choosing a form more understandable to North Africa, Augustine preaches, *s.* 37.14 (CCSL 41:459): "Videte quemadmodum neat, immo videte quemadmodum neiat–dum omnes instruantur, grammatici non timeantur–. Manus autem suas aperuit pauperi, fructum autem porrexit inopi."

who were highly educated, Augustine says that the simplicity and even the uneducated forms of Latin found in scripture have benefit. First, explaining who these people were who used what we might call the *sermo piscatorius* "fisherman's speech," Augustine preaches,

> It was men quite untrained in the liberal arts, and as far as secular disciplines go totally uneducated, unskilled in grammar, unequipped with the techniques of dialectic, it was fishermen whom Christ sent into the sea of the world with the nets of faith, and very few of them at that.[58]

These men were again the lower class of human according to Diomedes. They were the *humiliores* in distinction from Augustine's class of *honestiores*. That they were unskilled and uneducated only made them more effective for their task. To wit,

> And yet by their means he so filled the Churches with every kind of fish, that a great many even of the wise ones of the world, to whom the cross of Christ seemed so disgraceful, are signing themselves with it on the forehead, and setting up in the seat of shame the very thing they thought we should be ashamed of, and about which they used to taunt us.[59]

Why would these fishermen, the gospel writers, be able to gather every kind of fish? They can gather them because the speech they used influenced all who heard it.[60] To the extent that everyone is proud, the shame of the Cross is the antidote to pride. Even this had to be spoken in a way for all to understand, educated and uneducated alike. Yet, the speech itself was

58 *s.* 272A (= fragmentum Verbraken 38), (RB 84.265; WSA III/7, 303): "Ineruditos liberalibus disciplinis, et omnino quantum ad saeculi doctrinas pertinet impolitos, non peritos grammatica, non armatos dialectica, piscatores christus cum retibus fidei ad mare saeculi paucissimos misit."

59 *s.* 272A (= fragmentum Verbraken 38), (RB 84.265; WSA III/7, 303).

60 Although the provenance is disputed, Augustine may have stated a similar principle more succinctly in *s.* 298A (= Weidmann 12 = Ps.Aug. *s.* Mai 54, genuitas difficiliter accipitur), (PLS 2.1161): "Ecce ubique docent piscatores sapientiam, et errant grammatici et oratores sequentes stultitiam."

shameful for the educated who needed to learn humility even more than those already considered *humilior*. It was the language of fishermen which Christ used. The standard practice of the day was for emperors to choose the most eloquent speakers to herald their accomplishments.[61] In this case, Christ does the opposite because he came to teach humility.

The reason Christ chose fishermen to speak on his behalf to the world demonstrates Christ's power and his love for each. Augustine explains this more thoroughly in *s.* 43:

> "Give me," he says, "that fisherman, give me a common man, give me an uneducated man, give me one whom the senator doesn't deign to talk to, not even when he's buying fish. That's the one to give me," he says. "If I fill that one, it will be obvious that it's I who am doing it."[62]

Christ uses the fisherman to prove his power and to correct the pride of the senator. Augustine explains Christ's preference for the fisherman by saying, "The fisherman isn't in a position to boast about anything except Christ. Let him come first, to give a salutary lesson in humility. Let the fisherman come first; the emperor is best brought along through him."[63] In the Church, the fisherman comes first rather than the other way around. The Church has upside down values in comparison to the world and this is to demonstrate both Christ's power and Christ's love for all, including the otherwise overlooked fisherman.

When Augustine reads the scriptures and sees solecisms and barbarisms, he does not overlook them or excuse them, but he takes it as a cue for learning humility which is necessary for all who enter into the community of the Church as *rudes*. That Augustine did this serves to demonstrate the extent to which he is following the humble Christ. His speech now reflects in some ways the *sermo piscatorius* or the language of fishermen of the scriptures.

The instances from the sermons of Augustine have shown his direct engagement with barbarisms and solecism. One other form of rhetorical vice, a kind of solecism, can help clarify how Augustine thought differently

---

61 As Augustine was himself in *conf.* 6.

62 *s.* 43.6 (CCSL 41.510; WSA III/2, 242).

63 *s.* 43.6.

about certain rules of rhetoric and *auctoritas* in *Latinitas Christiana*. To this point we have seen how Augustine was willing to find meaning in barbarism and solecism which would not have been allowed in the standard *auctores*. The scriptures had become the new foundation for understanding what kind of speech was permitted. Several late ancient Latin grammars forbid another form of rhetorical vice known as *tapinosis*. The ancient grammarian forbid that any speaker would speak of something divine in a low form of speech. The word itself comes from the Greek word for humility, ταπείνωσις. Augustine transgresses this oratorical vice frequently when discussing the *sermo piscatorius* of the gospels, especially the Gospel of John.[64]

In two important grammatical treatise of the era, Diomedes (c. 400 CE) *Ars Grammatica*, and Donatus (320–380 CE) *Ars Maior*, the vice of *tapinosis* is forbidden.[65] Explaining this vice, Diomedes writes, "*Tapinosis* is the low presentation of something great, contrary to its dignity, as in *marcido dies sole pallet*, when *marcere* [to be weak or flabby] is properly used of earthly, rather than immortal things [i.e., *sole*, the sun]."[66] Not only Diomedes, but also Donatus, the former teacher of Jerome, describes the same phenomenon.[67] He defines the error of *tapinosis* as, "the setting low of a great thing with a sentence that does not indicate its greatness."[68] Two important manuals on rhetoric cite this as a critical error. One would not want to present something, or someone, divine in a manner "contrary to its dignity." How then does one

---

64 For a fuller treatment of Augustine's usage of *tapinosis*, see: Charles G. Kim, Jr "*Ipsa Ructatio Eungaleium Est: Tapinosis* in Augustine's Homilies," *Augustinian Studies* 50:2 (2019) 197–214.

65 Catherine Chin, "Imagining Classics," in *Grammar and Christianity in the Late Roman World* (Philadelphia: University of Pennsylvania Press, 2008), 11–38, has a sustained explanation of how the *artes grammaticae* formed "a specific and relatively consistent genre of educational writing in late antiquity." The vice of tapinosis is also cited by Charisius, *Ars Grammatica*, Book 4. ed. Karl Barwick (Leipzig: Dieter'sche Verlags-Buchhandlung, 1992), 357; Cledonius, *Ars Cledonii* (*Grammatici Latini*, 5.2, ed. Heinrich Keil [Leipzig: Teubner, 1855–1880], 79).

66 Diomedes, *Grammatici Latini* 1.450.1–1.451.20 (ed. Heinrich Keil, [Leipzig: Teubner, 1855–1880]; trans. Catherine Chin, in "Imagining Classics" [n.6], 32): "tapinosis est contra dignitatem magnae rei humilis expositio, ut est marcido dies sole pallet, cum marceant terrena, non inmortalia."

67 Cf. Jerome, *Apologia Contra Rufinum* 1.16 (CCSL 79:15), and Chin, "Imagining Classics" (n.6), 76.

68 *Grammatici Latini* 4.395.14–4.395.24 (trans. Chin, "Imagining Classics" [n.6], 32): "tapinosis est humilitas rei magnae non id agente sententia."

speak about a God who himself chooses to present himself in a manner that "does not indicate its greatness?"

When Augustine preaches about the incarnation of the *Verbum Dei,* he presents it defiantly in a manner contrary to its greatness. He uses coarse language which would be inappropriate if the Word did not choose to empty himself and take on the *forma servi.* On account of Christ's kenosis, Augustine now has biblical warrant to describe God in quite earthly terms. This is exactly what he does in several homilies on the belching fisherman who is one of the first to describe the incarnation. Augustine preaches about John, "'And how am I to understand his being God and Word?' May the one who gave the fisherman his fill also cause you to drink. Meanwhile, just listen to the one who's belching, believe his belching, so that you too may climb up on the ladder of faith and take your fill of lively understanding."[69] John belched the Gospel! All those gathered to hear Augustine speak from the bishop's seat now hear Augustine delighting in this rude expression to describe the Gospel itself.

This is not the sensibility that he learned from his oratorical manuals, like those of Diomedes or Donatus. Augustine deliberately exalts in this crass expression of the divine arrival on earth. Divinity is described contrary to its dignity because that is how the divine one chose to be remembered. Earlier in the same sermon, Augustine says, "It would be more advantageous for the Lord to gain an orator from a fisherman than a fisherman from an orator."[70] Why is it more advantageous? If the Lord wants to teach humility, it must be taught in a form consistent with its content. One must speak humbly to present humility well.

The Fisherman in the *City of God* vs. the *Sermons*

As a final way to demonstrate the kind of language Augustine uses to communicate with a broad audience, we will compare two different ways Augustine emphasizes the *sermo piscatorius.* Most frequently, Augustine

---

69 *s.* 341.5 [= *s.* Dolbeau 22.4] (EAA 147.559; WSAs, III/11, 287): "Et quomodo intellegam Deum et Verbum? Faciat te bibere, qui saturauit piscatorem. Interim modo audi ructantem, crede ructanti, ut et tu possis ascendens per gradum fidei uiuacitate intellegentiae saturari."

70 *s.* 341.5 (EAA 147.553–578; WSA, III/11, 283–309). "Salubrius itaque lucratus est Dominus oratorem de piscatore, quam piscatorem de oratore."

utilizes this framing of the Gospels in his sermons. One on occasion, however, he makes a similar move in *City of God*. Considering that *City of God* was composed for a literate pagan audience, we can see how Augustine changes the setting and language of a familiar trope.[71] One was meant to be read, and the other was meant to be heard. One was spoken off-the-cuff, the other was dictated to a scribe and likely edited before being included in the final manuscript.[72]

The comparison of these two short texts suggests that Augustine as preacher spoke differently than how he wrote.[73] Moreover, it evidences his ability to reach an advanced audience and also to communicate with a mixed audience, including many *rustici*. Christine Mohrmann described Augustine's homiletical style in terms of three main goals, first and foremost clarity, then expressiveness, and finally, weightiness.[74] This unique homiletical style we have seen to some degree in the way that he adapts the poor Latin quality of the biblical text to a preaching audience in the examples above.[75] We have

71 Gerard O'Daly, *Augustine's City of God: A Reader's Guide* (Oxford: Oxford University Press, 1999), 36–38.

72 In speaking about the difficulty of writing *City of God,* he laments,: "They laid a hand upon me, tore me away from other grounds for worry, and so bound me with their chains—so help me God!—that I did not know what I should admire in them more: the perfection of the priesthood, the teachings of philosophy, the ample knowledge of history, or the charm of eloquence, (iniecerunt manum, ereptumque aliis sollicitudinum causis, suis vinculis illigarunt [ta enim mihi Deus propitius sit], ut ego anceps sim quid in illis magis mirer, sacerdotii perfectionem, philosophiae dogmata, historiae plenam notitiam, an facundiae iucunditatem)," *ep.* 154.2 (CSEL 44.428; WSA III/2, 406).

73 Philip Burton illustrates a similar pattern in his article, "Augustine and Language," *A Companion to Augustine* (Oxford: Blackwell Publishing Ltd, 2012): 113–24.

74 Mohrmann writes,

"Within the framework of these observations, one better understands how St. Augustine has consciously created a homeletical style which was to meet the needs of popular preaching. In this style he seeks three things: first and foremost clarity, then expressiveness, and third gravity.

Mohrmann, "Saint Augustin prédicateur," in *Etudes Sur les Latin des Chretiennes* vol.1 (Rome, Italy: Edizioni di Storia e Letteratura, 1961), 396.

75 Gert Partoens emphasizes Mohrmann's point, "Die Klarheit ist in erster Linie die Wirkung einer stilisierten Version der gesprochenen Sprache, die durch einen relativ einfachen Wortschatz und eine ebenso klare Syntax gekennzeichnet wird." (The clarity is primarily the effect of a stylized version of the spoken language, characterized by a

seen these adaptations, without precisely naming it, in the sermons describing
the schoolroom of the church. Here, we will see the simpler charming speech
in the sermons in how Augustine compares the *piscator* with the *orator*.

In the *City of God*, Augustine contrasts Platonists and Christian beliefs
in terms of humility. Given that Augustine wrote the *City of God* for a more
highly educated audience, he naturally composes a higher register argument.
Before he can get to the incarnation, he makes a long statement of the beliefs
of the Platonists saying:

> In any case, since you also claim that there are in the heavens the
> immortal bodies of beings who are immortally blessed, why do you
> persist in the opinion that, for us to be happy, we must flee from all
> bodies? Why do you persist in this opinion, trying to make it look
> as though you have rational grounds for fleeing from the Christian
> faith, unless it is because—to say it again—Christ is humble and you
> are proud? Perhaps you are ashamed to be corrected? This, too, is a
> fault found only in the proud.

> Sed qualiacumque sint, cum incorruptibilia prorsus et immortalia
> nihiloque animae contemplationem, qua in Deo figitur, impedientia
> praedicentur vosque etiam dicatis esse in caelestibus immortalia
> corpora immortaliter beatorum: quid est quod, ut beati simus, omne
> corpus fugiendum esse opinamini, ut fidem christianam quasi ratio-
> nabiliter fugere videamini, nisi quia illud est, quod iterum dico:
> Christus est humilis, vos superbi? An forte corrigi pudet?[76]

For the purposes of the argument, it is necessary to place the Latin
beside the English. In order to make sense of the complex Latin syntax,
the translator has to break up the one long-winded sentence into several
sentences. This intentional use of a longer and more difficult structure also
includes other elements of higher register speech. We notice some elements
of the period style where Augustine contrasts the beginning section of the
question of "heavenly bodies" with the question of whether one ought to
flee all bodies.

relatively simple vocabulary and syntax that is just as clear). Partoens, "Augustinus Als
Praedigter," 245.

 76 *ciu.* 10.29 (CCSL 47.306; WSA I/6, 340).

In this passage, Augustine makes two short observations, "Christ is humble, and you are proud." He has varied his scheme for emphasis. The important stylistic point of this text which was to be read by the most educated is that Augustine uses a syntax more reminiscent of a Ciceronian sentence, long and drawn out through the use of multiple conjunctions. He rarely employs such a high style in his sermons.

He then moves to the central point, describing the humility required to hear the message fishermen proclaimed about the incarnation rather than orators. These learned men must bend their stiff necks and ignore their embarrassment:

> It is embarrassing, apparently, for learned men to turn from being disciples of Plato and to become disciples of Christ, who, by his spirit, taught a mere fisherman to understand and to say, In the beginning was the Word, and the Word was with God, and the Word was God. He was in the beginning with God. All things were made through him, and nothing that was made was made without him. In him was life, and that life was the light of men; and the light shines in the darkness, and the darkness has not comprehended it (Jn 1:1–5).

> Pudet videlicet doctos homines ex discipulis Platonis fieri discipulos Christi, qui piscatorem suo Spiritu docuit sapere ac dicere: In principio erat Verbum, et Verbum erat apud Deum, et Deus erat Verbum. Hoc erat in principio apud Deum. Omnia per ipsum facta sunt, et sine ipso factum est nihil, quod factum est. In ipso vita erat, et vita erat lux hominum, et lux in tenebris lucet, et tenebrae eam non comprehenderunt.[77]

These passages from *City of God* provide a place to consider the grammar in which they are presented, in addition to why humility is important. Augustine emphasizes the arrogance of the Platonists who would be ashamed to learn from fishermen. He does not speak directly about the fishermen or what this means for them, except to say that their lack of education created a stumbling block for the wise. Augustine does not elaborate further in this passage on

77 *ciu.* 10.29 (CCSL 47.306; WSA I/6, 340).

the nature of fishermen, but this moment in the great work finishes with the connection to Platonism. These two excerpts from *City of God* do not showcase the tight clarity and punchiness of the sermons. Rather, Augustine composes elaborate sentences for the more educated.

In a sermon preached at Hippo, just after Easter, Augustine highlights the lack of education of the fishermen. He preaches in *s.* 250:

> The Lord Jesus chose the weak things of the world to confound the strong (1 Cor 1:27), and so in gathering his Church together from the whole wide world, he didn't begin with emperors or senators, but with fishermen.

> Dominus Iesus infirma mundi eligens ut confunderet fortia, et colligens Ecclesiam suam de toto orbe terrarum non coepit ab imperatoribus aut a senatoribus sed a piscatoribus.[78]

Notice here that we have a straightforward purpose clause, ending with a little rhetorical charm. The content is similar in that Augustine still teaches about humility. When he preaches though, he uses more forceful straight forward clauses with a little word play. Imagine the audience at Hippo which included the *rustici*, the *piscatores*, in addition to the *urbani* and *dives*. They hear Augustine proclaiming that first in the kingdom are not those with wealth and status. He goes to great lengths to clarify that God chooses the weak for the sake of the strong and not the other way around. We even hear a bit of Augustine's favored rhyming scheme, homoeoteleuton, "non coepit ab imperatoribus, aut a senatoribus, sed a piscatoribus."[79] The rhyme was critical as not only a delight to the ear, but also a helpful memory device.[80]

---

78 *s.* 250 (SChr 116.308). It is worth noting, contra Dossey, Augustine speaks about the fishermen's elevated role around the time of Easter. This is not a sermon in which Augustine seeks to curry the favor of the educated urban elite. He, rather, corrects their arrogance.

79 Christine Mohrman says, "It achieves great expressiveness through the constant use of a limited number of stylistic figures, namely parallelism, antithesis, climax, dialectic, multiple plays on the sound of words (of which rhyme is the most striking) plays on words, etc." Mohrman, "Saint Augustin prédicateur," 396–97.

80 It may also have been a characteristic style of North African speech. Mohrmann, "Saint Augustin Écrivain," *Etudes Sur les Latin des Chretiennes* V.1 (Rome: Edizioni di Storia e Letteratura, 1961), 269–71.

In the end of his beginning section of the sermon, Augustine echoes what he says to Deogratias. The church encompasses the entire range of social classes. Now all can come into one body, as he says:

> Finally, at the present day there is equal access to the grace of God for nobles and commoners, for the educated and the illiterate, for the poor and the rich. For receiving this grace pride doesn't push itself ahead of the humility of the person who knows nothing, has nothing, is worth nothing. But what did he say to them? Come, follow me, and I will make you fishers of men (Mk 1:17). If those fishermen hadn't come first, who would have caught us? Nowadays a person is considered a great preacher man, if he can give a good explanation of what was written by a fisherman.

> Denique hodie ad gratiam Domini pariter accedunt nobiles et ignobiles, doctus et imperitus, pauper et dives. Ad istam gratiam accipiendam non se praeponit superbia humilitati, nihil scientis, nihil habentis, nihil valentis. Sed quid eis dixit? Venite post me et faciam vos fieri piscatores hominum. Si illi piscatores non praecessissent, nos quis cepisset? Modo magnus est quilibet orator si potuerit bene exponere de quo scripsit piscator.[81]

Those who fit the designation of proud do not get first access to grace, the fisherman does. In contrast, Christ says to the *piscatores*, "you all come first." And if they had not been first and written about their experience, how would any in the late-ancient North Africa know that Christ had come? In order to even know about this momentous event, the great orator, in this case Augustine, must be able to discern what had been written by fishermen.

In another sermon preached at an unknown location, Augustine contrasts the fisherman and the orator even further. *S.* 87, possibly preached at Hippo, begins with Augustine's attentiveness to the agricultural cycle and connects it to a parable about the harvest.[82] Moving on to discussing how God brings people to himself, he describes the role of the fisherman's gospel, John. Augustine preaches:

81 *s.* 250.1 (SChr 116.308; WSA III/7, 121).

82 Verbraken does not give a location (*Études Critiques,* 74). Gryson gives the possibility of Hippo (*Répertoire général des auteurs,* 236).

So we must put off, he says, these proud people, they need healing by
some solid sense. Give me first, he says, this fisherman. Come here, you,
poor man, follow me. You have nothing, you know nothing, follow me.
Common, uneducated poor man, follow me. There's nothing in you for
people to be frightened of, there's a lot of space in you that can be filled.[83]

The whole focus of the rhetoric is aimed at those which some would have
said were not even he present. Augustine calls out directly to the poor man,
the uneducated rustic. This calling of Augustine is not in his own voice, but
rather he imagines himself speaking in the voice of Christ, a tactic culled
from his rhetorical days known as *Prosopopoeia*.[84] Augustine's aim is to speak
in the voice of Christ directly to the people who would not believe that He
would call them. He says to them that they do not need to be educated to
follow God's call. God will fill them up with all they need.

The moment continues and crescendos in a delightful antithesis and
parallelism, "To such an abundant fountain an entirely empty vessel has to be
brought. The fisherman left his nets, the sinner received grace, and became a
divine preacher."[85] Mohrmann eloquently writes that the most characteristic
part of the Augustinian sermon is the antithesis in parallelism which returns at
each moment is results from a way of thinking which is proper to the phrase.[86]
The fisherman without training or schooling because of the grace of God can
become a divine orator. A position known for its social caché and prestige is
now inhabited by a humble fisherman. What great power of God! The way
Augustine uses his Latin makes the line stick in the memory with its playfulness.
Three sentences of three words all ending with the same sound "or": *piscator*,
peccator, and *orator*. An extemporaneous sermon which the *notarius* captured for
all posterity. We hear Augustine meeting his people where they are. He uses his
gift to make the Gospel clear. It is as Mohrmann says, a manner of thought
which is proper to the trait. The form matches the content.

---

83 *s.* 87.10 (PL 38.537; WSA III/3, 416).

84 *conf.* 1.17.27 (CCSL 27:15). Cf. Quintillian, *Institutio Oratoria* 9.2 (LCL
127.50–51).

85 *s.* 87.10 (PL 38.537; WSA III/3, 416). Dimisit retia piscator, accepit gratiam
peccator, et factus est divinus orator.

86 Mohrman, "Saint Augustin prédicateur," 397: "The most characteristic feature
is the antithetical parallelism which returns at every moment and which results from a
way of thinking which is peculiar to it."

Conclusion

As a summary, I will return once more to a quote from Mohrmann. The Latin of Augustine's sermons is not necessarily equivalent to what every vulgar person spoke. It has a certain quality of his education which cannot be wiped away. Though his language carries with it some of his long training, it is not at the expense of its comprehensibility to a broad swath of people. To this point, Morhmann argues that the language of Augustine's preaching was not simply vulgar Latin. It was stylized to be sure, but the style was simple and easy to understand by the common man. Without speaking exactly like them, he was accessible to people who spoke even at a lower level.[87] The language is simple enough to be understood even by a man of the people. Just as Christ came and called the fishermen in a way that they would understand, and beginning with them, Augustine's own sermon reaches all who came to hear him. Peter Brown remarks similarly, "his own superbly unaffected 'Christian' style was in reality a simplicity achieved at the other side of vast sophistication."[88] He speaks at a level which any could understand and all could enjoy.

The lyrical stylings of Augustine are part and parcel of his theological understanding of who Christ is. In this case, the simplicity of the language, with some charm, bespeak the truth of Christ coming in humility. Although of course the Son does not abandon his role in the godhead, *forma dei*, when he becomes man, he assumes the *forma servi* in the womb of a woman. What we have shown above in the style of Augustine's preaching is his way of communicating his deep Christology in way that connects with his audience, whether lettered or not in a way a kind of *forma servi*. The Son is both God and human, as Augustine and the church confess. In the language of rhetoric, the Son can be spoken of in both high and low forms. Augustine's theology in his preaching is suffused with his understanding of rhetoric passed down through centuries of grammarians, yet not without his own unique contribution. Augustine's marriage of theology with rhetoric leaves a mark on the

87 Mohrman, "Saint Augustin prédicateur," 396: "The language of the preaching of Augustine is not the vulgar Latin of its time, it is rather a highly stylized form of Latin as it was spoken in a cultured environment but which was, in its simplicity, easy to understand, even for the common man. Without descending to the level of the people, he speaks a language which remains accessible."

88 Brown, *Augustine*, 265.

discipline of rhetoric. To miss the theology in the rhetoric is to miss the whole project. He was at root a rhetorician inflamed with a love of wisdom which he found in the *humilis Deus* known through scripture.

In another treatise, Augustine argues that recognizing beauty, and by extension its enjoyment, leads one to want to learn more. He says, "The loveliness of such knowledge is now perceived in thought, and the thing so known is loved."[89] This is another way of saying that in order for something to be known well, its loveliness must be perceived. The purpose of the preaching of Augustine is not for those who hear to simply be impressed with Augustine. He wants them to come to love and enjoy the God he preaches. He thus calls out to all in a language they will understand and in which they might even enjoy. This enjoyment might spark a love of knowledge which will lead them to that end for which the whole of scripture and the Christian life seeks, the *beata vita*.

---

89 *de. Trin.* 10.1.3 (CCSL 50.122; WSA I/5, 289).

CHAPTER 5

AUGUSTINE'S ECCLESIOLOGY
Christ the Teacher in the School of the Church

Introduction

OUR THESIS FROM THE BEGINNING has been how Augustine shows the virtue of humility found in Christ in both the words and deeds of his sermons as the basis for his theology of preaching. This chapter will continue that research by relating Augustine's theology of preaching to his ecclesiology. Augustine's understanding of the church looms large in how Augustine's sermon functions within the *totus Christus* the body of the Christ, the church, with Christ its head. It will build off the research in chapter 2, by showing how Augustine rejected his former role as *magister* because of the humility modeled for him by Ambrose in Milan who listened to God speak in the scriptures. The means of seeing Augustine acting humbly requires a thorough investigation of the terms he uses and their larger historical contexts. That said, the language of school remains a critical component of his preaching, though modified for the context of the Church.[1]

The aim of this chapter will be to see Augustine at work modeling for his own congregation an example of humility. Augustine knew the power

1 Dolbeau, "Sermones," 258.

of models because he saw it in the theaters and in his own education. In Milan, the power of a different kind of *exemplum* in Ambrose moved him to consider Christianity in a way he had never imagined. Ambrose found his virtue in listening to the words of the humble Christ. Augustine would in turn do the same.

There are many potential ways in which Augustine does model humility for his congregation, but we will focus on the ways Augustine rejects and reimagines the role of the *magister*. For Augustine, one way to conceive of the church, his ecclesiology, is as a school where one learns to see Christ. We will first show how the relationship between a *magister* and a *discipulus* was understood in the ancient rhetorical schools. We will then turn to Augustine's redefinition of that relationship for the *schola Christi*, the school of Christ in the liturgy of the Church. Augustine the arrogant teacher renounces his position and becomes a pastor. Through his example, Augustine's preaching become a means of displaying for the faithful in the spectacle of the liturgy how all can listen to Christ the Teacher.

Sermon 23 and Christ the Teacher

s. 23 illustrates well the reimagined school of the body of Christ in Augustine's preaching. In the sermon, Augustine preforms a sermon humbly, without pridefully asserting himself as humble. In this sermon, Augustine states outright, drawing on James 3, "No one should wish to be called a teacher (*magister*)."[2] A man who once held the esteemed role of *magister* says this to the local church at Carthage in the Basilica Fausti. Presumably, the position of teacher was a celebrated position which came with quite a bit of authority and prestige. The *magistri* of the ancient world—although some merely freedman—held an important position as "guardians of language."[3] It was their job to train young noblemen to master classical texts and use the language found therein to form a culturally superior kind of human, the *vir bonus, dicendi peritus*. It was the teachers who knew the texts and how to speak that ornamented language so sought after for future magistrates

2 Although Jerome does call him "episcopus es, ecclesiarum christi magister." Jerome, *Epistula* 112.15 (CSEL 55, 384.21).

3 Robert Kaster's book, *Gaurdians of Language*, is a translation of one phrase used to describe a grammarian, *custos latini*.

and rhetoricians. In this very specific way, people revered *magistri* for their command of speech and erudition.

Augustine would have his hearers believe otherwise, "No one should wish to be a called a teacher." To begin to understand why this might be the case, Augustine cites a quote from Christ found in the Gospel of Mt 23:10, "Do not wish to be called masters; you have one master, the Christ." The full quote from the sermon proceeds as follows:

> We bishops are called teachers (*doctores*), but in many matters we seek a teacher ourselves, and we certainly don't want to be regarded as masters. That is dangerous, and forbidden by the Lord himself, who says Do not wish to be called masters (*magistri*); you have one master (*magister*), the Christ (Mt 23:10). So the office of master (*magistri*) is dangerous, the state of disciple safe. That's why the psalm says, To my hearing you will give joy and exultation (Ps 51:8). Hearing the word is safer than uttering it. That's why that man feels quite safe as he stands and hears him and rejoices with joy at the bridegroom's voice (Jn 3:29).[4]

The standard English translation glosses over the important technical terms in the Latin. Augustine describes the bishops as teachers, but the word is *doctors* "learned ones." A bishop was a learned one and he did do a form of teaching to be sure, but he did not want to be called a *magister*. Scripturally speaking, that would have been dangerous; as Jesus says, "do not wish to be called *magistri*." As the true teacher, Christ discourages this desire to be a *magister* in the *schola Christi*.

In the next section of this sermon, Augustine redraws the relationship between himself and those who hear him. As stated above, he is a *doctor*, the one addressing people who listen to him in a manner akin to what a *magister* does, as he would have known well. That said, he does not want to be called a *magister*. Although he speaks before a gathering of willing listeners as if

---

4 *s.* 23.1 (CCSL 41.309; WSA III/2, 57): "Doctores dicimur, sed in multis doctorem quaerimus, nec volumus nos haberi magistros. Periculosum est enim et prohibitum Domino ipso dicente: Ne velitis dici magistri, unus est magister vester Christus. Periculosum ergo magisterium, discipulatus securus est. Ideo psalmus: Auditui meo, inquit, dabis gaudium et exsultationem. Securior est enim verbi auditor, quam verbi prolator. Ideo ille securus stat, et audit eum, et gaudio gaudet propter vocem sponsi."

in a school, he redefines how this process should work in the *schola Christi*. He writes:

> The apostle had taken on the part of teacher (*doctoris*) because his stewardship obliged him to, and just see what he says about it: With fear and much trembling was I among you (1 Cor 2:3). So it is much safer that both we who speak and you who listen should realize that we are fellow disciples (*condiscipulos*) under one master (*sub uno magister*). Yes, it's unquestionably safer, and it helps enormously if you listen to us not as your masters (*magistros*) but as your fellow pupils (*condiscipulos*).[5]

The term which Augustine offers in this sermon is that he is a *condiscipulus*.[6] In common parlance of the time, there existed only a simple two-part relationship: *magister* and *discipulus*. Augustine imagines that the preacher plays an intermediate role between the teacher and the student. Just like Jesus Christ, he too is a *doctor*, learned in a certain way. He is also a member of the Church, and so he learns as a *condiscipulus*. He shares in some fashion the functions of the teacher and others as a student. In a creative reinterpretation, Augustine infuses old categories with new meaning.

By calling himself a *condiscipulus* and Christ the *magister* Augustine uses his words as an *exemplum* of humility. He does not just say "be humble," but instead shows them how to be humble by relinquishing his own esteemed title of *magister*. He puts himself in one single grouping of all those gathered as a *condiscipulus* before the *unus magister, Christus*. As we proceed, we will show just how great this renunciation was, but suffice it to say for now that Augustine is not merely speaking in humble words but is *illocuting*—performing his speech—in a humble example for all to see.

5 *s.* 23.1 (CCSL 41.309; WSA III/2, 57): "Et quia doctoris Apostolus susceperat dispensationis necessitate personam videte quid dicit: Cum timore et tremore multo fui apud vos 5. Tutius est ergo ut et nos qui loquimur, et vos qui auditis, sub uno magistro condiscipulos nos esse noverimus. Omnino tutius est, et hoc expedit ut nos non tamquam magistros, sed tamquam condiscipulos vestros audiatis."

6 Augustine uses the word 12 times in the *Sermones ad Populum* alone. *s.* 23 (CCSL 41.309), *s.* 134 (PL 38.742), *s.* 159B [= Dolbeau 21] (SL 41Bb.75), *s.* 257 (SChr 116.338), *s.* 258 ISChr 116.348), *s.* 261 (SPM 1.89), *s.* 270 (Pl 38.1237), *s.* 278 (PL 38.1273), *s.* 292 (PL 38.1319), *s.* 301A (MiAg 1.82), *s.* 340A (MiAg 1.566), *s.* 375C (MiAg 1.340).

Ancient Education from the Teacher to the Students

To appreciate the full context of this oratorical move, it is necessary to establish the broader societal context. Our point of departure is *s.* 23 and Augustine's claim that there is only one *magister* Christ. He situates this pronouncement within a broader explanation of how the bishops were in fact *condiscipuli* with those who would come to listen to the preaching from the *cathedra Christi.* It is thus evident that Augustine intends to use this term *magister* within its educational context, rather than the broader administrative uses.[7] To best appreciate how Augustine refashions the role of the teacher for the context of the church, we shall begin with the role of the *magister* in its pagan educational context. Robert Kaster's work on the *grammaticus* and his role in ancient education will help bring some clarity to their social status and function.[8] Furthermore, the first official imperial rhetor, Quintilian, wrote a sprawling 12 volume work, the *Instituto Oratoria,* which helpfully contrasts how Augustine describes the relationship between the teacher and the student (both *discipulus* and *condiscipulus*) in *s.* 23.

First, we will clarify the use of these terms within their ancient context. Although there was not the same sort of universally accepted age stratification and exact definition for levels of achievement in education, three main major steps in the process are discernible from the ancient sources. It appears that the first stage of education was the *magister ludi* "schoolteacher," where the students might learn letters and basic reading from the ages of 7–12. Second, the aspiring orator would go to the *grammaticus* to learn poetry and basic composition from 12–15.[9] This term is what Kaster calls the "Guardian of Language." The final stage was learning the *progymnasmata* from the teacher of rhetoric and culminating in a final declamation.[10] Quintilian uses the term *magister declamandi* "teacher of declamation," or *magister oratorum* "teacher of orators," for this final teacher.[11] It is thus evident that Augustine uses this

7 OLD V2., 1168–69.

8 Robert Kaster, "Part 1," in *Guardians of Langauge,* 3–230.

9 Kaster argues, "*grammatici* later more often belonged to the 'respectable' classes (**honestiores*), like the children they taught," in OCD, "*grammaticus,*" 646.

10 It's possible some of the steps of the progymnasmata were learned with the grammaticus: Marrou, *History of Education,* 172.

11 Quintilian makes the distinction between a "grammaticus" and a "magister declamandi" in *Institutio Oratoria* 2.1.3 (LCL 124.264). He also uses "magister" to refer to the rhetor in 2.2.13 (LCL 124.272). His other phrases for a teacher of rhetoric

word *magister* loosely. He certainly uses it to describe someone with a great deal of authority, as he applies this term first and foremost to Christ. I will argue it fits with some of the descriptions from Quintilian and thus likely referred to a teacher in either the second or third stage who had some social cachet and authority in a public setting.[12]

Regaining the visibility of this oft overlooked occupation, Kaster's study of the grammarian gives important perspective on the role of ancient education generally and those who provided it. Kaster's work *Guardians of Language* describes late ancient grammarians in detail, taking his title from a phrase of Seneca, calling *magistri "custos Latini sermonis"* (guardians of Latin language).[13] Summarizing their task, he writes:

> Their work was to lift the young nobility to their proper place in the hierarchy.... The student's experience was governed by three goals, pursued first in the grammarian's school, then in the rhetorician's: mastery of correct language, command of a fairly small number of classical texts, and an ability to turn the knowledge of language and literature to a facility in composition and speech.[14]

The various *magistri* received students from wealthy clients who wanted to learn to speak and compose well. The goal of this education was to provide "the language and mores through which a social and political elite recognized its members."[15] The children of noblemen rose through the levels of the school of the grammarian and of the rhetorician and acquired the proficiency in speech to be recognized as elite.[16] These descriptions from Kaster fit perfectly within what we have already discussed about Augustine's own education.

are, "magister eloquentiae" in 2.5.5 (LCL 124.302), "magister oratoris" at 2.8.15 (LCL 124.322), "magister eruditi" at 2.17.33 (LCL 124.390), 10.3.1 (LCL 127.336).

12 J.V. Muir writes, "*ludi magister* or *litterator, grammaticus,* teacher of rhetoric.... Probably from Diocletian's *Price Edict* 1:4:5. Quintilian held the first endowed Chair for rhetoric at Rome from Vespasian" ("education" in OCD, 509–10).

13 Sen. *Ep.* 95.65: "custos Latini sermonis." Aug. Solil. 2.19 (PL32.894): "vocis articulatae custos."

14 Kaster, *Gaurdians of Langaugi,* 11 cites Quintilian from *Institutio Oratoria* 1.4.2: "recte loquendi scientiam ei poetarum ennarationum."

15 Kaster, *Gaurdians of Language,* 14.

16 For Augustine's training in this education see chapter 2.

Turning to an ancient source on education, Quintilian, in his plan for the optimal orator's education, details an important distinction between a *magister* and a *discipulus*. In book 2, he writes, "The master does not have to speak to suit the pupil's judgment, the pupil has to speak to suit his."[17] Proceeding through various admonitions for the potential magister in this section of his work, Quintilian thinks it axiomatic that a teacher remember that their judgments are more important than the students. The basis of their judgment is the content and the quality of language.

Quintilian goes on to explain how this judgment works. The student will learn for themselves what constitutes good language from the teacher's assessment. He writes:

> The audience, therefore, as well as the pupil who is speaking, should keep their eyes on the teacher's face; they will thereby learn to distinguish what deserves approval from what does not, and will thus acquire judgment (*iudicium*) by listening as well as facility by writing ... this is what makes the declamation a success.[18]

As Quintilian imagines it, students will be gathered to give a declamation for each other and the teacher. Those who are not speaking on the chosen topic from the *magister* will learn from the judgment of the teacher the correct way to speak. If the teacher is pleased by what the student says, he will give the right kind of praise to the student. If the teacher finds the declamation lacking, he will either castigate the student or withhold praise.

Interestingly, Quintilian does use the word *condiscipulus* in his treatise, as Augustine did above, although it is not an especially common term in Quintilian's writings.[19] Quintilian recognizes that sometimes students are more likely to mimic each other rather than follow the example of the teacher. He thus warns the teacher of rhetoric:

17 *Institutio Oratoria* 2.2.13 (LCL 124.272–73), "Non enim iudicio discipulorum dicere debet magister sed discipulus magistri."

18 *institutio oratoria* 2.2.12 (LCL 124.272–75), "Vultum igitur praeceptoris intueri tam qui audiunt debent quam ipse qui dicit: ita enim probanda atque improbanda discernent; sic stil facultas continget, auidtione iudicium. . . . Id mutuum est et ibi declamationis fortuna."

19 The word appears 272 in the *Library of Latin Texts* search of the lemma condiscipul*, 42 in sources other than Augustine, 40 times in Augustine alone, which comprises nearly 1/7th of its uses.

But, while rivalry nurtures literary progress when it is more firmly established, beginners and the very young find imitation of their fellow pupils more agreeable than imitation of their masters, because it is easier. Elementary students will scarcely dare raise themselves to any hope of reproducing what they believe to be a crowning achievement of eloquence; they will prefer to embrace what is closest to them, just as vines trained on trees climb to the top by first taking hold of the lower branches.[20]

Students may despair of their ability to match a master's eloquence since they are less skilled. These students will in turn emulate the lesser forms of rhetoric they see in those around them. In a sense, it might be said that Augustine takes this to heart by identifying himself as a *condiscipulus* so as not create so wide a gap between himself and his. He does not show all of his learning and progress in the spiritual life but returns to the place of the majority of his hearers. By condescending to be a *condiscipulus* rather than *magister*, Augustine's position is closer to the hearers. This is similar to what Christ does by taking on the *forma servi*. The rhetorical conceit of calling himself a fellow student suggests that Augustine's speech is suffused with his theological commitments. Just as Augustine had exhorted Dioscorus in *ep.* 118 quoted above, the great teacher shows in his actions what he commended in his words. Augustine imitates Christ as his fellow students imitate him, a perilous position indeed.

We have seen that in the ancient literature, there was a firm divide between the *magister* and the *discipulus*. The goal of education was to learn from the *magister* how to speak in an elevated fashion, being encouraged in this through the judgments of the well-qualified *magister*. Even though the students might want to imitate their *condiscipuli*, they still need to heed the judgments of the magister to reach the heights of a well-educated orator. The preacher, in the case of the sermon, can be a *condiscipulus*, and help the student in their path of following the one teacher, Christ.

---

20 *Instutio Oratoria* 1.2.26 (LCL 124.93–95): "Sed sicut firmiores in litteris profectus alit aemulatio, ita incipientibus atque adhuc teneris condiscipulorum quam praeceptoris iucundior hoc ipso quod facilior imitatio est. Vix enim se prima elementa ad spem tollere effingendae quam summam putant eloquentiae audebunt: proxima amplectentur magis, ut vites arboribus adplicitae inferiores prius adprendendo ramos in cacumina evadunt."

The *Introduction* and *the Capture of Goodwill* of Sermon 23

Drawing on what we learned from Quintilian, we have a new perspective on the setting of Augustine's *s.* 23. This will permit us to see better how Augustine *illocuted* humility without naming it as such and modeling it for his hearers. We see it specifically in the role of judgment in the relationship between a teacher and a student. Augustine discusses who does the judging in the *proemium* of *s.* 23.[21] To fully appreciate what Augustine attempts to do with this imagery, context is helpful. The former teacher of rhetoric delivered this sermon in the latter half of his preaching career in the city Carthage. It was likely preached on or near the anniversary of the ordination of Augustine's great friend Aurelius the bishop of Carthage in a series of sermons which probably included, *ss.* 111, 23, 53, 277, likely in that order.[22] The subtitle of the sermon from folios first collected and edited by the Maurists suggest that this sermon was preached at a well-known church on the edge of Carthage called the Basilica Fausti, known today as the Basilique de Damous El Karita in Tunisia.[23]

Nearly 30 years before, Augustine went before a large audience in Milan to praise the emperor. It should have been a source of delight for

---

21 The *proemium* is one of four (or five, depending on the source) significant parts of *dispositio* in the formal rhetorical structures Augustine would have been familiar with in his traditional education. The four parts of *dispositio* were: *prooemium, narratio, argumentatio,* and *conclusio.* Augustine discusses these in *doc. Chr.* 4.2.3, 4.4.6 drawing them from his great classical exemplar Cicero who writes of them in *de oratore* 2.307–332. The five preparatory elements of rhetorical composition were: *inventio, dispositio, elocutio, memoria,* and *pronunciatio* or *actio.* For a further study on the role of structure in the preaching of Augustine, see: Joost van Neer, "Language and Scripture as Structuring Principles of Augustine's 'Sermones' 186 and 187," *Augustiniana* (Vol. 63, No. 1/4 [2013]):189–229.

22 For a full summary of the history of scholarship related to dating this particular sermon see Drobner, *Sermones 22–34,* Patrologia Beiträge zum Studium der Kirchenväter, Band XXV v.2 (Frankfurt am Main: Peter Lang, 2016), 774–76. His assessment is that this sermon should be considered undated due to the fragmentary nature of the evidence of the sermon. That said, the scholarly consensus of the last 100 years is that it was preached on January 20th, 413.

23 Duval Noël "Études d'architecture chrétienne nord-africaine," *Mélanges de l'école française de Rome Année* (1972 84–2), 1071–72. Alfred Louis Delattre, *Archéologie chrétienne de Carthage: Fouilles de la basilique de Damous-El-Karita* (Aux bureaux des Missions catholiques, 1888). Heimo Dolenz, "Two annex buildings to the Basilica Damous-el-Karita in Carthage. A summary of the excavations in 1996 and 1997" (Antiquités africaines Année 2000 36), 147–59.

the rising star of rhetoric, but it was the opposite. As the imperial orator, Augustine characterizes his work thus: "[the] fact was not for me a source of joy but only the means by which I sought to curry favor with human beings: I was not aiming to teach them but only to win their favor."[24] That was one of the low points in his life when he felt that a drunk beggar had more joy than he did. He experienced no joy, nor was he able to teach, a key component of Augustine's understanding of the aim of rhetoric from *On Christian Teaching* 4.12.27.

In the presence of Aurelius at a well-known basilica in the largest city of North Africa, Augustine now must speak, and he can truly teach the truth, not merely persuade. He can teach because it is Christ the Teacher who teaches both Augustine and his hearers as the Word. In the beginning of the sermon, Augustine uses this fact to draw in his hearers.

It is difficult to determine a succinct thread which holds the sermon together.[25] Augustine declares that the theme will be taken from the Psalm which had been previously canted, Psalm 72:24, but he does not actually take up a discussion of this until paragraph five. Not spending much time on Psalm 72, Augustine quickly progresses to the unusual word *pignus*, the down payment of the Holy Spirit given to Christians. After three paragraphs, 6–8, focused on this theme, he further explains the love of God and its down payment. Ultimately this leads to the crescendo in the *peroratio* "conclusion" where Augustine makes clear that the goal of the sermon, and the Christian life, is the beatific vision. He ends the sermon this way, "so in order to be able to see God, let us cleanse our hearts with faith, let us heal them with love, let us strengthen them with peace, because this thing with which we love each other has already come from him whom we are longing to see."[26] To some extent, this sermon provides a microcosm of his own theological structure for the sermon, the way of humility culminating in Christ.

24 *conf.* 6.6.9 (CCSL 27.79; WSA I/1, 144).

25 Paul Kolbet notes, "We lack an adequate theory that explains the homily as a discrete task with its own explicit criteria for effectiveness a theory that explains the structural characteristics of the homilies including their digressive repetitive, and exegetical features." Kolbet, "Formal Continuities Between Augustine's Early Philosophical Teaching and Late Homiletical Practice" *Studia Patristica* 43 (2006): 152. Dolbeau notes that likely the organization of the sermon had much to do with the kind of repetition necessary in Cicero's theory of a well-organized speech ("Sermones," 252).

26 *s.* 23.18 (CCSL 41.319; WSA III/2, 66).

Returning to the *prooemium* and the relationship between the teacher and student, Augustine preaches from an elevated position and says,

> May [God] take our minds up to a clear understanding, and assist us with his mercy and grace: me as I talk, you as you judge. For although to all appearances I am standing in a higher place than you, this is merely for the convenience of carrying my voice better, and in fact it is you who are in the higher place to pass judgment, and I who am being judged.[27]

A study of the basilica shows that Augustine probably spoke from an even more elevated position than he would have at Hippo.[28] He uses this height to rhetorical effect to discuss his separation from his people and what that means for how they should listen to them. Rather than use his height to intimidate his audience he uses it to make a vastly different point.

Although he is elevated, he is the one in danger, not the people. This quote comes right before the paragraph on the danger of being a teacher cited above. Notice the different roles of Augustine, the one speaking like a *magister* and the listener, like the student. Augustine tells his hearers that they will judge him.[29] Quintilian advised teachers of rhetoric to do exactly the opposite. The *magister* does not have to be concerned with the student's judgment but the other way around. In the context of the Church, the primary speaker, the *praedicator*, ought to be concerned with the judgment he will face from his hearers. He does not get to assume the role of *magister* which belongs first and foremost to Christ. Neither is he simply a student insofar as he is the one doing most of the speaking. He takes a difficult position between Christ, the teacher, and the gathered church, judging his sermon.

27 s. 23.1 (CCSL 41.309; WSA III/2, 57).

28 Heimo Dolenz, "Two annex buildings to the Basilica Damous-el-Karita in Carthage. A summary of the excavations in 1996 and 1997" (Antiquités africaines Année 2000 36): 147–59.

29 Drobner thinks that this passage and introduction indicate that Augustine had something which displeased those who heard him preach the previous sermon. Drobner writes, "Wie nämlich aus dem Text hervorgeht, war Augustinus offenbar für eine seiner Äußerungen in einer vorhergehenden Predigt heftig kritisiert worden, so dass er, bevor er weiter lehren kann, erst einaml die Atmosphäre reinigen d. h. das Verhältnis zwischen ihm und seinen Hörern klarstellen muß" (*Predigten zu den Psalmen* II, 777).

This tactic fits with what we know from Augustine's writing on how to begin a speech in *On Christian Teaching* 4. In the beginning of that work, Augustine offers a summary of *dispositio* "organization." From his training, he knows the import of getting the hearers on the speaker's side early. He argues,

> Rhetoric, after all, being the art of persuading people to accept something, whether it is true or false, would anyone dare to maintain that truth should stand there without any weapons in the hands of its defenders against falsehood; that those speakers, that is to say, who are trying to convince their hearers of what is untrue, should know how to get them on their side, to gain their attention and have them eating out of their hands by their opening remarks, while these who are defending the truth should not?[30]

Although Augustine understands persuasion differently as we will argue in the following chapter, he relies on the importance of a good introduction. A speaker must find a way to attract his hearers.

Ancient rhetoricians called this a *captatio benevolentiae* (capturing the goodwill). Augustine does not name it as such, but certainly he seems to describe something similar. The purpose of certain rhetorical moves like Augustine exhibits here is to gain the favor and interest of those hearing. One scholar defines it this way, "In an oration, the introduction in particular is of special importance: it has to provide the listener with information, and attract his attention, but also put him into a benevolent frame of mind."[31] This appears to be what Augustine does in his *proemium*. He establishes his role as what we might call a submagister to Christ for the moment, but in reality, all of them are learning from one teacher. More to the point, Augustine offers them a model for humility, in contrast to the spectacles of the amphitheater where pride takes center stage.

The life of Augustine and this action in particular showcase the virtue of humility. This former *magister declamandi* now asks to be judged by his hearers. That was his position and function for many years in Carthage and Milan. He puts himself in a dangerous position by his willingness to speak publicly and be judged by the students, but also to be judged by the one

---

30 *doc. Chr.* 4.2.3 (CCSL 32.117; WSA I/1, 202).
31 L. Calholi Montefusco, "Captatio Benevolentiae," *Brill's New Pauly*, 1080.

teacher who also has the right to judge. Despite this perilous predicament, Augustine carries on with his task of trying to help those gathered catch a glimpse of the divine vision.

He finishes this *proemium* of *s.* 23 showing how even his own understanding of how persuasion functions differently. He puts the emphasis on truth:

> So what you have to do is not only listen to us speaking, but also feel for us dreading; in this way for whatever we say that is true (since every-thing true is from Truth) you will praise not us but him, and wherever being human we slip up, you will pray to the same him for us.[32]

He desires that whatever words he can speak which lead them to the Truth will end in praise of the God, who is truth. The rhetorical conceit of the schoolroom challenges the distinctions which society created through their educational system.

The *magister* Augustine now calls himself a *condiscipulus*. He begs, "it helps enormously if you listen to us not as your masters but as your fellow pupils."[33] By bringing himself down to the level of *condiscipulus*, Augustine rejects the separation between earthly *magistri* and *discipuli*.[34] All become *condis-cipuli* in what Augustine calls the *schola christi*.[35]

To sum up this conversation about the *prooemium* of *s.* 23, it is worth noting how another scholar identifies Augustine's change in emphasis in rhet-oric from his pagan predecessors. A classicist who has studied the change in persuasion from pagan to Christian authors, Sarah Spence writes:

> Instead of insisting on the absolute power and verity of language and reason, the Christian persuader must remain part of the audi-ence even while assuming temporarily what is objectively the role

---

32 *s.* 23.1 (CCSL 41.309; WSA III/2, 57).

33 *s.* 23.1 (CCSL 41.309; WSA III/2, 57).

34 Though again, Drobner asserts the opposite, "He begins with establishing his position: 'Leading and teaching is dangerous, being a student though is safe.' Even the choice of words 'teacher' and 'student' puts the listener in a certain position. In the manner of a *captatio benevolentiae*, he quotes one of his typical theologumena that all students are of the one teacher, Christ, and that a preacher might encounter something challenging, and the students should pray for him" (*Predigten zu den Psalmen* II, 777).

35 Pierre Adnès, "Humilité a L'École de Saint Augustin," *Revue de Ascétique et de Mystique* 31 (1955), 28–46.

of teacher. There is consequently a reorganization of the hierarchy implicit in classical rhetoric, for no matter how much the Christian teacher or preacher is like the classical orator, he is also like the Ciceronian audience. Such power as the classical orator has over his audience—a power possible only if a distance exists between them—is thus denied.... The shift in pragmatics is thus a shift in underlying assumptions: the Christian orator must persuade laterally, not from on high, and all that he says is subject to a higher authority.[36]

The passage does not draw from sermon 23, but one could easily apply it here. Spence describes how Augustine wanted to persuade from the same position, rather than above. In *s.* 23, although Augustine speaks from an elevated position, he emphasizes that he is standing on the same ground as his hearers. The quote even begins with the very mechanism by which an ancient orator would have asserted their dominance over their social inferiors, language and logic. As we have already noted in chapter two, the young orators learned from their *magistri* how to speak a language which made them so far above the *rudes* that they were another class of human. Augustine begins a campaign for preachers to do the opposite of what orators would do in terms of their ability to use language and logic to create a chasm between themselves and their hearers.

The aim of the entire sermon comes into focus in *peroratio* of *s.* 23; Augustine reveals what humility brings. He directs his fellow students:

So in order to be able to see God, let us cleanse our hearts with faith, let us heal them with love, let us strengthen them with peace, because this thing with which we love each other has already come from him whom we are longing to see.

To catch a vision of God, the *beatific vision*, they must cleanse their hearts of pride as Augustine so aptly describes in his Confessions. All the *condiscipuli* if they will learn the humility Augustine has performed before them, notably without calling attention to his own humility by name, they can see the one who came humbly in the form of human flesh, the *Verbum Dei*.

---

36 Spence, *Rhetorics of Reason and Desire: Vergil, Augustine, and the Troubadours* (Ithaca, NY: Cornell University Press, 1987), 76.

Learning from Christ the Teacher

We have shown that Augustine offered himself as a model by renouncing his title as magister and called himself a *condiscipulus*. Learning in the *schola Christi* required listening to one teacher Christ. The students followed their intermediate example the *praedicator* as he showed all those who are gathered the *via humilitatis*.

We see this same pattern repeated in other sermons exemplifying how Augustine leads people to learn from Christ through preaching. How exactly does one learn from Christ the Teacher through the preacher? This one aspect of Augustine's *s.* 23 can be better explained in other sermons which mention Christ as sitting on the *cathedra in caelo*.[37] *S.* 23 demonstrated that Augustine did not see his role as the primary teacher and sought to gain the goodwill of his hearers through his use of the new designation *condiscipulus*. Where does that one teacher teach? In several places, Augustine will say that Christ the teacher teaches "inside," that is from his *cathedra in caelo*.[38] This imagery combines for Augustine the spiritual nature of preaching with the external act. That is, the words Augustine preaches, he draws from the words of scripture. He offers externally to the people those words and then encourages them to pray and meet Christ for themselves through the means of scripture which reveal Christ, the Word. As we have quoted before, Augustine preaching from the Psalms explains:

> There is but one single utterance of God amplified throughout all the scriptures (*unus sermo dei in scripturis omnibus dilatatus*), dearly beloved. Through the mouths of many holy persons a single Word makes itself heard, that Word who, being God-with-God in the beginning, has no syllables, because he is not confined by time. Yet we should not find it surprising that to meet our weakness he descended to the discrete sounds we use, for he also descended to

37 *s.* 179 (CCSL 41Bb.619); *s.* 261.2 (SPM 1.89; WSA III/7, 210); *disc. chr.* 9; 14 (CCSL 46); *ep. Io. tr.*3. (PL 2004.39).

38 *s.* 179.1.1–2.2, (CCSL 41Bb.619): "verbi dei enim inanis est forinsecus praedicator, qui non est intus auditor. nec ita aversi ab humanitate et fideli consideratione sumus ut pericula nostra non intelligamus, qui verbum dei populis praedicamus.... nam ut noveritis, fratres, quam tutiore loco stetis quam nos... ego qui vobis assidue loquor ... tunc solidum gaudeo, dum audio."

take to himself the weakness of our human body. The psalm which we are studying has already given rise to many words on our part. Mysteries were concealed in it to be opened to those who knock, and these mysterious verses occupied us for no little time over several days, as they were read out and your attention was directed to them, as they were shown to hold more than met the eye, and as their meaning was drawn out and interpreted.[39]

When Augustine goes to speak the words found in scripture, no matter which passage, he speaks the one speech of God. That speech is the Word made flesh, eternally begotten before time. He had to become human so that imperfect humans could hear him. For Augustine, the very words of scripture contain mysteries which must be opened. As a preacher and teacher, Augustine will guide the people through opening those words for deeper realities. For the people to access that on their own, they must look "inside."[40] As we quoted from Augustine above, he recognizes that the greatest effect his words as a preacher can have on his people is to force them to confront Christ in the words of scripture and pray to encounter him on their own. So, Christ is the teacher whose chair of authority is in heaven. By attending to the preaching of Augustine, all those who gather can learn how to listen for Christ who is the Good Teacher.[41] We will explain this further in the coming chapter, but it is important that Augustine does not think that the goal of his preaching is to provide a perfect explanation of every biblical text. He wants to guide the people to pray and learn from Christ themselves in the scriptural text, which speaks the one Word of God.

In. *s.* 261, Augustine explains how all the fellow Christian students can learn from their master teacher who teaches from the chair of authority in heaven.[42] The humility which Augustine shows through his speech by listening also appears in several other sermons. Augustine encourages his audience to listen with him taking the posture of a humble learner with his people. He creates a dialogue with someone who would not agree with him:

39 *en. Ps* 103.4.1 (CCSL 40.1521; WSA III/19, 168).

40 Recall Augustine's famous dictum, "Tu autem eras interior intimo meo et superior summo meo" *conf.* 3.6.11 (CCSL 27.33).

41 *s.* 102.2 (PL 38.611): "Redite ergo ad cor: et si fideles estis, invenietis ibi Christum; ipse vobis loquitur ibi. Ego enim clamo: ille vero in silentio plus docet."

42 Preached in the same Basilica as *s.* 23 (Dolbeau, "sermones," 303).

Look, I'll tell you, I won't cheat you. You're asking what sort of God Christ is? Listen to me, or rather, listen with me; let's both listen together, both learn together. I mean, just because I'm talking and you're listening, it doesn't mean that I'm not listening with you. So when you hear "Christ is God," you ask, "What sort of God is Christ?"[43]

He imagines his opponent saying, "what sort of God is Christ?" Augustine then embodies the way of humility by showing that the way to learn from Christ is by listening to the scriptures and not asserting what he thinks as if it is based on his authority. It is what Jean Louis Chretien, the French philosopher, describes as the "event of listening."[44] Chretien argues that when Augustine calls the Church to listen with him, he asks that they all be transformed by the Word which they all hear together. This is more than the reception of information. Augustine preaches, "let's both listen together, both learn together." He enacts the *via humilitatis agendo* by his willingness to take authority from the humble scriptures and the God who speaks therein. All gathered, preacher and congregation alike, learn from the Word as one in Christ.

To what do they listen? Augustine, in *s.* 261, turns their focus to a frequently referenced passage, John 1. He preaches: "In the beginning was the Word. Where? And the Word was with God. But words are something we're used to hearing every day. Don't think about this one in the way you're used to hearing; The Word was God (Jn 1:1)."[45] He explains the nature of the

43 *s.* 261.2 (SPM 1.89; WSA III/7, 210): "Audi mecum; non, inquam, me audi, sed mecum. In hac enim schola omnes sumus condiscipuli. Caelum est cathedra magistri nostri." cf. *s.* 340A (= Guelferbytanus 32), (MiAg 1.566): "audiat, non me, sed mecum; simul audiamus, simul in una schola condiscipuli ab uno magistro Christo discamus, cuius cathedra ideo est in caelo, quia prius crux fuit in terra." *s.*108.6 (PL 38.635) "Audite non a me, sed mecum simul." *s.* 60.6 (CCSL 41Aa.246): "Nos diximus et vos audistis, immo ille dixit et simul audivimus. Praestet adiutorium faciendi qui dedit consilium corrigendi."

44 Jean Louis Chretien summarizes this idea by saying, "Because listening is an event: it is not about the simple perception of meaning, nor the reception of information, but about a transformation by the word that we hear. This word happens to us, it happens in us, and it is only thus that it is understood," *Saint Augustin et les actes de parole*, 29.

45 *s.* 261.2 (SPM 1.89; WSA III/7, 210).

verbum which is not just the typical word that his hearers are accustomed to hearing. All those gathered listen for the God speaking in scripture. Augustine offers his congregation someone to imitate. He is their *exemplum* now, but only insofar as Augustine images listening to Christ in the scriptures. He says in the same section, "In this school, you see, we are all fellow students; heaven is our professor's chair."[46] Although he is both an under teacher and fellow student, the true teacher is the one whose chair is in heaven.

The term *cathedra* holds much weight in the thought of Augustine as we have tried to show. Augustine first learns the authority of the *cathedra* from his teachers at school who sought to teach him a kind of language that made him appear a more virtuous kind of human than those around, simply by the use of his tongue. Eventually, he comes to take up this cathedra himself as a teacher of rhetoric, encouraging in his students the same kind of pride. Although this does not satisfy Augustine for long, he does teach it for several years. Over time it becomes to him a symbol of pride and the kind of life he does not want to live and so calls it the *cathedra mendacii*. After his conversion, he is willing to take a position on the *cathedra Christi*, but he has to find a way to use it well. He imitates Ambrose who listens first to another teacher who is the head of the Church. Augustine now terms this the *cathedra in caelo*. This is the one true teacher and so constrains Augustine to humbly submit to the teaching of Christ which is known in the humble scriptures. The Ciceronian Augustine had to learn from the *humillimo genere loquendi* (the most humble genre of speaking) in the scriptures because that is where Christ speaks to his heart.[47]

This *preomium* to *s.* 261 suggests Augustine's action in his words. Returning to SAT for a moment, what we see with Augustine is that his words showcase the humble posture he has assumed. Neither *s.* 261 nor *s.* 23 are obvious sermons treating the Christian virtue of humility. The nature of humility is such that one is no longer humble if they call themselves humble. Thus, the best texts to look for evidence of humility might be ones where the author does not speak about humility. At the very least, they provide case studies to see humility at work.

---

46 *s.* 261.2 (SPM 1.89; WSA III/7, 210). Cf. *s.* 153.1: (CCSL 41Ba.49): "Nos loquimur, sed erudit Deus; nos loquiumr, sed Deus docet"; *s.* 34.2 (CCSL 41.424); and *s.* 298.5.5 (SPM 1.99).

47 *conf.* 6.5.8 (CCSL 27:78–79; WSA I/1, 142).

Ss. 261 and 23 provide exactly this kind of evidence. They both share a self-described theme of helping those gathered to purify their hearts so that they might be able to see God. Augustine says midway through *s.* 261, "I mean, do you want to see? It's a good thing, a great thing that you want. I'm encouraging you to want it. Do you want to see? *Blessed are those of pure heart, because it is they who will see God* (Mt 5:8)."[48] Similarly in *s.* 23, "because this thing with which we love each other has already come from him whom we are longing to see." The goal of Augustine's preaching is to provide a means for those gathered to learn how to see God. Augustine embodies the practice of listening for the words of Christ in scripture so that the heart would be cleansed to see God. The words Augustine uses come first from scripture, the *locution*. As he offers that locution in his words (the *illocution*), they become an action which embodies the humility of a man who once used his words to draw all attention to himself. Now he uses the words in his action to bring those listening into contact with the greater teacher in heaven.

Totus Christus

We will close with an examination of Augustine's doctrine of the *totus Christus*. Although the majority of this chapter has been on the image of schoolroom as Church for Augustine, one might wonder what makes it a church. Or to borrow a sarcastic quip from Victorinus, "it's the walls that make Christians, then?" What is it that makes all these separate people the one body of Christ? Augustine maintains that the humility of Christ unites all Christians, which came as an embarrassment to Victorinus himself. In this story of the conversion of Victorinus, Augustine highlights how the humility of Christ itself becomes a sacrament of the Word in the Church, a *sacramentis humilitatis Verbi tui*.[49] Augustine as preacher and bishop presents this sacrament of the humble Word in his preaching, establishing the school of Christ on earth who listens to Christ in heaven. In the liturgy, the Church receives a foretaste of the eschatological goal to which the Christian life, and Augustine's sermons, are directed. The One Word unifies the church through the sacrament of his humility.

48 *s.* 261.4 (SPM 1.90; WSA III.7, 211): "Videre enim vis? Bonam rem, magnam rem vis; hortor ut velis. Videre vis? Beati mundo corde, quia ipsi Deum videbunt."
49 *conf.* 8.2.4 (CCSL 27.116).

All those gathered by grace to receive this sacrament become participators in the *totus Christus*, the whole Christ, and so become unified. This is a critical doctrine which pervades all of Augustine's preaching. The *totus Christus*, as a sacramental doctrine, takes the *sacramentum* of the body gathered hearing the preaching of the Word as a sign of the *res*, the reality, which is the exalted Christ, body and head. When the Word is preached, all partake of the *sacramentum* which points to the eschatological reality of the resurrection.[50]

The doctrine of the *totus Christus*, as it is understood throughout the *Expositions on the Psalms*, has a particularly rhetorical character.[51] Augustine looks for the ways in which all are united to Christ in the reciting of the Psalms. As a means of explaining how Christians and their roles in the Church are related, Paul says, "For just as the body is one and has many members, and all the members of the body, though many, are one body, so it is with Christ. For in one Spirit we were all baptized into one body—Jews or Greeks, slaves or free—and all were made to drink of one Spirit. For the body does not consist of one member but of many" (1 Cor 12:12–14). The members of the body of Christ do not represent one stratum of society but come from everywhere. They become one through the Spirit. Paul describes this body as the body of Christ but does not extrapolate on the composition of the body as containing a head, as Augustine will. He simply leaves the rhetorical composition at the members of the body in 1 Cor 12, though he does call Christ the head Col 1:18.

Augustine takes the next step to explain that the fullness of Christ is understood through the unification of the head of the body. The addition of this explanation with that of Paul's becomes Augustine's doctrine of the *totus Christus*. Cameron explains:

More than a simple object of analysis within the text, for Augustine *totus Christus* was woven deeply into the fabric of the Psalter. The whole Christ was part of the psalms' content as fulfilled prophecy and so acted as a tight binding filament of scriptural unity. The whole Christ was the very means of salvation for readers, for the

---

50 Tarsicuis J. van Bavel, "Church," in *Augustine through the Ages*, 169–76.
51 Cameron, *Christ Meets Me Everywhere*, 165.

church saw itself and heard its own voice in the praises and prayers of the ancient text. Reading oneself in the whole Christ therefore was also a way of participating in God's saving action.[52]

The Church reads itself into the Psalms through the rhetorical practice of *prosopological* exegesis. Augustine saw Christ speaking the words of the Psalms in the Gospels, but especially on the Cross. This recognition encouraged Augustine to look for Christ speaking throughout the Psalms. When he came to places where the speaking of the Psalms did not seem to apply to the perfectly divine Christ, he recognized the speaking as Christ taking on human flesh and speaking for the body. The scriptures then become a univocal message of the unity of Christ and the body as the *totus Christus*, the whole Christ. When the church participates in this by speaking and reading, she becomes a participator in the sacramental speech of Christ.

Cameron is again helpful on the connection between sacramental preaching and the *totus Christus*. He explains it thusly, "Augustine had another term for it: sacrament. Christ's 'sacramental' will-to-death gave what it portrayed; and all other events, words, and signs were also sacramental insofar as they partook of it."[53] This partaking of the people is similar to what Augustine described in *s.* 272 on the Eucharist. It is the "Amen" which seals the unity of the body to the head. Augustine says, "So if it's you that are the body of Christ and its members, it's the mystery meaning you that has been placed on the Lord's table; what you receive is the mystery that means you. It is to what you are that you reply *Amen*, and by so replying you express your assent. What you hear, you see, is *The body of Christ*, and you answer, *Amen*. So be a member of the body of Christ, in order to make that *Amen* true."[54] This exhortation to respond with Amen, indicates Augustine's awareness of the power of speech to create a state of affairs in the world, beyond mere indication. The people's response speaks to the reality of their unification with Christ as his body. The people must say Amen to partake in the sacrament and so receive Christ in the sacrament which bestows what it represents. The Church becomes Christ.

52 Cameron, *Christ Meets Me*, 206.

53 Cameron, "*Totus Christus* as Hermeneutical Center in *Enarrationes in Psalmos*," in *The Harp of Prophecy: Early Christian Interpretation of the Psalms* ed. Paul Kolbet and Brian Daley, SJ (Notre Dame, IN: University Notre Dame Press, 2015): 205–26, 217.

54 *s.* 272. (PL 38.1247; WSA III/7, 301).

Cameron explains how the Psalm sermons were exercises of the soul: "These early psalms studies, and the later psalms sermons, were training exercises to help readers to practice this self-transposition into the text through Christ's gracious incarnation and death."[55] Preaching became an act of teaching the people to see themselves in the scriptural text and to see Christ's condescension in it. Christ speaks their words for them so that when people re-cite (say again what Christ quotes and David wrote) the Psalms they hear unite both their cry of dereliction and their reconciliation to Christ in the very words. This is seen especially in Psalm 22, but the *totus Christus* doctrine is found throughout Augustine's preaching corpus.

In another sermon in the *Sermons to the People*, Augustine, commenting on Psalm 67, writes:

> The whole body has not yet received it, because the head is in heaven, the members still on earth. Nor is the head going to receive the inheritance alone, leaving the body behind. The whole Christ (*totus Christus*) is going to receive the inheritance, the whole as man, that is to say, head and body. So we are members of Christ, we must be hoping for the inheritance.... Just as he promised life, bliss, the kingdom, an eternal inheritance without end to the saints, so with eternal fire he threatened the wicked. If we don't yet love what he promised, let us at least dread what he has threatened.[56]

The passage exemplifies the moment of preaching as a sacrament of Christ. The congregation learns to hope, and receive a down-payment (*pignus*) in the Holy Spirit, for their inheritance as it is proclaimed in the words of the sermon. The Church proclaims and hears the truth of the resurrection. All gathered learn to love their head who is resurrected in reality. Christians on their sojourn to eternity hold on to the promise which is Christ, the first-fruits of the dead and the head to whom they are united in prayer. When they pray

---

55 Ibid., 220.

56 *s.* 22.10 (CCSL 41.300; WSA III/2, 49): "Adhuc enim non totum corpus accepit, quia caput in caelo est, membra adhuc in terra sunt. Nec caput solum accepturum est hereditatem, et corpus relinquetur. Totus Christus accepturus est hereditatem, totus secundum hominem, id est, caput et corpus. Membra ergo Christi sumus, speremus hereditatem. Quia cum ista omnia transierint, hoc bonum accepturi sumus quod non transibit, et hoc malum evasuri quod non transibit. Aeterna sunt enim utraque."

to be taught and connected to their head through the words of preaching, they receive a foretaste of what is to come.

The Word who was made flesh did not receive eternal life as God, which he already possessed, but as man. If Augustine's hearers are connected to Christ in the body of Christ through the Holy Spirit, they too can hope for that reality which is to come. Augustine explains,

> Inasmuch as *the Word became flesh and dwelt among us* (Jn 1:14), he was reared and grew up. After suffering, dying and rising again, he received as his inheritance the kingdom of heaven. It was in being man that he received resurrection and eternal life. In being man he received it. In being the Word he did not receive it, because the Word abides unchangingly from everlasting to everlasting. So because it was that flesh, which rose again and being quickened ascended into heaven, that received resurrection and eternal life, this too is promised to us. We are waiting for that very inheritance, eternal life.[57]

The Spirit of Christ is given to the body to strengthen the body in its pilgrimage. In the liturgy of the Church, we come closer to that reality through the sacraments, even the sacrament of preaching which offers Christ, *tradere Christum*. The goal of preaching for Augustine was to offer Christ to his hearers and for them to receive it through their amen. The sermons become a place where Christ becomes one with his Body, through the preached word and the prayerful amen of the body.

Conclusion

As a means of concluding, I will draw together these three sermons to show that Augustine's sermons give evidence for his very theology of preaching, the *via humilitatis agendo*. Refusing to call himself *magister*, Augustine accepts the command of the Lord not to be a called a teacher. As a *captatio benevolentiae*, Augustine metaphorically returns to a previous station in the life of his education. He becomes a *condiscipulus* when he once rightfully claimed the title of *magister oratorum*. As he states in his *Confessions*, he must go down before going up. This action demonstrates that *via humilitatis* which he learned

---

57 *s.* 22.10 (CCSL 41.300; WSA III/2, 49).

from Christ's walking the way of humility by taking on the *forma servi*. In the very action of his words, Augustine puts this virtue into practice in order that it might be imitated by all those gathered. He acts in his words in the hopes that those who follow would not actually follow Augustine himself, but Christ.

In another way, *s.* 265 illustrates how all the *condiscipuli* must listen to Christ. This sermon is not simply a didactic explanation of the historical context of John. Augustine calls all of those gathered to listen with him to Christ the one true *magister* teaching from his *cathedra* in heaven. The locution, "In the beginning was the Word," comes from scripture itself. Augustine offers this to the congregation for them all to hear as Christ teaches through his words. The authority is in the locution of Holy Scripture, the word of God, not foremost in the man, Augustine.

Finally, we ended with tying these sermonic illustrations of Augustine's ecclesiology to some further observations more straightforwardly connected to his doctrine of the Church. We saw that in fact the *Schola Christi* is but one manifestation of Augustine's ecclesiology, insofar as it unites the Head to the Body as teacher and student. The preaching of Augustine sacramentally binds Christians to their head by demonstrating how one ought to learn from the one Teacher in heaven. The teaching is training for the gathered faithful in their eschatological longings by giving them a foretaste of the heavenly reality. It is not the walls themselves which instantiate the mystery, but rather the sacramental presence of the humility of Christ in the preaching of the Word and in the response of the people through their word.

For Augustine, the preacher listens to the Word of God. He preaches that Word to the congregation, while using his life and words as an example for them to follow. Finally, he must wait for God to act in those words. The locution comes from scripture. The illocution is how the preacher offers those words to the congregation. God performs the perlocution, working through and beyond the words of the preacher to reach the heart of the hearer.

CHAPTER 6

AUGUSTINE'S SOTERIOLOGY
The Grace of God Giving the Increase

Introduction

IN THIS FINAL CHAPTER, WE WILL BEGIN to look at the last category of speech act theory known as the perlocution. Such a framing will help us see the ways in which Augustine understood his words to lead to the participation of his audience with the divine.[1] The perlocution is the characteristic aim of the speech act. That is, the speaker has an intention for what he wants the speech to do to the person hearing the words. Searle pointed out that certain institutional conditions need to be present for this to be possible. In this case, Augustine's ordination as presbyter gives him proper authority for the speech act, but he learned from Paul's epistles that, for his to be successful, he needed something more to happen. Perlocution is, to some extent, out of Augustine's control, and this is precisely how Augustine understood the importance of the preacher's words. For the goal of preaching was not merely to give all the necessary information to the audience and fully script an uncontested reading of the scriptures.

---

1 For an introduction to the ways in which Augustine used the terms participation, see: David Meconi, "Saint Augustine's Early Theory of Participation," *Augustinian Studies* 27 (1996): 79–96.

On the contrary, Augustine knew that the preaching of the scriptures in the liturgy of the Church presented the possibility for each individual in the audience to participate sacramentally in the preaching moment through the presence of the Word of God, the *intus Magister,* (the interior Teacher). This chapter provides an account of the participatory aspects of the sermon, which moves the participant from prayer to vision, the process of salvation.[2] This happened primarily through the grace of participation in the sermon.[3]

As in the previous chapters, we will look at the theological import of participation in Augustine's preaching through sermons, *s.* 152, *s.* 179, and *s.* 126. Each offers a glimpse of how God gives the increase,[4] that is, how God uses grace in the moment of the sermon to aid the prayerful Christian in their desire for a participatory vision. Theologically, we must work through how grace functions in moving the hearer in the moment of the sermon through prayer from a hearer to seer. Following Paul (Phil 2:12), Augustine did not see salvation as a point in time but the entirety of the journey from birth to rest in God. The sermons demonstrate how God is at work bringing salvation and participation through the preacher preaching the Word.

Sermon 152 also presents a test case for an insight into how Augustine understood the sermon as an exercise for the spirit, *exercitatio animi,* through the prayerful desire to see.[5] All those involved in the Christian life learn to desire to see God and understand how the words of scripture point to the one Word. Adam Ployd calls this "the moral epistemology" of the mechanics of Augustine's engagement with his audience. That is to say, Augustine uses these exercises to train the audience to move from carnal thoughts to spiritual ones.[6] This desire is actually a prayer for understanding. The preacher

2 We will see the use of the language of participation begin with its more mundane usage, as one prays and listens, which can be called "participation." We will also move upwards in the more metaphysical forms of participation which Augustine also employed.

3 Meconi writes, "Grace removes each of us from the influence of the fallen Adam and brings us more and more into Christ: while the fullness of this Christ-life may not be realized until the resurrection, even not it is proceeded by the newness of the Spirit in the lives of Christian," *The One Christ,* 107.

4 1 Cor 3.17.

5 Marrou, *Saint Augustin et la fin de la culture antique,* 299–328.

6 Adam Ployd, *Augustine, the Trinity, and the Church* (Oxford: Oxford University Press, 2015): 29–37.

can only do so much from the outside. God must work within to give the increase—*incrementum dat deus*, as he will say later—to the soul straining towards the *beata vita*, the perfect vision and understanding of God.[7] The preacher and the parishioner must rely on the participation of prayer and God at work through grace in the spiritual exercise of both preaching and active listening through prayer to the preached word of God, effectively working out their salvation in the moment of the sermon (Phil 2:12).

We will use this frame to explore the final important element of the way of humility in the preaching of Augustine, the graced participation in the Word. We begin by looking at the work of Sarah Spence, a classicist who helpfully details the change in the word *oratio* "prayer" or "speaking" and its cognates, which developed as it became common Christian Latin. Then, we will consider the notion of prayer as desire for seeing which requires the humble dependence of the hearer on the Holy Spirit. To demonstrate how this works in the whole corpus of Augustinian preaching, we will look at passages from the sermons that show the way in which Augustine understands how God sows the words of the scriptures into the hearts of his hearers and in those who participate in the very act of preaching through prayer.[8] The

---

7 Jonathan Teubner describes the exercises of the soul, "First, certain metaphysical 'problems' or 'puzzles' become, for Augustine, eschatological 'exercises' ... the investigation's doxological climax still points to that which is beyond human existence, that is the *beata vita*," (*Prayer After Augustine*, 112). For additional engagement with these exercises of the soul, see: Michael Cameron, "Totus Christus and the Psychagogy of Augustine's Sermons," *Augustinian Studies* 36:1 (2005) 59–70, and Paul Kolbet, "Formal Continuities Between Augustine's Early Philosophical Teaching and Late Homiletical Practice" *Studia Patristica* 43 (2006) 149–54. Frederick Van Fleteren's article helpfully articulates the problem of whether Augustine believed a complete vision was possible in this life, in "Augustine and the Possibility of the Vision of God in This Life," *Studies in Medieval Culture, XI* (Kalamazoo: Western Michigan University Press, 1977), 9–16. We agree with Van Fleteren that Augustine's reading of 1 Corinthians 13:7, that we "see through a glass dimly" shapes his later understanding that our ability to see God completely has its limitations in the corruptible flesh this side of the resurrection. For a more recent consideration of Augustine's understanding of the Beatific Vision, see Lewis Ayres, "Remember That You Are Catholic (*serm* 52.2): Augustine on the Unity of the Triune God" *JECS* 8.1. (Spring 2000): 39–82, and Han Boersma's chapter on Augustine "Anticipation and Vision: Augustine on Theophanies and Ecstasy," in *Seeing God: The Beatific Vision in Christian Tradition* (Grand Rapids, MI: Eerdmans, 2018), 96–125.

8 We do this through his use of the Pauline phrase, *incrementum dat Deus.s.*102.2 (PL 38.611): "Ergo ipse inserat in corde vestro verbum meum."

second half of the chapter dives deeper into the notion of participation to capture the ontological means of seeing through "deified eyes," in the rhetorical trope of *ekphrasis*. We will look at *s.* 179 in particular, which demonstrates how Augustine led the congregation to see into the scripture in new ways while relying on God to provide grace for the encounter.

Prayer as Participation in Augustine's Theology

In 419 at Carthage, Augustine preaches a sermon, *s.* 152, on a difficult aspect of Paul's letter to the Romans.[9] Prior to this sermon, Augustine had tried to explain Rom 7:15–8:3 in several consecutive sermons. According to Augustine, he could only work through 10 verses up to 7:25 in the previous sermon but plans to continue his explication of the passage in *s.* 152, adding a few more verses from what had been read the day before. In this passage, Paul describes two laws, a law of sin and death and a law of the spirit. Augustine surmises that this might be difficult for his audience to understand. To explain how Christ fits under the law of sin, he spends most of the sermon exploring how the Son came into the world and "from sin condemned sin in the flesh; so that the justice of the law might be fulfilled in us" (Rom 8:3–4). Augustine raises the question of how exactly the perfect Son of God "condemn sin from sin?"

Before giving his own solution to the difficulty at the end of the sermon, Augustine suggests that the audience ought to do more than passively listen to the sermon. He asks that the church engage in a reciprocal give and take while they listen to him speak. He preaches,

> No difficulty in these obscure thoughts exists when the Spirit helps. May he help us therefore in your prayers (*orantibus*) because that very desire by which you want to understand, is itself a prayer (*oratio*) to God. From him therefore you should wait for help. I, though, just like a peasant (*rusticus*) in the field, am working on the outside. But if there was no one working on the inside, the seed wouldn't take root in the earth.[10]

9 Pierre-Patrick Verbraken, *Études Critiques*, 90.

10 *s.* 152.1 (CCSL 41Ba. 33–34; English, mine): "Difficultas non est in obscuris sensibus, quando adiuvat spiritus. Adiuvet ergo nos orantibus vobis; quia ipsum desi-

The Spirit helps by working inside those who pray for understanding a difficult passage of scripture. The audience wants to know what the ambiguous passage means and understand how this communicates to them something about God. Later in the sermon, Augustine will say there are several possible interpretations. Augustine takes this opportunity at the beginning to say that the sermon is not simply meant to give one single conclusive unambiguous interpretation of a passage. He will try to give his best answer, but he knows it will far short because the well of the Word itself is deeper than he can fathom.[11]

Furthermore, though the congregation may still lack an exact understanding, Augustine can proclaim to the congregation something far better. He offers them Christ, the Word, as we saw in the previous chapter.[12] In order for the congregation to receive the Word, they must depend on grace, the work of the Spirit. As Paul says, God gives the increase.[13] Through his preaching, Augustine offers a moment of encounter with Christ. We will elucidate how this can indeed be possible theologically in Augustine's conception by relying on the notion of participation central to his soteriology.[14] For

derium quod vultis intellegere, oratio est ad Deum. Ab ipso ergo oportet ut exspectetis auxilium. Nos enim, quomodo rustici in agro, forinsecus operamur. Si autem nullus esset qui intrinsecus operaretur, nec semen terrae figeretur." Cf. *en. Ps.* 37.14, *en. Ps.* 85, *In* 1 *Io.* 4.6.

11 *s.* 152.10.

12 Recall *doc.Chr.* 4.15.32 (CCSL 32:139): "traduntur pro Christo, cur non et in eis qui tradunt discentibus Christum."

13 1 Cor 3:17. This quote from Paul becomes one of the characteristic riffs or refrains in the *Sermones ad Populum* of Augustine. Cf. *s.*4 (CCSL 41.39), *s.* 43 (CCSL 41.512), *s.* 81 (PL 38.500), *s.* 104 (SPM 1.57), *s.* 152 CCSL [Ba] 41.34, *s.* 152 (CCSL [Ba] 41.34), *s.* 198 [Dolbeau 26] (EAA 147.378), *s.* 224 (RB 79.203), *s.* 260B [Mai 89] (MiAg 1.330), *s.* 292 (PL 38.1326). We also find this phrase in two of Augustine's treatises on the Beatific Vision *ep.* 120 and 147.

14 There will always be a tentative nature to this suggestion as no one can fully script how God might come to present to his people. This recognition is part of the reason that Augustine does not want to over define the nature of God's work in the sermon. This recalls the famous Augustinian phrase, "Si tu comprehendis non est Deus," (if you understand it, its not God) (*s.* 117 [RB134.221]). The lack of comprehension does not prohibit Augustine from saying anything positively about the character of God because God has chosen the words of scripture to reveal himself to people. The preacher must struggle to say something, while recognizing that he or she cannot say everything. One might say that this is the task of theology in general.

it is in the grace of salvation that one can participate in the Word. For Augustine, as for Paul, salvation has a present as well as an eschatological character.

The act of praying pervades every aspect of the preaching moment in the Church. Before the preacher even begins to preach, he must become a prayer before a speaker (*sit orator antequam dictor*).[15] The sermon often ended with a specific prayer, the *conversi ad dominum* (turned to the Lord), found at the end of many of Augustine's sermons.[16] Even in the midst of Augustine speaking to the church as preacher, he encourages his hearers to pray while they listen.[17] Augustine understood the moment of the sermon to unite God, preacher, and congregant through the preaching of the Word. The word for prayer used in the sermon underwent a shift in meaning from the Latin of Cicero to that of Augustine, who retains a sense of both meanings. The words *oratio* and *orare* are the basis for the words dealing with public speaking, oration and orator.[18] When Augustine's audience heard him, they did not assume that they were all encouraged to speak out loud.[19]

For an example which indicates this change in the meaning of the word *oratio*, Augustine says in *s.* 80, "if you are desiring always, you are praying always."[20] Early in the sermon, Augustine says we follow the Lord's command not to be garrulous by having recognized what prayer is. In this maxim, he explains that prayer is now nearly synonymous with desire. One can thus pray always and not always be talking. On a simple, linguistic level this demonstrates that Augustine did not intend that his hearers speak aloud but desire God in their hearts through prayer. They are rather to be speaking inside in their prayers to God. By their participation in the divine illumination, God

15 *doc. Chr.* 4.15.32 (CCSL 32:138; WSA I/11, 219).

16 F. Dolbeau, "Sermons inédits de saint Augustin prêchés en 397 [5ème série]," *RevBen* 104 (1994): 34–76, esp. 72–76.

17 Harrison, commenting on Augustine's emphasis on being an *orator* before a *dictor*, notes, "The preacher's prayer could become their prayer; his direct conversation with God could be made their own through listening to him attentively; his words, which were at once God's and his own, could also become, through overhearing, the words of his hearers, uniting them in a single prayer," in *The Art of Listening*, 199.

18 "Oratio," OLD V.2, 1389–1390.

19 However, it is an interesting footnote that they certainly did speak aloud. Even more to the point, the word *sermo* indicates a kind of conversation. Cf. Harrison, *Art of Listening*, 152.

20 *s.* 80.7 (PL 38.498; WSA III/3, 356): "Si semper desideras, semper oras" (if you desire always, you pray always).

speaks to them as well. In Augustinian understanding, the sermon was a spiritually charged encounter with God in prayer.

Before the advent of Christianity, the kind of person most likely to orate would have been the person educated in the orator's art. Cicero, the paradigmatic Latin orator, made his way in the Roman political system through his oratorical training. Noblemen learned this art as children to inaugurate them into the new genus of person who could be recognized by their skill in the Latin language.[21] It is worth noting of course that Augustine uses many words for prayer throughout his writing corpus, but the focus for this section will be on the most common, *orare*, because of its relationship to the occupation of orator.[22]

Spence has argued that the term *oratio* as used by Christian speakers, becomes a category for the participation of the audience in the moment of Christian oration, known as preaching.[23] In Christian Latin, the person who spoke before the gathered audience no longer can be said to *orare*, but *praedicare* "to preach." *Orare* becomes the domain of communication with the divine for all Christians, rather than just the preacher. Spence explains the movement from secular "oration" to Christian "oration" this way:

> Prayer may thus have been seen at first as form of oration, maybe even specifically Christian oratory, and the *orans* can be understood not just as someone praying but also as someone orating.... While classical rhetoric attempts to persuade its audience through language, Christian prayer tries to convince through participation in faith.[24]

21 Christine Mohrman, "we have severely excluded from Christian vocabulary all that was charged with a cultural sense derived from paganism.... To designate prayer, the first generations of the faithful sought a special word, *oratio*, derived from *orare,* an ancient term, unusual in first century of our era," ("Notes sur le latin liturgique," *Etudes sur le latin des chretiens, t. 2,* [Roma, 1962] 102).

22 Augustine, a good rhetor, utilized many words for prayer (*precari, clamare, invocare, petere,* etc.) as Monique Vincent notes in "Le vocabulaire de la prière chez saint Augustin," *Augustiniana* (41.1, 1994), 783–804.

23 Spence use of "participation" does not necessarily include the metaphysical meaning as employed later in this chapter. In a sense, Spence lays the groundwork for the deeper participation by showing how it connects to a more straightforward English usage.

24 Spence, *Rhetorics of Reason and Desire: Vergil, Augustine, and the Troubadours* (Ithaca, NY: Cornell University Press, 1987) 65.

Notice how the pagan vocabulary shifts when Augustine begins to encourage all the baptized to orate publicly. All can now orate, not just those trained in the orator's art. In the classical usage of the term, Augustine asked all to participate in the moment of the public speech by speaking out loud. In the Christian era, they will orate silently, as Augustine encourages them to do so in *s.* 152. The preachers, like Augustine, will not orate, strictly speaking but *praedicat.* For the Christian sermon, God does the work, while the preacher merely works the field.[25] Persuasion works differently in that it becomes participation. As we shall see, the journey from persuasion to participation ends for Augustine in vision.

Spence explains this change in persuasion by comparing how Augustine and Cicero thought differently about the way a speaker might influence an audience. Her explanation of the contrast between Ciceronian persuasion and Christian persuasion is worth quoting in full:

> Yet in a permanent audience, language is now directed and used in a different way. Instead of being used to convince other men of the truths achieved and conceived through the rational powers language has given us, language now becomes a means for pursuing the higher, and eminently non-rational, truths of God. As audience we need convince no one but ourselves, as active participants we need to follow out those possibilities that language offers to us, but those possibilities are now aimed in a different direction. All language is one Word; all life is now aimed at understanding that Word.[26]

Although Augustine might not have said that the truths of God are "non-rational," Spence does correctly emphasize that through prayer the Christian speaker and the Christian audience are expected to take action in response to the speech.[27] Augustine recognizes that he cannot close the loop

---

25 Again, he draws on the language of Paul from 1 Corinthians 3.

26 Spence, *Rhetorics*, 83.

27 Another way of saying what Spence argues comes from Kennedy who remarks: "The word for 'preach' in Mark 13:10 and commonly in the New Testament, is *kerusso*, which literally means 'proclaim.' It is what a herald (*keryx*) does with a message, a law, or a commandment. The message is a *kerygma*, or proclamation, and constitutes the gospel ('good news' *euangelion*). Christian preaching is thus not persuasion, but proclamation, and is based on authority and grace, not on proof. . . . Its truth must be apprehended

to perfect understanding. He alone cannot make the hearer participate in the divine understanding through prayer. The audience must engage with God on their own through prayerful oration.

The language which Augustine speaks, as we discussed in chapter four, comes from scripture which is the locus to interact with the one Word. As Augustine says elsewhere, "The divinely inspired readings are all so connected with each other, that they almost make one reading, because they all proceed from one mouth. Many are the mouths of those who exercise the ministry of the word; but he that fills the ministers has only one mouth."[28] The sermon provides space for any to hear the one Word through the preaching of many ministers. The fact that the whole of scripture comes from one divine mouth means that Augustine will not hesitate to draw other scriptures in to explain confusing passages. Scripture interprets scripture.[29] Recall again that the majority of the population likely did not read but were indeed capable of learning the scriptures and encountering God through memorizing the scriptures in the repetitions of the liturgy.[30] Augustine does not encourage them to wait passively but to seek God mystically in the divine readings.

Although a further analysis of the precise understanding of the sacramental nature of preaching will come below, it is worth noting here how prayer functions in individual reception. For Augustine, the hearers could also be said to receive the words of the sermon through prayer. In a sermon on the sacraments, Augustine explains how the combination of the Eucharistic physical elements with the word makes it a sacrament. He preaches:

> Take away the word, I mean, it's just bread and wine; add the word [amen], and it's now something else. And what is that something else? The body of Christ, and the blood of Christ. So take away the

by the listener, not proved by the speaker. The reaction of a person in the audience to the *kerygma* is like his reaction to a miracle, the direct embrace of authority: he believes it or he does not," (*Classical Rhetoric*, 127).

28 *s.* 170.1 (CCSL 41Bb.434; WSA III/5, 239).

29 Christoph Schäublin, "Homerum ex Homero," *Museum Helveticum* (V. 34.4, 1977) 221–27.

30 Cf. Stanley P. Rosenbergy, "Besides Books: Approaching Augustine's Sermons in the Oral and Textual Cultures of Late Antiquity," in Anthony Dupont, Gert Partoens, and Mathijs Lamberigts ed. *Tractatio Scripturarum: Philological, Exegetical, Rhetorical and Theological Studies on Augustine's Sermons* (Turnhout: Brepols, 2012) 405–43.

word, it's bread and wine; add the word and it will become the sacrament. To this you say, *Amen*. To say *Amen* is to add your signature.
Then comes the Lord's prayer, which you have already received and
given back.[31]

Augustine explains that the people say "Amen" to add their agreement with
the words combined with the elements. Something akin to this happens in
the preaching itself. If the words of the preacher come from the scriptures,
the Church receives them as Christ through prayer and Christ's word for
them. He concludes by saying that the Lord's prayer itself is "received and
given back." The sermon, like all the elements of the liturgy, require the
work of the people of receiving and giving back. Prayer is the receiving and
giving back of the sermon.[32] Recall that the sermon always ended with the
full congregation praying the *conversi ad dominum* prayer.

This critical aspect of preaching and persuasion encourages a deeper
engagement than a Ciceronian oration, which aims to settle all disputes and
perfectly deliver the meaning for the audience. In contrast to Cicero, Augustine
does not presume that every text has one simple meaning. Spence observes,

> While Cicero sees the argument of the speech as the establish-
> ment of a structure that encloses the right meaning and exiles the
> wrong, Augustine sees reading as the motion from one to the other,
> a motion that recognizes both poles, acknowledges the existence of
> each, and asserts that the true reading, the charitable reading, is that
> which will acknowledge the difference between the two, as well as
> the path from one to the other.... We are thus asked to participate
> in the text to the extent of identifying a passage as ambiguous and
> then finding the charitable other to cover this rift.[33]

In the places where Augustine discusses the ambiguity of scripture, he
leaves room for multiple interpretations to encourage the hearer to enter
the conversation.[34] The conversation concerning scriptural meaning exists

---

31 *s.* 229.3 (MiAg1.130; WSA III/6, 267).
32 *s.* 229.3.
33 Spence, *Rhetorics*, 101.
34 In three of his major works, Augustine grants there can be differing opinions

not only between two people who might have differing opinions about its meaning, but in fact the God who speaks the one Word. It is God speaking in the scriptures. The human inability to provide a perfect reading is exactly God's intention for the scripture. It encourages the Christian to pray and seek what Spence calls "the charitable other." The gap in total comprehension provides the space for a mystical encounter with another.[35] The possibility of meeting the Word through the words of scripture is presumably far greater than a flawless reading of a text.

In defense of her position, Spence reexamines Augustine's conversion in the *Confessions* and argues that it was not only the garden scene so much as the ascent at Ostia, which should be understood as the definitive moment of Augustine's conversion. In fact, Augustine writes *Confessions* 9 in such an open ended and even halting way because he expects that the reader will take over and participate themselves in a kind of ascent.[36] Recall that the Latin meaning of the word conversion is a turning towards. Augustine desires that all turn towards the light that comes from God through the grace of the Holy Spirit. Spence contends:

> This scene [*conf.* 9.25] is exactly what it should be: the open-ended silence that allows for audience participation. Augustine offers us not one but two conversion scenes, two turning points in the text, one which is programmed and virtually explained [book 8], one of which is left shrouded in mystery. This narrative takes over after

on what the author intended. This need not mean they conflict with the truth. Indeed, the differing interpretations can all potentially be helpful in leading people to desire more understanding, so long as they conform to the *regula fidei*. See also: *conf.* 12.14.17; *doc. Chr.* 1.36.41 and 1.37; and *ciu.* 11.33. For the most recent discussion of Augustinian hermeneutics, see: Michael Cameron, "Augustine's Rhetorical Reading of Genesis in *Confessions* 11–12" in *Augustine and Tradition* eds. David G. Hunter and Jonathan P. Yates (Grand Rapids, MI: Wm. B. Eerdmans, 2021) 3–27.

35 We will explore this more fully below.

36 We could add that Augustine does not see the point of the *Confessiones* as merely telling his story of how he became a Christian. Indeed, his aim as one recognizes when the whole work is read is to prayerfully encourage all his readers to seek God and open themselves up for greater love for God. It is through the difficulty of trying to understand that the room in the soul for God to fill up becomes greater. There is a unity to the work which is not captured by the simplicity of naming the genre of the work "autobiography."

the conversion and moves into a reading of Genesis. This is the truly new text, the text that reads, interprets, and leaves meaning up in the air.[37]

The first conversion of *Confessions* 8 matches closer to the Ciceronian ideal where everything is detailed perfectly, and every moment is drawn out. *Confessions* 9 on the other hand leaves the reader feeling like they have not had everything explained. This is the point. Augustine wants to carry the reader on as far as possible until she can take over and ascend to God on her own prayerful desire for the mystery of God. It is not up to Augustine to tell the reader exactly how to experience the mystical delight of the ascent to God. No one person can. Nor can Augustine determine how God might speak to that person. Prayer is a two-way conversation in Augustine's understanding.

In summary, we have shown how *oratio* has become an action for every Christian. All can now pray and speak in their own internal words to God. The language of scripture is a sign pointing to the one Word which is not perfectly understood by all. Rather in it is ambiguity and mystery, it encourages the reader to *orare*, pray, and so participate in the moment of the sermon. Spence traces Augustine's movement and understanding of *oratio* from his first encounter with it as a Ciceronian to the scripturally infused concept of the divine Word. She writes, "while words can lead to the threshold of knowledge, beyond that, language is to no avail—truth must come to the audience like a flame kindled by a leaping spark."[38] This truth cannot be controlled by the *praedicator*. In fact, how people experience their participation in the liturgy might be wildly different, which is critical for all who are involved to move closer to the beatific vision, that for which all Christians strive.

Humility in Striving for the Blessed Life

To this point, we have followed the transformation of the Latin words in *oratio-orare* in its usage by Christian and pre-Christian sources. For Augustine, prayer is a kind of speech that all can address *to* God based on a fundamental a desire to participate *in* God through the sermon.[39] This section will unpack

---

37 Spence, *Rhetorics*, 85.
38 Spence, *Rhetorics*, 90.
39 As this desire for God is possible at all times, Augustine can make sense of

how this desire for participation prepares the soul for the eschatological fulfillment of those goods which all Christians desire, the *uisio dei*, or *beata vita*.[40] In a theological sense, the sermon does more than merely provide information to all who are gathered. To the contrary, for Augustine the *incrementum dat Deus* happens in the sermon which does not fully explain the scriptural text.[41] The human participation depends on the grace to achieve that which is modeled both by the preacher and by Christ.

This desire for participation can also be explained in terms of a desire for understanding. Recall our quote from *s.* 152: "No difficulty in these obscure thoughts exists when the Spirit helps. May he help us therefore in your prayers (*orantibus*) because that very desire by which you want to understand, is itself a prayer (*oratio*) to God." *Intelligere*, "to understand," means for Augustine to have an enlightened vision and clarity from God. Above we discussed the importance of the preacher offering a space through giving a reading of scripture for the Christian to participate. Now we will think about this participation in terms of a desire for understanding. This a kind of *exercitatio animi* is a training for the soul as she seeks the enlightenment that comes from seeing God.

This section will explore this *exercitatio animi* from the perspective of the preacher and the congregation as all strive together in Christ for the

passages like 1 Thess. 5:17 "pray without ceasing" if one desires without ceasing. Furthermore, this desire for understanding helps us see that for Augustine the "*cor* functions within the remit of *mens*. Although an intellectual/affective disjunction must be avoided, it is important to notice the shift in the terminology within the locus of prayer." Teubner, *Prayer*, 61. See also: Carol Harrison, *Augustine; Christian Truth and Fractured Humanity* (Oxford: Oxford University Press, 2000), 158–93.

40 Augustine uses many different expressions for this fundamentally unknown good: "In regard to our theme, such phrases as *frui deo, adhaerere Deo, beata vita, perventurum ad summum bonum, cognitio Dei, videre Dum, intellectus Dei*, and *contemplatio dei* indicate in Augustine's terminology the proper end of terminal intellectual union with God. Some of these phrases emphasize the eudaemonistic character of his thought; other phrases underscore the teleological element; still others illustrate the cognitive aspect. Yet several times Augustine indicates the basic equivalence of these terms in designating the terminal and habitual intellectual union of man with God," (Van Fleteren, "Augustine and the Possibility of the Vision of God in This Life," 9).

41 *doc. Chr.* 4.16.33 (CCSL 32.138; WSA I/11, 221): "So in the same way the assistance of sound doctrine provided by a human teacher is only then any good to the soul when God is at work to make it any good, seeing that he was able to give the gospel to man, even without its coming from men or through man."

eschatological vision. We will continue to draw on *s.* 152 as a model sermon in which Augustine provides an analysis of a scriptural text that leaves the exact interpretation open ended. The preacher provides enough explanation to elongate the desire to see God, which he knows can only be fulfilled interiorly and sacramentally now in *spe* but which increases the hope of an exterior, bodily resurrection, of which the resurrected Christ is the *res*.[42]

Beginning with the quote stated above, Augustine explains the role of prayer as the means for understanding. Then, the preacher demonstrates the *exemplum* he finds in Christ for the benefit of those gathered. Modeling humility, Augustine calls himself, the former orator, a *rusticus in agro*—which I translated as "peasant" above based on the typical condescending and derogatory usage in Latin—dependent on God to do the critical work.[43] Following the section of the sermon on the *rusticus*, Augustine explains God's action:

> But if there was nobody working from the inside, the seed wouldn't take root in the earth, nor would the treetop rise in the orchard, nor the sapling grow stout and hard and become a tree trunk, nor branches nor fruit nor leaves ever be produced. That's why the apostle himself said, to distinguish between the work of the workers and of the Creator, "I myself planted, Apollo watered; but it was God who gave the growth." And he added, Neither the one who plants nor the one who waters is anything, but only God who gives the growth (*incrementum dat Deus*) (1 Cor 3:6–7). If God is not giving any growth from within, then this sound reaching your ears is just worthless. But if he is giving it, then what I am planting and watering has some value, and my efforts are not worthless.[44]

God works on the Church gathered by offering them an increase of space to be filled through their desire for understanding for the scripture passage in question. Indeed, both the preacher and the parishioner must act humbly in the moment of the sermon. The preacher humbly recognizes their lack of

---

42 Teubner, *Prayer After Augustine,* 101–11. He distinguishes Christ as having two kinds of *exemplum*, both having an influence on the contemporary moment and pointing towards the eschatological resurrection.

43 OLD, V.II, 1843: "Having a countryman's lack of refinement, uncouth in manner or lifestyle, coarse, unpolished, boorish, etc."

44 *s.* 152.1 (CCSL 41Ba.31; WSA III/5, 59).

control in persuasion. The parishioners must rely on God to complete their understanding because the preacher cannot explain the one Word of God without remainder.[45] In this, they increase their trust in the Holy Spirit to complete their movement towards the eschatological fulfillment of the *beata vita*. How exactly does the Spirit aid in the moment of the sermon?

One way of saying it is that both are dependent on grace. Verwilghen calls Christ the *sacramentum-exemplum*. Not only does Christ gives us the example, which we saw in the previous chapter in the performance of Augustine, but also the *sacramentum*, the grace and the means to achieve that which was modeled.[46] Grace works in the preacher and the parishioner who recognize their inability to understand and explain completely on their own. They need the illumination of grace.

This sermon has an obvious connection to the role of desire in the movement of the soul towards the *beata vita*. Augustine says that their desire (*desiderium*) is an *oratio* itself. As we noted in the section above, the desire in prayer is part of the reception of the word. In a sermon on the 1 John, Augustine says, "The entirety of the good Christian life is a holy desire (*tota vita christiani boni, sanctum desiderium est*)."[47] Indeed, this desire comprises the entirety of a good Christian life. It is a desire because it has not come to the fulfillment in the *beata uita*. The sermon, as we shall continue to see, is one arena to learn and increase this desire for *uisio dei*.

Returning to the central sermon of the chapter, the lector has read a portion of Paul's letter to the Romans (Rom. 7:25–8:1–4) that all agree has some difficulty for understanding. When Augustine gets to the passage about Christ's relationship to sin, he says a curious thing, "So from what sin did he condemn sin? Some people, trying to understand, have arrived at a sense

45 In *s.* 32.9, Augustine suggests that the divine imperative carries with it grace saying, "And in order to appreciate that it is grace which achieves this, none of you, brothers, should rely on his own powers. In this way you rely on the grace of God. You see, God is calling you and ordering you to do something, and he himself gives you the strength, so that you are able to carry out his orders. What you have to provide is a large faith, humbling yourself under the flood of grace, beseeching God, trusting not a whit to yourself, stripping yourself of Goliath, putting on David," (CCSL 41.403; WSA III/2, 142).

46 Verwilghen, *Christologie et Spiritualité*, 295. See also: Studer, "'Sacramentum et exemplum' chez saint Augustin" *Recherches Augustiniennes et Patristiques* 10 (January, 1975): 87–141.

47 *ep. Io. tr.* 4.6 (PL 35.2008; English mine).

that is certainly not to be rejected out of hand. And yet, as far as I can see, they have not really been able to fathom what the apostle has said. However, they have said something that is not bad in itself."[48] The question of Christ's relationship to sin has several answers. Augustine does not name who proffered this other explanation for what is going on this passage, but he says it is not "bad in itself." In making this move, Augustine indicates that there are multiple legitimate interpretations of this obscure passage. While offering the reading he takes to be correct, he nonetheless does not give the once and for all, definitive answer to the question. Augustine wants to give space for the Holy Spirit to operate.[49]

What Augustine the preacher wants is for his people to pray rightly and he wants to stir within them a desire for understanding. This is the *exercitatio animi*. In fact, the most effective thing that Augustine can do as a preacher at this precise moment is to open the text for multiple readings. Multiple readings generate uncertainty in the listener so that they will turn inward to pray and allow God to give the increase—an increase in understanding as well as an increase in their capacities. God elongates their desire, which creates the possibility for more joy in the fulfillment. It is the greater the capacity for understanding that brings delight the greater the delight itself is.

Augustine can best facilitate an encounter with God through the scriptures by creating some uncertainty in what the text precisely means.[50] Jonathan Teubner in his work *Prayer after Augustine*, explains it this way, "Participation occurs in this age through placing faith in the *scientia* of Christ, but *scientia* can only become *sapientia* through 'failure,' or rather only at the point where the human person reaches her limit and is left with no other device or scheme than to trust the Holy Spirit's 'groaning' in completing her *scientia*."[51] Scientia is the complete knowledge—or all-encompassing vision—of Christ

---

48 *s.* 152.10 (CCSL 41Ba.43; WSA III/5, 55).

49 Michael Cameron puts it this way, "A strong community gathered around the text hears a call, not to generate biblical position papers that only reveal correct answers from the back of the holy Book, so to speak, but to give counsel and training in how to read with love," in "Augustine's Rhetorical Reading of Genesis in *Confessiones* 11–12," 23.

50 It is worth noting that he completely rejects a Manichean reading of an early section. There are wrong readings, but that does not mean there is only one right meaning. Augustine solves this problem with the *regula fidei*, which rules out some readings entirely.

51 Teubner, *Prayer*, 107.

that is impossible in this age. There is a limit to human knowing, a failure. For Teubner's reading of Augustine, *sapientia* is possible but only through reliance on the Holy Spirit. The goal of the Christian life is Christ himself, though of course that can only come at the consummation of time.[52] Thus, the sermon becomes the arena where the soul can recognize that which it lacks and call upon the Holy Spirit through her desire to understand the ultimate *res,* Christ.

This very training to rely on the Holy Spirit plays out in other arenas of life. If those gathered can begin to see the need to pray and rely on the Holy Spirit for understanding of a scriptural passage, they can do the same for moments of their lives outside of the liturgy. The Holy Spirit does more than merely give understanding but cooperates with souls as they seek to carry out the scriptural commands to live justly.

With that in mind, we will focus on Augustine's use of *oratio,* which does seem to match Teubner's understanding of prayer in Augustine.[53] The orating which the congregation does, in Augustine's mind, fits well with the definition which Teubner draws out in his work. This prayerful desire to understand connects the listener internally to the God who meets them in their desire for understanding, and critically in their failure of understanding. It is in this prayer of longing that God works in their soul. Teubner correctly attributes this work uniquely to the Holy Spirit, "The groaning of the Holy Spirit in us, that which emerges through creaturely failure, does not shift the suppliant from mortal to immortal prayer. Rather, remaining firmly planted on this earth, the supplicant waits in *patience.*"[54] The creaturely failure for the listener may be great or small depending on their education or natural abilities. Their very lack is precisely what they need. It is then that they can depend on the Holy Spirit to intercede for them and ground them in patience until the reception.

---

52 Marrou cautions against creating too strict of a semantic boundary for Augustine, "Nothing shows this better than the floating character of his terminology. He does not know how to forge a technical vocabulary, there is not an Augustinian terminology as there is with Aristotle, St. Thomas, or Kant" *Saint Augustin et La Fin de la Culture Antique* (Paris, 1958) 245–246. Marrou shows at the end of *Saint Augustin et La Fin de la Culture Antique* that even the words *sapientia* and *scientia* are used at times as synonyms within the corpus of Augustine (561–569).

53 Teubner's analysis relies too heavily on another Latin word, *precari,* for the kind of prayer we discuss here as dependency. It is not a stretch to say that Augustine uses different words for similar concepts, as he was a trained rhetorician. We will thus apply Teubner's explanation of *precari* for *orare* (Teubner, *Prayer,* 20).

54 Teubner, *Prayer,* 92.

Now they are not self-reliant but humble. Any person listening can be put in the breach of the failure to understand and not the educated only. In his previous understanding of the role of rhetoric and philosophy, Augustine thought that only certain people could attain to the divine vision. Mark Clavier notes, "previously, the uneducated continued to live in darkness; unlike Augustine they had not been enlightened by the divine light that had come down on him through the liberal arts and Neoplatonic philosophy."[55] It is the brilliance of Augustine's reimagining of the role of preaching to provide a place for any present to hear a sermon and listen for the Word to illuminate them in ways hitherto unimaginable outside an advanced philosophical education.

The orator in classical usage gets all the credit and all the blame when their speech fails to persuade. More to the point, only certain people were even capable of understanding a Ciceronian oration, and these orations were developed for an educated aristocracy. The half step from Cicero's understanding of an oration to Augustine's preaching comes in the person of Marius Victorinus. As Clavier notes, "Someone like Victorinus, who combined philosophical learning with rhetorical training, could provide the tools of enlightenment that would free people to seek to rise above this world."[56] Augustine develops this notion and in his own preaching opens the possibility that any gathered can, through prayerful dependence on the Spirit, be brought to the kind of enlightenment Victorinus still only imagined for the philosophically inclined. Because Augustine waits on the Holy Spirit for the illumination, God gets the praise one way or another. The success of the sermon depends entirely on God for it to grow, as well as on the congregation to desire to learn in their prayers to God.

As he does in this passage from Romans, Augustine encourages his readers to look for Christ the head in this passage on his relationship to sin. Moving beyond merely a question of mental recognition, Augustine wants his people to grasp internally how Christ acts in their place by becoming sin for them. Meconi explains it this way:

55 Clavier, *Eloquent Wisdom*, 106. The section of the quote gives a full background as to how one achieved true wisdom and vision in the Neoplatonic tradition and through the liberal arts (*Eloquent Wisdom*, 100–12). Our purpose through this book, especially the section on the sermons, has been to show how Augustine sought to teach and shape many more people than had the means and time to study philosophy for this kind of ascent.

56 Clavier, *Eloquent Wisdom*, 49.

Augustine here commits himself to the view that the historical Christ also reveals himself as the mystical Christ and thus able to include all who truly bear his name. Christ has chosen to involve each human person in his own birth, toil, persecutions, and his final victory over death.[57]

Augustine teaches the gathered faithful to read the text through the lens of the Christ who humbly takes on our sin. Christ envelops us in every aspect of his own sinless life, which culminates in victory over sin.

This moves the conversation beyond mere comprehension into learning to always see the Word in the word. Cameron summarizes this kind of spiritual exercises of seeing Christ despite the noetic effects of sin by explaining, "In short, Augustine's sermons are spiritual exercises that train Christians to read Scripture as Christ. When they do, the Law grants them what it commands because of Christ's grace, and Prophecy reveals to them what it signifies because of Christ's truth."[58] These words of the scripture are to be read as Christ. Augustine is merely teaching them how to do that as *praedicator*. He trains their souls in the exercise of seeing Christ in the text and recognizing their desire for Christ in understanding him as he is.

Augustine ends *s.* 152 by reminding his people what true happiness is. He asks in conclusion, "So what's the solution? Your love, strain towards this great mystery: you will be happy, if you will have loved understanding and you will have come to love."[59] In a sense, Augustine is saying that he knows they will not all attain to the perfect understanding of this difficult passage of Paul's letter—not all are philosophers. The most important thing is to desire to understand and learn from that desire that the love of the thing you desire is the proper end.[60] He wants them all to understand, but he knows that not

57 Meconi, *The One Christ: St. Augustine's Theology of Deification* (Washington, DC: Catholic University of America Press, 2012), 205.

58 Cameron, *Christ Meets Me Everywhere*, 288.

59 *s.* 152.11 (CCSL 41Ba. 45; English translation my own): "Intendat Caritas vestra magnum altumque mysterium. Felices eritis, si intellectum dilexeritis, et ad dilectum perveneritis." Edmund Hill's translation of this is particularly deficient, "So what's the solution? Would your graces please pay close attention to a great and profound mystery. You will be truly blessed if you cherish it once you have understood it, and attain to it once you cherish it" (WSA III/5, 55).

60 Two preeminent Augustinian scholars, Lewis Ayres and Thomas Humphries,

all can come to that same depth of knowledge. Rather, all of them can at least come to loving that for which they have strained to understand, Christ. This is the power of prayer and the exercise of the soul which all undergo in the midst of the proclamation of the Church: all gathered come to love the God (*caritas*) who is the *telos* of the whole of the liturgy and all of life.

Ekphrasis and the Grace to See

As a final way to think about participation in the moment of the sermon, we will look at another rhetorical strategy that has a theological character in its use in the church's liturgy. We have been thinking about the *exercitatio animi* and how the sermon "works" to create desire and participation between God and church. This final section will see how participation in Christ and the grace he offers changes the one listening into one seeing God.

The only remnant of Augustine's life are of course his words, and some of these words are from the transcription of *notarii* present at the preaching of Augustine. The introduction of this study began with a quote from Possidius who noted the profit one could gain from those who could "hear him speak in church and see him with their own eyes." With words as all we have to work with it might seem difficult to draw on the second half of this statement about those who could "see him with their own eyes." Yet, Augustine, as a trained rhetorician, likely knew the rhetorical strategy outlined in the Progymnasmata, *ekphrasis,* which denotes the ability for words to become like a vision. As a master of this rhetoric and a preacher, Augustine combines this rhetorical technique with a deeper insight about vision and grace, thus combining his rhetorical ability with theological acumen. We can both look at Augustine preaching and look with Augustine through his preached words at the telos of his preaching, the humble Christ.

---

define Augustinian hermeneutics, thusly, "Augustine's insistence on the value of the figurative here is famously found also in the second book of his *On Christian Teaching*. In that book, as soon as Augustine offers the comment that the figurative stimulates greater delight and thus better rouses the soul towards its true love, he offers us an account of the various stages through which the soul ascends or grows," [Lewis Ayres and Thomas Humphrey, "Augustine and the West to AD 600," in *The Oxford Handbook of Sacramental Theology*, ed. Hans Boersma and Matthew Levering (Oxford: Oxford University Press, [2001], 226).

In the simplest terms, *ekphrasis* was the art of using words to describe something which created an image in the mind of the listener. Any who studied rhetoric in the ancient world would have been familiar with such a strategy, no less Augustine himself, as we shall see. The technique of *ekphrasis* offers the possibility of seeing with words. To be able to see through words lies deep at the heart of Augustine's theology of preaching. In Augustine's weekly (sometimes daily) preaching, he took the recorded words of scripture and preached them to an audience. Not even the best rhetorician could make everyone see what Augustine saw when he read the words of scripture, but it was incumbent upon him to use the capabilities at his disposal to bring the hearer as close as possible to sight.[61]

The modern reader of Augustine cannot see him as Possidius did, but the reader can begin to see the scriptures through the vision created by the words of Augustine. Augustine relied on his abilities as a rhetorician to offer to his hearers more than the words of the text itself, but to create an image from the text of scripture. What we will find is that Augustine did as much as he could with his own words, but as a theologian he understood that it was the power of grace that enabled his hearers to see the humble Word with "deified eyes."[62]

To grasp the power of this kind of rhetoric, it will be beneficial to first lay out the classical art of *ekphrasis* briefly. Classicist Ruth Webb writes, "Ekphrasis can be of any length, of any subject matter, composed in verse or prose, using any verbal techniques, as long as it 'brings its subject before the eyes' or, as one of the ancient authors says, 'makes listeners into spectators.'"[63] The last line is the *sine qua non* of ekphrasis. By listening to a gifted and practiced speaker, a listener can be transformed into a spectator. Whatever is described through the abilities of speaker becomes something to behold, not merely heard.

Webb distinguishes between simple description and *ekphrasis*, which unites the speaker and the listener-cum-spectator. It encapsulates the connection between speaking and hearing, not merely recording a written word.

---

61 Carol Harrison notes that in Augustine's reading of Cyprian of Carthage, he learned the ability to see with the preacher, *The Art of Listening* (102).

62 We will expound on this notion below, but it comes from *s.* 126.14 and the phrase "oculis deificatis."

63 Ruth Webb, *Imagination and Persuasion in Ancient Rhetorical Theory and Practice* (Surrey, England: Ashgate, 2009), 8. Nikolaos, *Progymnasmata*, p. 68, ll. 11–12: [ἔκφρασις] πειρᾶται θεατὰς τοὺς ἀκούοντας ἐργάζεσθαι.

There is a give and take between the listener and the speaker. The speaker engaged in creating *ekphrasis* does not only describe what they see as a picture. This would, in a sense, separate the speaker from the one listening. In fact, the ancients linked the description of something with the virtual image, or the image of the inner eye, which was created in the listener-cum-spectator. The bond between the speaker and the hearer cannot be severed. That is to say, the power of *ekphrasis* is that it does not focus only on the words which describe a painting or an object, but the ability of the words chosen to transform a hearer, one present to the speaking of the words, into a spectator.

As we have done throughout this study, we will draw on Augustine's predecessors in the art of rhetoric, Quintilian and Cicero, to illuminate *ekphrasis* further.[64] Quintilian's explanation of *ekphrasis* in his manual for the orator, *The Orator's Education*, takes Cicero as his guide and example. In his explanation of this practice, Quintilian describes Cicero's use of *ekphrasis* as "putting something before our eyes, instead of stating *that* an event took place, we show *how* it took place, and that not as a whole, but in detail."[65] The emphasis is on the detail and showing rather than telling. Both Quintilian and Cicero were pillars of Augustine's own education, and he shows considerable familiarity with them.

For an example of what this might look like, Quintilian again draws on Cicero, though this time from one of his declamations *in Verrem* 5.161, he cites, "Then he made for the marketplace, on fire with mad and wicked rage, his eyes blazing, and cruelty showing clearly in every feature of his face."[66] How did the man come into the forum? "On fire with mad and wicked rage" and "his eyes blazing" with "cruelty showing clearly in every feature of his face." Cicero offers a visual interpretation of the events. The listener-now-spectator is invited through these words to look with Cicero at the event. It is as much vision as hearing.

Returning to Augustine, the skill of *ekphrasis* made the scriptures come alive for the audience of his sermons.[67] In chapter three above, we went to

---

64 Quinitilian also translates ekphrasis as evidentia, *Instituto Oratoria* 4.2.64; 6.2.32, 8.3.61. The Latin translation comes from the preposition *ex* and the verb *videre*, literally indicating "to see from."

65 Quintilian *Instituto Oratoria* 9.2.40 (LCL 127:56–57); Quintilian cites Cicero *De Oratore* 3.202.

66 Cicero, *In Verrem*, 5.161 (LCL 221: 123).

67 We also see a similar phenomenon in the Syriac preaching tradition. According

great length to study the audiences present at the sermons of Augustine. With the consideration of *ekphrasis* in view, we can understand better what made Augustine's speeches so captivating, not only to the lettered urbanites but also to the greater portion of those unlettered and less philosophically inclined. Ekphrasis presents a helpful way to consider how illiterate people could be trained to see and understand the scriptures as through the preaching of someone like Augustine.

The only means of becoming a spectator in an ancient church was through the words of the preacher to create an image in the minds of the hearers during the liturgy of the church. Augustine could not play a video, but he could use his words and skill with language to transform his hearers into spectators. When the faithful gathered on a Sunday for the liturgy, all at once they viewed one story through the gifted preacher's deployment of *ekphrasis* to create a visual image of the scriptural text. As an illustration of Augustine's own abilities in *ekphrasis*, we will turn to one recurrent example, the story of Mary and Martha.[68]

Mary, Martha, and the Humility of the Better Part

On several occasions in his preaching career, Augustine told the story of Mary and Martha recorded in Luke 10 to offer a visual representation of humility and the delight of truth. The lectionary for the day when the African bishop preached *s.* 179 included a reading from James 1:22, which Augustine takes as an occasion to tell the story of Mary and Martha.[69] The details of the story are quite simple as recorded in Luke 10:38–42, Jesus comes to the home of Mary and Martha. While the text records that Martha welcomed Jesus into her home, it was Mary who receives the surprising praise at the end of the text. Jesus commends Mary saying, "Mary has chosen the better part ... which shall not be taken away from her (Luke 10:42)."[70] Much to

to Jeffrey Wickes, Ephrem the Syrian did this in his *madrashe*, "the poet fixes his attention on small narrative scenes within larger biblical books and presents these scenes as objects for his audience to look upon," *Bible and Poetry in Late Antique Mesopatamia* (Berkeley: University of California Press, 2019) 86.

 68 *io. eu. tr.* 15.18; 49.4; *ss.* 103, 104, 69, 255.

 69 Some commentators have chosen a date of 409 for this sermon, Gryson *Répertoire général des auteurs ecclésiastiques latins de l'Antiquiteé*, 241.

 70 *s.* 179.4 (CCSL 41Bb.621; WSA III/5, 301).

the annoyance of Martha and to the confusion of some readers, Jesus does
not praise Martha for preparing the table, but Mary for sitting at his feet.
Augustine finds in this surprising commendation an occasion for *ekphrasis*
and reflection on the nature of the active and contemplative lives. He poses
this question to his congregation, "What are we to make of this [the praise
of Mary], my brothers and sisters?"[71]

To answer his question and give the hearers something on which to
reflect, Augustine expounds on the scant details of the text. The sermon
begins by encapsulating the simple story saying, "this is the part that Mary
also chose for herself, who sat at the Lord's feet and listened at leisure to
his word, while her sister was serving them and was distracted with all the
serving." He goes on a little later to describe Martha who was "worrying
and slogging away, and taking care of all sorts of things."[72] In this narration,
Augustine follows the details given in the biblical text.

In contrast to Martha, however, Augustine penetrates deeper into what
Mary did in the Lord's presence. The great preacher weaves insights from
other scriptures. His words direct those listening to look closer at the story
and why Mary might be sitting:

> What was Mary enjoying while she was listening? What was she
> eating, what was she drinking?.... Let's ask the Lord, who keeps
> such a splendid table for his own people, let's ask him. *Blessed, he
> says, are those who are hungry and thirsty for justice, because they shall be
> satisfied* (Mt 5:6). It was for this wellspring, from this storehouse
> of justice, that Mary, seated at the Lord's feat, was in her hunger
> receiving some crumbs.[73]

The scripture does not mention that Mary "enjoyed" anything or was "hungry."
Augustine uses his imagination to probe the text and see something beyond
the text in question. And a little further on, "What was Mary enjoying? What
was she eating, what was she drinking so avidly with the mouth of her heart?
Justice, truth. She was enjoying truth, listening to truth, avid for truth, longing
for truth. In her hunger she was eating truth, drinking it in her thirst. She was

71 *s.* 179.4 (CCSL 41Bb.621; WSA III/5, 301).
72 *s.* 179.3 (CCSL 41Bb.620; WSA III/5, 300).
73 *s.* 179.5 (CCSL 41Bb.623; WSA III/5, 302).

being refreshed." Augustine admits that he has gone beyond the text, saying "I'm lingering on the point because I'm enjoying it too."[74] The sketch of the text and the detail from Augustine draw out a deeper truth from a simple story.

The Latin in Luke 10 gives little detail about Martha and Mary, so Augustine elaborates and embellishes details about the characters. In the description of Martha, we get, "Martha satagebat circa frequens ministerium" (Martha worried herself with much serving). And then the Lord describes her, "solicita es et turbaris erga plurima" (worried and trouble on account of many things). Augustine as we have shown above gives his own interpretation by glossing the infrequent Latin word "satagebat" with "occupata" and adds "laborante, multa curante" (working, worrying about many things). To aid his hearers into becoming seers, Augustine provides extended explanations and glosses of the Latin text. He draws a contrast between Mary and Martha to illuminate the "better part" which Jesus indicated above. Step by step, Augustine leads his hearers into a deeper vision of the text and what one sees when one looks to Christ.

Further working out what Augustine sees in the text, he portrays the humility of Mary which prepared her for the truth she was about to receive. Mary "vacabat, sedebat, et audiebat" (was doing nothing, sitting, and listening). The verb "vacabat" is part of the ekphrastic embellishment. For Augustine, the fact that Mary "sedebat" indicates that she was practicing humility, "For standing signifies humility and sitting, humility (Stato enim significat humilitatem, sessio humilitatem)."[75] And most significantly for Augustine's own reading, "From what did Mary take delight, as I said? What was she eating, what was she drinking with the throat of our keen heart? Justice and Truth, by Truth she was delighted (Unde ergo Maria, ut dixi, delectabatur? Quid manducabat, quid bibebat, avidissimis cordis faucibus? Iustitiam, veritatem. Veritate delectabatur)."[76] From these short 4 verses of scripture, Augustine sees a spectacle of humility which leads to a delight in a truth on the part of the woman Mary, sitting and listening to the Lord. This delight in the truth is but a foretaste of their heavenly *patria* ("fatherland") to which they sojourn together. The power of the contemplative life is the ability to enjoy a foretaste of that which is to come. Jesus calls himself the "bread of life" in addition to the "truth" in the Gospel of John and is therefore the food Mary

74 *s.* 179.5 (CCSL 41Bb.623; WSA III/5, 302).
75 *s.* 179.3 (CCSL 41Bb.620 WSA III/5, 300).
76 *s.* 179.5 (CCSL 41Bb.623; WSA III/5, 302).

consumes. Augustine uses these other scriptural verses to make sense of the narrative and the dominical saying that Mary had chosen "the better part."

In the text which follows, a record remains of Augustine himself enjoying the moment. He writes, "I am delaying because I am enjoying it (Immoror, quia delector)." It appears that the congregation wondered why he spent so much time dwelling on the image he constructed. Not hesitating to commune with his audience, Augustine admits of his delight in what he was doing. Augustine demonstrates for his people his own enjoyment of the scripture and seeing the biblical story illuminated. The words of the sermon provide a window back in time to see Augustine in his element enjoying the moment of preaching, recorded by a scribe without any editing by Augustine.

Not only does Augustine delight in catching a glimpse of the Truth, but the text indicates that his hearers themselves have become seers. Slightly further on down the text, Augustine speaks directly to the gathered faithful, *Quid est enim modo quod omnes attenditis, omnes auditis, omnes excitamini, et quando verum aliquid dicitur, delectamini?* "What is it that you all have grasped, heard, been excited by and when something true was spoken, you delight."[77] He asks them to what they are paying attention and hearing which has made them excited and truly, delighted? He is only some 15 minutes into the sermon, but clearly, they were enjoying what they were hearing. As if explaining *ekphrasis* in action, Augustine changes his language from audition to vision. He asks, *quid vidistis? Quid tenuistis?* "What have they seen and what are they beholding?" The audience have become spectators. They now see the story, rather than merely hear it.[78]

To dispel all doubt that Augustine means vision, he draws out the contrast between physical and mental vision. He asks, "What color has appeared before your eyes, what form, what shape, what figure, what lines and limbs, what beauty of body? None of these things. Yet you love it."[79] It would seem that he is contradicting the notion that they see, but we must understand what he means. He continues, "I mean, when would you have applauded like that, if you didn't love it? When would you have loved it, if you hadn't seen anything?" It is the fact they love it and are delighted in it which indicates that they have grasped it, that they have seen with their

---

77 *s.* 179.6 (CCSL 41Bb.625; WSA III/5, 303).

78 Cf. *in Io. Ev.* 7.6.20; 117.3.5; *en. Psalm.* 32.2.25; *en. Psalm.* 36.2.8; *en. Psalm* 146.4; *s.* 49.11; *s.* 51.1.2; *s.* 168; *s.* 229s; *s.* 301; *s.* 313a.

79 *s.* 179.6 (CCSL 41Bb.625; WSA III/5, 303.)

inner eye. As we saw above in this very chapter, Augustine's goal for his sermons was that the audience would come to "love" through the experience of following his lead in the sermons. This is the *via humilitatis agendo* at work. Augustine acts out the way of humility for all to follow as they come to love the Word. By seeing and delighting in the vision of Jesus made possible through the sermon, Augustine can encourage his congregation that they have begun to see the Word in the word.

They have seen something, just not physically with their eyes. Augustine believes they are seeing with "deified eyes." He goes on, "And so, though I am not showing you any form of a body, any lines, color, beautiful movements, though I'm showing you nothing, you all the same are seeing, loving, applauding. If this delight in the truth is lovely now, it will be much lovelier then."[80] They do see, but they see through love. There is a conversation between the preacher and the congregation as they catch a glimpse of the Truth. He speaks, using the rhetorical tool of *ekphrasis* and the audience responds with applause. This was no silent congregation. We know of whom it was composed from chapter 3.

We will close this section with a comment on how Augustine encouraged his audience through this interaction. We have seen the great eloquent psychagogue at work in that Augustine stops mid sermon to commend his audience for their excitement. He leads them through his words to delight in seeing deeper into the scriptural text. Augustine uses the moment of the sermon to train his audience to see through his ekphrasis and encouragement. But of course, that is not the only factor in what takes place in the moment of the sermon. So far, we have limited ourselves to Augustine's part in the interaction between preacher and hearer. We will follow along as Augustine explains the theological elements of this rhetorical strategy.

Grace in the Vision of a Sermon

Participation, prayer, and vision are all critical touchstones for Augustine's soteriology as evidenced in his sermons. The language of loving from *s.* 179 opens an avenue for a deeper understanding of Augustine's soteriology and how theologically, more than rhetorically, the congregation can become partakers in the divine nature to see Christ. We began this chapter by talking

80 *s.* 179.6 (CCSL 41Bb.625; WSA III/5, 303).

about the participation of prayer. The congregation prays, desiring to behold the Humble Christ. Augustine preaches and gives voice to what he sees as a biblical interpreter using the tools of eloquence. The final portion is the graced participation offered by Christ which unites the whole of the *totus Christus*, body, preacher, and head, to become mystically one.

Although Augustine does not go into depth about grace in *s.* 179, in *ss.* 126 and 136 he explores how grace fosters love in the hearts of those who believe and allows them to see. For our purposes, we are using the language of vision to capture the moment of the sermon where Augustine moves from his own eloquence into the realm of its source. As Clavier sums up well, "Whereas for Victorinus the orator is a vehicle only for wisdom, in Augustine he is the vehicle for wisdom and eloquence, both of which find their true source in God."[81] In the theology of Augustine, salvation offers the gift of grace to truly see. Without it, the eyes and the ears of the flesh will fail. It is through grace that this carnal vision is healed to see the Christ as God, to look beyond the *forma servi* to the *forma dei*. Augustine calls this seeing with "deified eyes."[82]

The lectionary of the day for *s.* 126 came from John 5:19 and presented some difficulties in its relation to the doctrine of the Trinity. In the Gospel, Jesus says he cannot do anything on his own, but only what he sees the Father doing. Augustine tries to head off potential confusion by beginning the sermon with his famous dictum drawn from Isaiah 7:9, "unless you believe, you shall not understand."[83] The people must believe in order to see and understand.

In the difficult section of the sermon, Augustine tries to explain the obscure comment from John, "the Son cannot do anything except what he sees the father doing." Augustine leads his congregation through some difficult theological reasoning, asking them to consider God *in se* "in himself." The language in the sermon is *forma dei*. When Jesus says that he only does what he sees the Father doing, he means what takes place in the mystery of the Trinity, not in his physical human person, the *forma servi*.[84] This form of the servant though is not the only thing that Augustine believes the faithful

---

81 Clavier, *Eloquent Wisdom*, 84.

82 *s.* 126.14 (RB 169.189; WSA III/4, 278).

83 *s.* 126.1 (RB 169.183; WSA III/4, 270). This is from Isaiah 7:9 in Augustine's *Vetus Latina*.

84 *s.* 126.13 (RB 169.189).

can observe. He tells them, "Put aside, put aside, I say for the time being the form of a servant. Observe the form of God, in which he was before the world was made, in which he was equal to the Father."[85] The form of God is what he is guiding them to understand and strain their reasoning powers towards. The congregation would have been following his logic orally. If they are unable or struggle to follow him, Augustine reminds them, "do our sort of eyes find a place in him—and I don't mean our bodily eyes, but the eyes of devout and loving hearts? After all, *blessed are the clean of heart, for they shall see God* (Mt. 5;8)." The kind of vision Augustine has in mind is hastening towards the eschatological beatific vision. While this is intellectually difficult, it is not only for the knowledgeable.[86] The way to see is through a cleansing of the heart. Coupled with this cleansing, it is the work of God that transforms the heart to be able to see, not with bodily eyes, but deified eyes.

Some of those present at the time of Christ's earthly sojourn could not see him because, according to Augustine, sin had clouded their vision. This unbelief becomes evident in the inability to see the form of God, "*Show us the father and it is enough for us.* And there he stood, in front of the eyes of a servant, in the form of a servant, saving the form of God for deified eyes, and he said to him, *Am I with you all this time, and you do not know me? Whoever sees me also sees the Father* (Jn 14:8–9)."[87] While it may appear that Augustine understands the Son to be "saving" the form of God for the eschaton, he implies in the section quoted above that they do indeed have the possibility of a foretaste of that vision now. The "saving the form of God" he has in mind, is that this vision is kept for the pure in heart. Not many, or not all, may see now, but the pure in heart can. It is this deification, participation in the divinity of Christ, that allows the believer to see in a way not possible even for their physical eyes. Some of those who saw Jesus Christ on earth

---

85 *s.* 126.13 (RB 169.189).

86 One thinks of Monica in the Ascent of *conf.* 9 and her role in the Cassiciacum dialogue. John Peter Kenny sates, "Monica represents an affront to the Platonic contemplative ideal. However unpromising she may be as a philosopher, she achieves certain knowledge of transcendental Wisdom. . . . Her success is not a function of her intellectual preparation, nor, given her own story of gradual moral development. . . . It is instead a function of the Spirit within her" (*The Mysticism of Saint Augustine: Rereading the Confessions* [New York: Routledge, 2005], 112).

87 *s.* 126.14 (RB 69.190; WSA III/4, 279).

were unable to see, or perceive, the fact that he was also divine. For Augustine, one must be born in love to become divinized and see who God is.

The phrase, "deified eyes," only occurs this one time in the writings of Augustine. As such, the comment deserves further attention. It might be thought that Augustine posits a kind of fully realized eschatology here.[88] Though we now "see through a glass dimly, we will see him face to face." Could it be said that "deified eyes" mean Beatific Vision in the present? Lewis Ayres explores the question of what kind of vision Augustine meant in *ep.* 120, and finds: "the mature Augustine does allow for a possible vision of God in this life. However, the following observations are important: such a vision is only possible if we are taken by God out of the body as if we were dead; the vision is of God insofar as God can be seen by a created being; the vision is indescribable in corporeal terms; the vision takes place through the Trinitarian structure of God speaking his Word and is of the consubstantial Trinity."[89] Both *ep.* 120 and 139 give a fuller account of what Beatific Vision means for Augustine. What it makes clear though is Augustine had a category for this worldly vision of God in certain circumstances. Let's return to the context of the quote in *s.* 126.

One also ought to recall that Augustine says that it is the *forma dei* which is seen by the *oculis deificatis*. That is to say, in Augustinian Christology, only those participating in God through grace come to see the *forma dei* which Christ came to lead the way towards in the *forma servi*. Augustine the preacher provides space through his sermon for those gathered to look with him and consider with him the *forma dei* as he describes what he has seen on the *via humilitatis*. He opens up the possibility for any that they too can have this vision. It is however only the *incrementum* which God alone gives that provides the deep illumination to see beyond the *forma servi* into the *forma dei*.

For Augustine, it is love that makes possible this seeing. He writes, "Let charity (caritas) bring you to birth, charity rear you, charity perfect you,

88 Michel Barnes is more reticent to expound on the possibility of a Beatific Vision this side of Christ's return, "The Visible Christ and the Invisible Trinity: Mt 5:8 in Augustine's Trinitarian Theology of 400," *Modern Theology* (Summer 2003):10, "The eschatological location of the turning over of the Kingdom is a consistent part of Augustine's reading of the Pauline text; eschatological, but not wholly unrealized."

89 Lewis Ayres, "'Remember That You Are Catholic' (s. 52.2): Augustine on the Unity of the Triune God" *JECS* 8.1 (2000) 39–81; n. 70 page 69.

charity stiffen you, so that you may see the seeing of the Word, and that the
Word is not one thing, and another his seeing; but that what the seeing of
the Word is, that is what the Word is too."[90] *Caritas* gives birth to the seeing
of faith that cleanses and forms eyes once darkened by the mist of sin and
pride. These sins build over time and obfuscate the vision of the Word.[91]
The illumination of grace moves those so imbued by it to be able to see
something previously unknown.[92]

When we consider his further comments on the power of vision, we
see that grace furnishes the power to see in a way that is deeper than even
that of the flesh. The grace of God makes people to see with their mind's
eye, what some did not see with their eyes of flesh. While Augustine uses
the rhetorical technique of *ekphrasis* to help those listening understand the
story, he concedes that he cannot give them the power to see as only Christ
can through the power of grace. What Augustine wants more than to be a
good rhetorician is that all might become pure in heart and behold Christ,
the Truth. What begins as a simple rhetorical technique becomes the very
means to know God. Augustine moves his audience from depending on
the eyes of the flesh to see and use the eyes of the heart.[93] Once they have
joined him in this journey all await the movement of God to give them the
lasting vision.

To bring this analysis full circle, we recall that Augustine, following Paul,
relied on "God to give the increase." One way to read this is to see that the
"increase" is grace. Grace allows those listening to become spectators of the
truth, more so than they ever could be even with their physical eyes. This is

90 *s.* 126.14 (RB 69.190; WSA III/4, 279).

91 Augustine recognizes this mist of sin in his own vision in *conf.* 8.11. A similar
point is made in *s.* 88.5 (CCSL 41Ab.468; WSA III/3. 432): "Whatever points are
made by God's holy scriptures, this is their ultimate point, to help us purge that inner
faculty of ours from that thing that prevents us beholding God." Also: *s.* 88.14 (CCSL
41Ab.480; WSA III/3. 429): "The eye is healed, you see, when it understands Christ's
divinity. Your graces must try to grasp this; pay attention to the sublime mystery I am
trying to explain."

92 In *s.* 166.4, Augustine preaches, "God wants to make you god; but not by
nature, as he is the one bore you; by his gift and adoption. Just as he is made a participator in your mortality through humanity; so also he made you a participator of his
immortality through exaltation" (CCSL 41Bb. 315; translation my own).

93 Augustine explains this in *en. Psalm.* 37.11.

salvation for Augustine. It is the healing of the sin-sick soul to see that to which it was formerly blind.

Furthermore, it is through sharing in the humility of Christ that one has the possibility or power to see with deified eyes. Augustine teaches the virtue of humility, which he learned from Christ, through his words and deeds as preacher. The preaching moment also presents the possibility to rely humbly on God to give the increase, both for the preacher and the parishioner. Augustine cannot give the definitive interpretation of a scriptural passage, but he can present the possibility of a humble encounter with the Word. The parishioner must humbly receive the divine illumination, a gift of vision. The *via humilitatis agendo* of Augustine the preacher relies on the action of the preacher the divine action. It is only a possibility to follow the via to the head because of the intervention of grace. As Augustine preached in *s.* 121, Christ is the way and the destination. Salvation is in *spe* of the final *re*. The sacramental nature of preaching the Word offers the Christian a foretaste of the delightful vision of the Truth. Christ is present uniquely in the preaching of the Word for all to participate in him and come to a sure hope that the love made known in the moment of preaching will finally last forever.

To return to the phrase, *via humiliatis agendo*, we might say that in the end, this way of humility is acted out both in the words of the speaker and the hearts of the listeners. Augustine as preacher leads through the words of Christ to the Word and those participating in Christ, both oratorically and metaphysically, travel that same via. Thus, the phrase *via humiliatis* refers to more than just the preacher, but the parishioners as well. If this training in the way of humility is successful, the *totus Christus* shares in their vision of God by grace.

For Augustine, the spectacle in the liturgy—because it occurs through the participation of prayer and gift of grace—becomes in fact more powerful than that of the theater. Those who gather at the shows merely see with their human eyes. Through the power of the grace to save and purify the sinful eye of the mind, those who participate in the moment of the sermon can see more deeply and more truly. Some who were present in the earthly sojourn of the Word could not see past the *forma servi* to the *forma Dei,* much like those entertained in the theater. All have the possibility through grace to behold Christ in spirit and in part now as a foretaste of that which is to come in the final eschatological vision.

Conclusion

This more theologically influenced chapter has shown that Augustine recognized the necessity of God's intervention in the moment of the sermon. Although Augustine spoke before his congregation and attempted to persuade them, he did so very differently than his former hero, Cicero. For Augustine, persuasion worked differently as it required the participation of the audience in the speech of the *praedicator*. That participation occurred in the form of prayer, a desire for understanding. The word for prayer in Latin had undergone a shift in meaning in the centuries in between Cicero and Augustine. When Augustine encouraged his audience to pray, he asked them to do something which would not be done out loud, nor was it simply the purview of the educated elite.

When the congregation participated in the moment of the sermon through prayer, they too depended on the grace of illumination. This was possible for all of those gathered to hear Augustine, even the unlettered. Augustine offered to them the words of Christ so that they could pray to be taught by the inner teacher, as we described in chapter 5. The moment of the sermon was a moment of exchange, of conversation between God, the preacher, and the church. The goal of this conversation was to increase the understanding of those gathered, so that they might expand their desire for a greater vision of God. This increased longing opened the soul up for greater enjoyment by their greater capacity for the presence of God. The sermon can be aptly described as *exercitatio animi*.

We also saw through Augustine's reading of the story of Mary and Martha the deployment of the rhetorical strategy of ekphrasis. While on one level, it is simply a strategy any orator could use, in the hands of Augustine the preacher, ekphrasis became a tool dependent on God to allow all to see Christ through "deified eyes." The necessity of understanding the rhetorical tropes is quite evident, but to leave it there would be to miss the theological component of God at work through grace. We were able to both see Augustine at work and see how Augustine understood God to be at work in the moment of the sermon.

As Christ the head of the body spoke through the preacher to the Church, the whole body of Christ was united to its head in the *totus Christus*. The Church sacramentally participated in the risen Christ whose resurrection was an *exemplum* of every Christians eventual bodily resurrection. By listening to the words of the preacher mined from the text of scripture, the Church heard the one voice of Christ. Augustine knew that this was only possible if *incrementum dat Deus*. The *totus Christus* relied on the grace of God to make Christ present to them.

More succinctly, Augustine encourages his hearers, "So for the time being treat the scripture of God as the face of God. Melt in front of it."[94] The present is the time of hope and the sacrament which points to the real Christ. Similarly, Augustine says, *In spe gaudemus, nondum in re* "in hope we rejoice, not yet in the thing itself."[95]

94 *s.* 22.7 (CCSL 41.297; WSA III/2, 47).
95 *s.* 360A ([= Dolbeau 24] *EAA* 147.239).

CONCLUSION

*"Let us avoid the assumption that rhetoric is a vice of manner,
and endeavour to find a rhetoric of substance also,
which is right because it issues from what it has to express."*[1]

—T. S. Eliot

THIS HAS BEEN A STUDY OF THE ROLE of humility in the preaching of St. Augustine of Hippo. Though the young Augustine was trained in ancient rhetoric, a discipline which placed little value on humility, the virtue of humility came to permeate his preaching. We looked at speech at the level of the words understood as a species of action. Augustine used humbler words to demonstrate the virtue of humility in the liturgy of the Church. Despite lowering his language and criticizing rhetorical training, Augustine still engaged in rhetorical practice. However, Augustine wedded these rhetorical ideas to his pursuit of Truth and so buttressed his own theological understanding with rhetorical elements.

In a sense, we can see Augustine "plundering the Egyptians" with respect to rhetoric, insofar as he employed rhetorical strategies though layered with theological insight.[2] The incarnation of the Word liberates the preacher from relying on his own genius because the Word speaks through the words of the preacher. In fact, he knows he cannot. If the congregation is to see God in the scriptures through the preaching of the scriptures it is a work of the Spirit. The preacher is thus free to use the tools at his disposal but not worry lest they might fail.

1 Eliot, T. S., "The Sacred Wood," in *The Complete Prose of T. S. Eliot: The Critical Edition: The Perfect Critic, 1919–1926* (Baltimore: The Johns Hopkins University Press and Faber & Faber Ltd, 2014): 83–91, 85.

2 *doc. Chr.* 2.40.60.

The modern world has taught us to be suspicious of rhetoric, which seems to be forced and unnatural. When we speak of politicians and public figures, we often dismiss what they say as "merely rhetoric." Or we might think of "rhetorical tricks" or "semantics." To trivialize the creative endeavor of a well-constructed speech and argument ignores that the form as well as the content serve an important function. In some cases, the medium is the message. Eliot is right to remind us that some rhetoric is a rhetoric of substance. What makes it right and good? If it springs from what it desires to express. Is there a better way to characterize what Augustine was up to in his preaching?

Augustine's calling was to preach the Word. If the Word came in the form of a humble servant, then the speech about that Word had to be humble. Christ the Word chose fishermen to witness his first advent. Augustine loved to remind his hearers of this because of how shocking it was. The Word through whom all things were made, the divine Word chose the least eloquent wordsmiths. Christ chose fishermen rather than orators. The Roman emperors chose orators, like Augustine, for the purpose of imperial propaganda. The power of the emperors paled in comparison to the power of the almighty Creator. If, however, the way to understanding and entering communion with that God required humility, he had to speak in a form that matched the content.

As we have seen, at times, Augustine's rhetoric looked quite simple. At other points, it could be quite complex. In every instance, Augustine knew the truth which Eliot highlights. Good rhetoric issues from what it has to express. If God is the almighty creator, there must be instances where it is necessary to use the heights of eloquence. When Augustine preached to audiences of less education, the ornamentation had to change. For the preacher of a smaller coastal city, speaking in the *sermo piscatorius* so that all might know the truth was in itself a rhetoric deriving from the Humble Word. Christ was born in the town of Bethlehem. Why would God be born in such a lowly place if not to teach humility?

In some respects, what we ought to see from this study focused on the *Sermones ad Populum* of Augustine, is that Augustine should be thought of as a kind of rhetorical theologian. That is to say, rhetoric is endemic to Augustine's thought world as man of words and public speaking. This does not mean that Augustine must only be considered for his rhetoric, but he does not speak or think as someone merely trained in theological reasoning, as his later interpreters were. Even Augustine's *exempla*, Cicero and Ambrose, lovers of philosophy as well, were in fact first public orators. The hope in the study was to capture some of the lyrical nature of Augustine's preaching to appreciate it for precisely how charming it could be. To miss this part of Augustine's output is to miss what made him so winsome to the tens of thousands of people who heard him speak.

It is also not to say that Augustine was simply a man of his time. As we proposed throughout, Augustine bent his rhetorical rules to the task at hand, which was submission to the humble God made known in the scriptures. Rhetorical categories helped lead us into his own thought world, but once arrived, we found ourselves looking through those means to a new reality, a God who chose the fishermen to herald the Creator. This is in fact not a flattening out, but an enlarging of techniques to capture a profoundly different reality.

Our study has tried to elucidate Augustine's theology of preaching in two parts. In the first, we established the necessary contextual features which would situate the latter three chapters. In chapter 1, we defined Speech Act Theory and how Augustine's own theory of language could accommodate a similar notion. Augustine reminded his readers in *On Christian Teaching* that *agit cum dicit*, "one acts when one speaks." The public speech of orators and preachers has an effect on the audience, greater than the simplistic notion of focusing on the delivery of information. SAT has three main components which we used in chapter 2 and part 2: locution, illocution, and perlocution. Chapter 2 was a historically focused study on the education of Augustine and his two exemplars of oratory and preaching. Cicero used his words for the perlocutionary effect of fame and glory. It worked and it inculcated in Augustine his own desire for a similar fame and fortune to Cicero. Along the way, Augustine ran into another speaker who was no rhetorical slouch, St. Ambrose. Ambrose encouraged Augustine to consider that humility might be a virtue and thus the scriptures themselves might hold a deeper meaning than Augustine ever thought possible. Moved by Ambrose's speech, Augustine listened to the scriptures and heard the divine author, the Humble Word speaking to him.

Knowing that the Word came to a humble place, Augustine had no fear of living himself in a smaller city in North Africa. Chapter 3 assessed the historical situation of Hippo and North Africa broadly. We argued that despite some scholarship to the contrary, most of Augustine's hearers must have been unlettered, but not necessarily unintelligent. The *Sermons to the People* show a preacher conversant with a wide variety of people in differing social stations.

Each chapter in Part 2 was based around a commonly found phrase in the sermons of Augustine. By looking at these leitmotifs, we provided a sense of what it was like to hear Augustine preach on a regular basis. One could call these leitmotifs "riffs," as one would play in music. Carol Harrison captures the difficulty of finding a precise term for this. She writes:

> The particular intertexts, language, images, and examples were like familiar chords or themes, which the congregation had heard over and over again, in many different contexts, in relation to innumerable passages of Scripture, to elucidate a wide range of points. They would inevitably resonate with the text in hand, and the mere fact of voicing them again would sometimes suffice to convey the preacher's meaning.[3]

We strummed these familiar chords to capture both the character of Augustine's preaching and as cues to his understanding of the act of preaching.

We divided part 2 into three categories for heuristic purposes based on the tripartite structure of SAT. Chapter 4 considered the *sermo piscatorius*, the speech of fishermen and how Augustine's language changed. He was willing to use barbarism, solecism, and *tapinosis* to good effect. He began to speak humbly, and his rhetoric reflected this. Once a *magister oratorum*, the erstwhile *magister* assumed the role of *praedicator* which required some rethinking. In chapter 5, we looked at how Augustine reconsidered the public speech of a preacher who had to listen to the One Teacher Christ. Augustine taught his hearers how to learn from the One Teacher by listening to the inner teacher whose *cathedra in caelo est*. Finally, in chapter 6, we looked at the way in which God works in the moment of the sermon. The *totus Christus* has to wait as *incrementum dat deus*, God must give the increase. God must be at work in the *oratory* of both the *praedicator* and *orator*.

---

3 Harrison, *The Art of Listening in the Early Church*, 172. In her preface, Harrison cites the influence of Harmless in her own conception of the preaching of Augustine. Both heavily utilize jazz music as a point of comparison in the preaching of St. Augustine. See Harrison, *Art of Listening*, ix.

This study moves the conversation on Augustine's theology of preaching forward by considering speech as action. It shows that Augustine's recognition of the virtue of humility was not merely something he discussed in his theological treatises but practiced in his preaching. As he says in *On Christian Teaching* his *forma vivendi* (form of living) is a *copia dicendi* (great source of speech). The manner of living is itself an abundance of speaking. His manner of life matched his manner of speaking. In smaller ways, we showed that Augustine's philosophy of language is more complex than some have assumed. Moreover, we have been able to discern that the majority of his audience must have been able to understand him, even if they were unlettered. Finally, we tied all of this into the Augustine's understanding of the goal of the Christian life, the *beata vita*.

As far as future studies go, one might consider how the next generations of preachers used Augustine's words. The influence of Augustine's preaching does not stop with the immediate audience of Hippo. His sermons were transcribed and edited for centuries after his death and used across Europe. One might consider how the theology of preaching changes when the preacher merely reads the words of a former preacher. The effect of the moment of the sermon might be different.

One way to assess the claims made throughout this work, especially the influence of Augustine's deeds through words is to consider the kind of example Augustine presented to those within his close orbit. Throughout this work we have encountered several different protegees of Augustine: Possidius, Antoninus, and Dioscorus. Possidius presented Augustine as a man who had a profound influence on those around him by the power of pairing his actions with his words. It is of course too simple to merely take Possidius at his word, and that is why we tried to see what the record of Augustine's language left as the only evidence of his claim. That said, Possidius's dedication to his former teacher in terms of cataloguing his works and remaining with him on his deathbed as the Vandals came down from the north at least suggests that his former teacher inspired a great affection in Possidius.

In the story of Antoninus from chapter 1, we saw a less than glowing example of the influence of Augustine. Augustine rushed Antoninus into the pulpit at Fussala before the young lector had reached any kind of spiritual maturity. To some extent, this shows that Augustine was not beloved by all and that his influence did not always end with devoted preachers devoted to their calling in service to the church, but instead sought to use their position of power to horde wealth.

While not much remains of the story of Dioscorus, we see in Augustine's letter to him, a man determined not to let the faults of his own youth be repeated in the next generation. Augustine pleaded with Dioscorus, as he did to some extent with Antoninus, to remember that the Christian faith rises and falls with the humility of its adherents. Dioscorus had more wealth and opportunity at his disposal, as well as a love for philosophy, but Augustine implored him to remember that without humility, all knowledge is vanity.

Others within Augustine's circle like Alypius, Aurelius, Nebridius, or Evodius could all be mentioned as within the broad circle of Augustine in Africa. Nebridius both aided Augustine in his own conversion, and Augustine in return encouraged Nebridius and his family to be baptized before his death.[4] Another North African whom we know less about, Aurelius of Carthage, helped Augustine found his monastery at Hippo and received frequent communication from Augustine.[5] Still another friend who spent time with Augustine at Cassiciacum which prodded him to the priesthood was Evodius of Uzalis.[6] We thus see that Augustine cast a tremendous shadow across the Christianity of North Africa in all of these figures, lesser known to history, nevertheless they demonstrate how Augustine's example exerted its influence on a great many church leaders. Among those who knew Augustine both before and after his conversion like Nebridius, is Alypius, well known from his role in *Confessions* 6. Not only did Ambrose baptize Alypius with Augustine and Adeodatus, but they followed many of the same intellectual movements from Manichaeism to Christianity. In the end, Alypius took up the bishopric of Thagaste after spending some time in the monastery at Hippo.[7] Despite having at least one follower reject his example, many others prove the contrary.

To encapsulate the way Augustine was remembered by those closest to him, we will draw from a lesser-known sermon by another man whom Augustine took under his care. Augustine, like Valerius before him, chose a successor before his full retirement. Fortunately, the first sermon given by

---

4 *conf.* 6.10.17 and *conf.* 9.3.6.

5 *ep.* 22.1

6 *ep.* 158–64.

7 *ep.* 22 and *Vita Augustini* 3.1–2.

this successor, Eraclius, remains to this day. The sermon is quite short, but within it we see the manner one of Augustine's disciples wanted his legacy to be remembered and followed by those who would listen. Aware of the difficulty of following so great a preacher, Eraclius says, "the cricket clamors, while the swan remains silent."[8] Despite his own humility, we can see in his words why so many men followed through on their own calling to serve the church. I will let the successor for Augustine have the last word on Augustine's example of the Way of Humility. Eraclius preached:

> I think, brothers, that you sense the heavy load of my task. And I seek that you lift me up while I am laboring under so great a weight as if your prayers are lifting up my shoulders. For the very blessed Father, who put this heavy weight on me, I know that he does not stop praying for me. He would not place this on me by his command alone and desist from pious prayer. Without a doubt, brothers, the one who requested I bear it, prays that I will complete it. What is that he requested, except to dare ignorance in the presence of wisdom, and to speak ineptitude in the presence of silent knowledge? And when scripture says, "speak, elder, for it is fitting for you" (Eccli. 32:5); Father says, "speak junior: for it delights me." You know, however, brothers, that even before now I have begun to speak for you all the word of God.
>
> Recently, I have undertaken what was compelled by the necessity of office: because I was not able to flee this duty. But it is easy in the absence of the teacher for a student to fill his place; it is arduous and difficult to teach the fellow students under the teacher; especially under such a teacher, whose great authority comes from words, which brings with the teaching tongue a life to match. For every good which is offered to us by the word of erudition, it is preceded by an example of life. It does go before us. I add; would even that we might follow. For whatever in this man that at which we marvel, admire, embrace, then it is truly to be loved by us, if we would not tire to imitate. Each one of us tends towards him in our own little way, what arises from the root of his heart are so many branches of virtue that each of us can grab ahold of one.

8 PL. 39.1718

Whoever can, let him follow his eloquence, and if they cannot, let him hold to his restraint. Whoever can, let him be filled with his authority, who cannot, let him pursue his humility. Whoever can, let him achieve his wisdom; who cannot, let him follow his patience. And in all the ways of the Lord, whoever can, let him walk with him. Who cannot, let him learn from him. Let us rejoice brothers, according to the outpouring of divine gifts to have ourselves in itself, what we do not have in ourselves. For whatever we see in him, it is ours, if we will love.[9]

9 PL 39.1717–1719. Translation my own.

BIBLIOGRAPHY

Primary Sources

Ambrose. *De Jacob. Seven Exegetical Works.* Translated by Michael McHugh. The Catholic University Press, Washington, DC: 1977.

Augustine. *Confessiones.* CCL 27. Translated by Maria Boulding in WSA I/1. Hyde Park, NY: New City Press, 1997.

———. *De Ciuitate Dei.* CCL 47–48. Translated by William Babcock in WSA I/6–7. Hyde Park, NY: New City Press, 2012–13.

———. *De doctrina Christiana.* CCL 32. Translated by Edmund Hill in WSA I/11. Hyde Park, NY: New City Press, 1996.

———. *De fide et symbolo.* CSEL 41. Translated by William Harmless, *Augustine in His Own Words.* Washington, DC: The Catholic University of America Press, 2010.

———. *De Magistro. Against the Academics and the Teacher.* Translated by Peter King. Indianapolis, IN: Hackett Publishing, 1995.

———. *De Ordine.* CCSL 29. Translated by Robert Russell in FC 1. New York: Cima, 1948.

———. *De Trinitate.* CCL 50/50A. Translated by Edmund Hill in WSA I/5. Hyde Park, NY: New City Press, 1991.

———. *Enarrationes in Psalmos.* CCL 38–40. Translated by Maria Boulding in WSA III/15–20. Hyde Park, NY: New City Press, 2000–2004.

———. *Epistulae.* CSEL 34, 44, 57, 58, 88. Translated by Roland Teske in WSA II/1–3. Hyde Park, NY: New City Press, 2001–5.

———. *In epistulam Iohannis ad Parthos tractatus decem.* PL 35.1977–2062.

———. *In Joannis euangelium tractatus.* CCL 36. Translated by John Rettig in FC 78, 79, 88, 90, 92. Washington, DC: The Catholic University of America Press, 1988–95.

————. *Sermones ad populum.* PL 38–40. *Sermones de Vetere Testamento: I–L.* Edited by Cyrillus Lambot. CCSL 41. *Sermones in Matthaeum I: LI–LXX.* Edited by P.P. Verbraken, L. De Coninck, B. Coppieters 't Wallant, R. Demeulenaere, F. Dolbeau. CCSL 41 Aa. *Sermones in Epistolas Apostolicas I: CLI–CLVI.* Edited by Gert Partoens. CCSL 41 Ba. *Sermones in Epistolas Apostolicas II: CLVII–CLXXXIII.* Edited by Shari Boodts. CCSL 41Bb. Translated by Edmund Hill in WSA III/1–10. Hyde Park, NY: New City Press, 1990–95.

Cicero. *De Officiis.* Translated by Walter Miller. LCL 30. Cambridge, MA: Harvard University Press, 1913.

————. *De Oratore.* Edited and translated by E. W. Sutton. Cambridge, MA: Harvard University Press, 1948.

————. *De inventione.* Edited and translated by H. M. Hubble. LCL 386. Cambridge, MA: Harvard University Press, 1960.

————. *Orator.* Edited and translated by H. M. Hubbell. LCL 342. Cambridge, MA: Harvard University Press, 1939.

————. *Pro Quinctio. Pro Roscio Amerino. Pro Roscio Comoedo. On the Agrarian Law.* Translated by J. H. Freese. Loeb Classical Library 240. Cambridge, MA: Harvard University Press, 1930.

Diomedes. *Ars Grammatica. Grammatici Latini* 1.299.

Jerome. *Epistulae* 120–154. Edited by Isidorus Hilberg. CSEL 56. Vienna: F. Tempsky, 1918.

Possidius. *Vita Augustini: zweisprachige Ausgabe eingeleitet, kommentiert und herausgegeben.* Edited by Wilhelm Geerlings. Paderborn: Ferdinand Schöningh, 2005. Translated in English by Frederick R. Hoare. *The Western Fathers.* New York: Sheed and Ward, 1954.

Quintilian. *Institutio oratoria.* Edited and translated by Donald A. Russell. LCL 124, 125, 126, 127, 494 [2001 edition]. Cambridge, MA: Harvard University Press, 2001.

Rhetorica ad Herennium. Edited and translated by Harry Caplan. LCL 403. Cambridge, MA: Harvard University Press, 1977.

Sidonius. *Poems. Letters: Books 1–2.* Translated by W. B. Anderson. Loeb Classical Library 296. Cambridge, MA: Harvard University Press, 1936.

Secondary Sources

Adnès, Pierre. "Humilité a l'École de Saint Augustin," *Revue d'ascetique et de mystique* 31 (1955): 28–46.

Allen, Pauline and Bronwen Neil. *Crisis Management in Late Antiquity (410–590 CE): A Survey of the Evidence from Episcopal Letters.* Supplements to Vigiliae Christianae. Leiden: Brill 2013.

Arendt, Hannah. *Human Condition.* Garden City, NY: Doubleday, 1959.

Arnold, W.H. and P. Bright. *De Doctrina Christiana: A Classic of Western Culture.* Notre Dame, IN: The University of Notre Dame Press, 1995.

Auerbach, Erich. *"Sermo Humilis." Literary Language and Its Public in Late Latin Antiquity and in the Middle Ages.* Translated by Ralph Manheim. New York: Pantheon, 1965. 25–66.

Austin, J. L. *How to do Things with Words.* Cambridge, MA: Harvard University Press, 1975.

Ayres, Lewis, and Thomas Humphrey. "Augustine and the West to AD 600." *The Oxford Handbook of Sacramental Theology.* Edited by Hans Boersma and Matthew Levering. Oxford, England: Oxford University Press, 2001.

Ayres, Lewis. "Remember That You Are Catholic (s. 52.2): Augustine on the Unity of the Triune God" *JECS* 8.1 (2000): 39–81.

Barfield, Owen. *Poetic Diction.* Middletown, CT: Wesleyan University Press, 1987.

Barnes, Michel Renee. "The Visible Christ and the Invisible Trinity: Mt. 5:8 in Augustine's Trinitarian Theology of 400" *Modern Theology* Summer 2003

Bartelink, G. J. M. "Sermo piscatorius. De wisserstaal van de apostelen." *Studia Catholica* 35 (1930): 267–73.

Baumann, Notker. *Die Demut als Grundlage aller Tugenden bei Augustinus.* Frankfurt am Main: Peter Lang, 2009.

Boersma, Gerald. "Augustine on the Beatific Vision as ubique totus." *Scottish Journal of Theology* 71 (2018): 16–32.

Boersma, Hans. *Seeing God: The Beatific Vision in Christian Tradition.* Grand Rapids, MI: Eerdmans, 2018.

Boersma, Hans and Matthew Levering. *The Oxford Handbook of Sacramental Theology.* Oxford: Oxford University Press, 2001.

Bouton-Touboulic, Isabelle. "Body Language in Augustine's *Confessiones* and *De doctrina christiana*." *Augustinian Studies* 49:1 (2018): 1–23.

Brown, Peter. "Augustine and a crisis of wealth in Late Antiquity," *Augustinian Studies* 36 (2005): 5–30.

———. *Power and Persuasion in Late Antiquity: Towards a Christian Empire.* Madison: University of Wisconsin Press, 1992.

———. *Through the Eye of a Needle.* Princeton, NJ: Princeton University Press, 2012.

Burns, J. Patout. *Augustine's Preached Theology: Living as the Body of Christ.* Grand Rapids, MI: Eerdmans Press, 2022.

Cameron, Averil. "Redrawing the Map: Early Christian Territory after Foucault." *The Journal of Roman Studies* 76 (1986): 266–71.

———. *Christianity and the Rhetoric of Empire: The Development of Christian Discourse.* Berkeley: University of California Press, 1991.

Cameron, Michael. "Augustine and Scripture." In *The Wiley-Blackwell Companion to Augustine.* Edited by Mark Vessey, 200–214. Oxford: Wiley-Blackwell Publishing, 2012.

———. *Christ Meets Me Everywhere: Augustine's Early Figurative Exegesis.* New York, NY: Oxford University Press, 2012.

———. *"Totus Christus* as Hermeneutical Center in *Enarrationes in Psalmos."* In *The Harp of Prophecy: Early Christian Interpretation of the Psalms.* Edited by Paul Kolbet and Brian Daley, SJ, 205–26. Notre Dame, IN: The University of Notre Dame Press, 2015.

———. "Augustine's Rhetorical Reading of Genesis in *Confessions 11–12." Augustine and Tradition.* Edited by David G. Hunter and Jonathan P. Yates, 3–27. Grand Rapids, MI: Eerdmans, 2021.

Cardascia, G. "L'apparition dans le Droit des Classes D'«Honestiores» et d' «Humiliroes»." *Revue historique de droit français et étranger* V. 27 (1950): 461–85.

Cary, Philip. *Outward Signs.* Oxford: Oxford University Press, 2008.

Castelfranchi, Christiano, and Isaeblla Poggi. "Lying as Pretending to Give Information." In *Pretending to Communicate.* Edited by Herman Parret, 276–89. Berlin: Walter de Gruyter, 1994.

Catherine Chin, *Grammar and Christianity in the Late Roman World.* Philadelphia: University of Pennsylvania Press, 2008.

Cavadini, John. "Pride." *Augustine through the Ages.* Edited by Allan D. Fitzgerald, 679–85. Grand Rapids, MI: Eerdmans, 1999.

———. "Simplifying Augustine." In *Educating People of Faith: Exploring the History of Jewish and Christian*. Edited by John H. Van Engen, 63–84. Grand Rapids, MI: Eerdmans, 2004.

Chadwick, Henry. *Augustine of Hippo: A Life*. Oxford: Oxford University Press, 2009.

Chin, Catherine. *Grammar and Christianity in the Late Roman World*. Philadelphia: University of Pennsylvania Press, 2008.

Chretien, Jean-Louis. *Saint Augustin et les actes de parole*. Paris: Presses Universitaires de France, 2002.

Clark, E. G. "Pastoral Care: Town and Country in Late-Antique Preaching." In *Urban Centers and Rural Contexts in Late Antiquity*. Edited by Thomas S. Burns and John William Eadie, 265–85. East Lansing: Michigan State University Press, 2001.

Clavier, Mark F. M. *Eloquent Wisdom: Rhetoric Cosmology and Delight in the Theology of Augustine of Hippo*. Turnhout: Brepols, 2014.

Courcelle, Pierre. *Recherches sur les "Confessions" de saint Augustin*. Paris, Boccard: 1950.

Daley, Brian. "Christology." *Augustine through the Ages*. Edited by Allan D. Fitzgerald, 165–69. Grand Rapids, MI: Eerdmans, 1999.

Deferrari, Roy J. "Verbatim Reports of Augustine's Unwritten Sermons." *Transactions and Proceedings of the American Philological Association* 46 (1915): 35–45.

———. "St. Augustine's Method of Composing and Delivering Sermons." *American Journal of Philology* 43 (1922): 97–123, 193–219.

Delattre, Alfred Louis. *Archéologie chrétienne de Carthage: Fouilles de la basilique de Damous-El-Karita*. Algiers: Aux bureaux des Missions Catholiques, 1888.

Dolbeau, Francois. "Sermons inédits de saint Augustin prêchés en 397 [5ème série]." *RevBen* 104 [1994]: 34–76.

———. *Vingt-six sermons au peuple d'Afrique*. Paris, France: Institut d'études augustiniennes, 2009.

Dolenz, Heimo. "Two Annex Buildings to the Basilica Damous-el-Karita in Carthage. A Summary of the Excavations in 1996 and 1997." *Antiquités africaines Année* 36 (2000): 147–59.

Dossey, Lesslie. *Peasant and Empire in Christian North Africa*. Berkeley: University of California Press, 2010.

Drobner, Hubertus. "The Chronology of St. Augustine's *Sermones ad populum*." *Augustinian Studies* 31:2, 2000; 211–18.

———. *Sermones 1–5,* Patrologia Beiträge zum Studium der Kirchenväter, Band VII. Frankfurt am Main: Peter Lang, 2000.

———. *Sermones 13–21.* Patrologia Beiträge zum Studium der Kirchenväter. Band XXV. V.1. Frankfurt am Main: Peter Lang, 2016.

———. *Sermones 148–150.* Patrologia Beiträge zum Studium der Kirchenväter, Band XXVI. Frankfurt am Main: Peter Lang, 2012.

———. *Sermones 196/A-204/A.* Patrologia Beiträge zum Studium der Kirchenväter, Band XXII. V.1. Frankfurt am Main: Peter Lang, 2010.

———. *Sermones 22–34.* Patrologia Beiträge zum Studium der Kirchenväter. Band XXV. V.2. Frankfurt am Main: Peter Lang, 2016.

———. *Sermones 336–340/A.* Patrologia Beiträge zum Studium der Kirchenväter. Band IX. Frankfurt am Main: Peter Lang, 2003.

———. *Sermones 35–41.* Patrologia Beiträge zum Studium der Kirchenväter. Band XIII. Frankfurt am Main: Peter Lang, 2004.

———. *Sermones 42–50.* Patrologia Beiträge zum Studium der Kirchenväter. Band XXIX. Frankfurt am Main: Peter Lang, 2013.

———. *Sermones 6–12.* Patrologia Beiträge zum Studium der Kirchenväter. Band X. Frankfurt am Main: Peter Lang, 2003.

———. *Sermones 94/A-97.* Patrologia Beiträge zum Studium der Kirchenväter. Band XIX. Frankfurt am Main: Peter Lang, 2007.

Dunnington, Kent. *Humility, Pride, and Christian Virtue Theory.* Oxford: Oxford University Press, 2019.

Dupont, Anthony. *Gratia in Augustine's Sermones Ad Populum During the Pelagian Controversy: Do Different Contexts Furnish Different Insights.* Leiden: Brill, 2013.

Duval, Noël. "Études d'architecture chrétienne nord-africaine." *Mélanges de l'école française de Rome Année* (1972 84–2): 1071–172.

Frend, W. H. C. "Fussala: Augustine's Crisis of Credibility (Ep. 20*)." In *Les lettres de saint Augustin.* 251–265. Paris: Etudes Augustiniennes, 1983.

Fuhrer, Therese. "Orator Humilis." In *Paul as Homo Novus: Authorial Strategies of Self-Fashioning in Light of a Ciceronian Term.* 251–66. Göttingen: Vandenhoeck and Ruprecht, 2018.

Getty, Marie. *The Life of the North Africans as Revealed in the Sermons of Saint Augustine.* Washington DC: The Catholic University of America, 1931.

Glare, P. G. *Oxford Latin Dictionary.* 2 Vols. Oxford, England: Oxford University Press, 2012.

Gowans, Coleen Hoffman. *The Identity of the True Believer in the Sermons of Augustine of Hippo: A Dimension of His Christian Anthropology.* Lewiston, NY: Edwin Mellen Press, 1998.

Glowasky, Michael. *Rhetoric and Scripture in Augustine's Homiletic Strategy.* Leiden: Brill, 2021.

Gronewoller, Brian. *Rhetorical Economy in Augustine's Theology.* Oxford: Oxford University Press, 2021.

Green, R. P. H. "Augustine's De Doctrina Christiana: Some Clarifications." *Respublica Litterarum* 15 (1992): 101–2.

Gryson, Robert. *Répertoire général des auteurs ecclésiastiques latins de l'Antiquiteé et du Haut Moyen Âge / Tome I, Introduction, Répertoire des auteurs: A-H.* Freiburg : Verlag Herder, 2007.

Hamman, A. G. *La vie quotidienne en Afrique du Nord au temps de Saint Augustin.* Paris: Hachette, 1979.

Harmless, S.J, William. "A Love Supreme: Augustine's 'Jazz' of Theology." *Augustinian Studies,* 43:1/2 (2012): 149–77.

Harris, William V. *Ancient Literacy.* Cambridge, MA: Harvard University Press, 1989.

Harrison, Carol. *Art of Listening in the Early Church.* Oxford: Oxford University Press, 2013.

———. *Augustine; Christian Truth and Fractured Humanity.* Oxford: Oxford University Press, 2000.

———. "The Rhetoric of Scripture and Preaching." *Augustine and His Critics.* Edited by Robert Dodaro and George Lawless, 213–30. New York: Routledge, 2000.

Herdt, Jennifer. "The Theatre of the Virtues: Augustine's Critique of Pagan Mimesis," in *Augustine's City of God: A Critical Guide.* Edited by James Wetzel, 111–29. New York: Cambridge University Press, 2012.

Hombert, Pierre-Marie. *Nouvelles recherches de chronologie augustinienne.* Paris: Institut d'Études Augustiniennes, 2000.

———. "Rhétorique et Théologie. La prédication sur le Verbe incarné dans les sermons d'Augustin pour Noël." In *Ministerium Sermonis. Philological, Historical, and Theological Studies on Augustine's Sermones ad populum.* Edited by Grett Partones, Anthony Dupont, and Mathijs Lamberigts, 221–42. Turnhout: Brepols, 2012.

Johnson, W.R. "Isocrates Flowering," *Philosophy & Rhetoric.* v.9.4 (Fall, 1976) 217-231.

Kannengiesser, C. "The Interrupted *De Doctrina Christiana.*" In *De Doctrina Christiana.* Edited by W.H.Arnold and P. Bright, 4–14. Notre Dame, IN: The University of Notre Dame Press, 1995.

Kaster, Robert. *Guardians of Language.* Berkeley: University of California Press, 1988.

Kenny, John Peter. *The Mysticism of Saint Augustine: Rereading the Confessions.* New York: Routledge, 2005.

———. *Contemplation and Classical Christianity : A Study in Augustine.* Oxford: Oxford University Press, 2013.

Kennedy, George A. *Classical Rhetoric and Its Christian and Secular Tradition from Ancient to Modern Time*s. 2nd ed. Chapel Hill: University of North Carolina Press, 1999.

Kim, Jr., Charles G. "*Ipsa Ructatio Eungaleium Est: Tapinosis* in Augustine's Homilies," *Augustinian Studies* 50:2 (2019): 197–214.

Kolbet, Paul. "Formal Continuities Between Augustine's Early Philosophical Teaching and Late Homiletical Practice." *Studia Patristica,* 43. 2006: 149–54.

———. *Augustine and the Cure of Souls : Revising a Classical Idea.* Notre Dame, IN: University of Notre Dame Press, 2010.

Macdonald, C. "Introduction," *Pro Sulla.* LCL 324.

MacMullen, Ramsey. "A Note on *sermo humilis.*" *Journal of Theological Studies n.s.* 17 (1966) 108–12.

MacMullen, Ramsey. "The Preacher's Audience [AD 350–400]." *Journal of Theological Studies n.s.* 40 (1989): 503–11.

Madec, Goulven. *Introduction Aux "Révisions" et à la Lecture des Oeuvres de Saint Augustin.* Paris: Institut d'Études Augustiniennes, 1996.

Marec, Erwan. *Hippone le Royale: Antique Hippo Regius.* Algers, Alegeria: Dir. de l'Intérieur et des Beaux-Arts,1954.

Markus, R. A. "St. Augustine on Signs." *Phronesis* 2.1 (1957): 60–83.

Marrou, Henri-Irenée. *A History of Education in Antiquity.* Translated by George Lamb. New York: Sheed and Ward, 1956.

———. *Saint Augustin et la Fin de la Culture Antique.* Paris: Editions E. De Broccard, 1958.

Mazzeo, Joseph Anthony. "St. Augustine's Rhetoric of Silence." *Journal of the History of Ideas* V. 23, No. 2 (1962): 175–96.

McCarthy, M. C. "Augustine's Mixed Feelings: Vergil's 'Aeneid' and the Psalms of David in the 'Confessions.'" *The Harvard Theological Review,* 4, (2009), 453–79.

Meador, Jr, Prentice A. "Quintilian's '*vir bonus*.'" *Western Speech* 34.3 (1970): 162–69.

Mechlinsky, Lutz. *Der Modus Proferendi in Augustins Sermones Ad Populum/* Paderborn: Ferdinand Schöningh, 2004.

Meconi, David, SJ. "The Incarnation and the Role of Participation in St. Augustine's Confessions," *Augustinian Studies* 29:2 (1998): 61–75.

———. *On Self-Harm, Narcissism, Atonement, and the Vulnerable Christ.* New York, NY: Bloomsbury, 2019.

———. *The One Christ: St. Augustine's Theology of Deification.* Washington, DC: The Catholic University of America Press, 2012.

———. "Saint Augustine's Early Theory of Participation." *Augustinian Studies* 27 (1996): 79–96.

Merdinger, J.E. *Rome and the African Church in the Time of Augustine.* New Haven, CT: Yale University Press, 1997.

Mohrmann, Christine. *Etudes Sur les Latin des Chretiennes.* V.1, V.2. Rome, Italy: Edizioni di Storia e Letteratura, 1961.

———. "Das Wortspiel in den augustinischen Sermones," in *Études sur le latin des chrétiens,* Vol. 1 (Roma, Edizioni di Storia e Litteratura: 1961): 323–49.

———. "St. Augustine and the Eloquentia," *Etudes sur le latin des chrétiens* Tome 1 (Rome, 1958) 351–70.

Montefusco, L. Calholi. "Captatio Benevolentiae." *Brill's New Pauly.* 1080.

O'Daly, Gerald. *Augustine's City of God: A Reader's Guide.* Oxford: Oxford University Press, 1999.

O'Donnell, James J. *Augustine: A New Biography.* New York: Ecco, 2005.

———. *Confessions.* 3 Vols. Oxford: Oxford University Press, 1992.

Ochs, Peter. "Outward Signs: The Powerlessness of External Things in Augustine's Thought." *Modern Theology* 27, no. 1 (January 2011): 206–8.

Olivar, Alexandre. *La Precicacion Cristiana Antiqua.* Barcelona: Editorial Herder, 1991.

Palanque, Jean-Rémy. *S. Ambrose et l'Empire Romain.* Paris: E. de Boccard, 1933.

Partoens, Gert. "Augustin Als Praediger." In *Augustin Handbuch.* Tübingen: Mohr Siebeck, 2007.

Ployd, Adam. *Augustine, the Trinity, and the Church.* Oxford: Oxford University Press, 2015.

Pontet, Maurice. *L'Exegese de S. Augustin Predicateur.* Paris: Aubier, 1944.

Randolph, Jacob. "Salvation and Speech Act. Reading Luther with the Aid of Searle's Analysis of Declarations." *Perichoresis* 15, no. 1 (Spring 2017): 101–17.

Rapp, Claudia, *Holy Bishops in Late Antiquity: The Nature of Christian Leadership in an Age of Transition.* Berkeley: University of California Press, 2005.

Rebillard, Eric. "Sermons, Audience, Preacher." *Preaching in the Patristic Era.* Leiden: Brill, 2018.

Rist, John M. *Augustine: Ancient Thought Baptized.* New York: Cambridge University Press, 1994.

Robinson, Thomas A. *Who Were the First Christians?: Dismantling the Urban Thesis.* Oxford: Oxford University Press, 2017.

Rosenberg, Stanley P. "Beside Books: Approaching Augustine's Sermons," *Tractatio Scripturarum: Philological, Exegetical, Rhetorical, and Theological Studies on Augustine's sermons.* Edited Anthony Dupont, Gert Partoens, Mathijs Lamberigts, 405–42. Turnhout: Brepols, 2012.

Rousseau, Phillip. "The Preacher's Audience: A More Optimistic View," *Ancient History in a Modern University. Volume 2 Early Christianity, Late Antiquity and Beyond.* 391–400. Grand Rapids, MI: Eerdmans, 1998.

Ruddy, Deborah Wallace, "A Christological Approach to the Virtue of Humility," PhD diss., Boston College, 2001.

Sanlon, Peter. *Augustine's Theology of Preaching.* Minneapolis: Fortress Press, 2014.

Schaffner, Otto. *Christliche Demut: des Hl. Augustinus Lehre von der Humilitas.* Würzburg: Augustinus-Verlag, 1959.

Schäublin, Christoph. "Homerum ex Homero." *Museum Helveticum* (V. 34.4, 1977), 221–27.

Searle, John. "Austin on Locutionary and Illocutionary Acts." *Philosophical Review* 77 (Oct. 1968): 405–24.

Searle, John. *Expression and Meaning: Studies in the Theory of Speech Acts.* London: Cambridge University Press, 1969.

Searle, John. *Foundations of Illocutionary Logic.* New York: Cambridge University Press, 1985.

Searle, John. "How Performatives Work." *Linguistics and Philosophy* 12(5), (1989): 535–58.

Searle, John. *Speech Acts: An Essay in the Philosophy of Language.* New York: Cambridge University Press, 1970.

Shaublin, Christophe. "*De Doctrina Christiana*: A Classic of Western Culture?" In *De Doctrina Christiana*, edited by Arnold and Bright, 47–67.

Smith, James, K. A. *Who's Afraid of Relativism*. Grand Rapids, MI: Baker Academic Press, 2014.

Spence, Sarah. *Rhetorics of Reason and Desire: Vergil, Augustine, and the Troubadours*. Ithaca, NY: Cornell University Press, 1987.

Stead, G. C. "Augustine's "De Magistro": A Philosopher's View," Studia Patristica, 63–73.

Stefaniw, Blossom. *Christian Reading: Language, Ethics, and the Order of Things*. Oakland: University of California Press, 2019.

Studer, Basil. "'Sacramentum et exemplum' chez saint Augustin." *Recherches Augustiniennes et Patristiques* 10 (January, 1975): 87–141.

Taylor, Daniel J. "Varro and the Teaching of Latin." *The Classical Outlook* 92.1 (2017): 9–14.

Teske, Roland J. *Paradoxes of Time in Saint Augustine*. Milwaukee, WI: Marquette University Press, 1996.

Teubner, Jonathan. *Prayer after Augustine: A Study in the Development of the Latin Tradition*. Oxford: Oxford University Press, 2018.

Thane, Marcus. "Speech-act theory to enhance Karl Barth's homiletical postulation of a sermon's 'revelatory compliance.'" *Scottish Journal of Theology* no. 2 (2015): 187–200.

Too, Lee Yun, "Education, Grammar, and Rhetoric," *Augustine in Context*. Cambridge: Cambridge University Press, 2017.

Van den Boer, W. "Tapeinos in Pagan and Christian Terminology." In *Tria Corda: Scritti in onore di Arnaldo Momigliano*. Biblioteca di Athenaeum 1. Como: Edizioni New Press, 1983.

Van der Meer, Frederick. *Augustine the Bishop: The Life and Work of a Father of the Church* Trans. Brian Battershaw and G.R. Lamb. London: Sheed and Ward, 1961.

Van Fleteren, Frederick. "Augustine and the Possibility of the Vision of God in This Life." *Studies in Medieval Culture, XI*. 9–16. Lansing: Western Michigain University Press, 1977.

Van Neer, Joost. "From Pride to Humility, from Impasse to Resolution, from Day to Day: Structure and Argument in Augustine's Nativity Sermons 195 and 196 with a Division into Five Parts." *Sacris Erudiri* 53 (2014): 69–98.

———. "Language and Scripture as Structuring Principles of Augustine's 'Sermones' 186 and 187." *Augustiniana* Vol. 63, No. 1/4 (2013): 189–229.

Vanhoozer, Kevin. *The Drama of Doctrine: A Critical-Linguistic Approach.* Louisville, KY: Westminster John Knox Press, 2005.

———. *Is There a Meaning in This Text?* Grand Rapids, MI: Zondervan, 1998.

Vasaly, Ann. "Cicero's Early Speeches." In *Brill's Companion to Cicero.* Edited by James M. May, 77–111. Leiden: Brill, 2002.

Verbraken, Pierre-Patrick. *Études critiques sur les sermons authentiques de saint Augustin.* Steenbrugis: Abbatia Sancti Petri, 1976.

Verwilghen, Albert. *Christologie et Spiritualité selon Saint Augustin.* Paris, France: Beauchesne, 1984.

———. "Jesus Christ: Source of Christian Humility," *Augustine and the Bible.* Edited and translated by Pamela Bright. Notre Dame, IN: University of Notre Dame Press, 1986.

Vincent, Monique. "Le vocabulaire de la prière chez saint Augustin." *Augustiniana* 41.1 (1994): 783–804.

Webb, Ruth. *Imagination and Persuasion in Ancient Rhetorical. Theory and Practice.* Surrey: Ashgate, 2009.

Wickes, Jeffrey. *Bible and Poetry in Late Antique Mesopatamia.* Berkeley: University of California Press, 2019.

Wilbrand, W. "Zur Chronologie einiger Schriften des hl. Ambrosius." *Historiches Jahrbuch, XLI* (1921): 1–19.

Wilcoxen, Matthew. *Divine Humility: God's Morally Perfect Being.* Waco, TX: Baylor University Press, 2019.

Wilken, Robert Louis, and Ramsay MacMullen. "The Second Church: Popular Christianity A.D. 200–400—By Ramsay MacMullen," *Conversations in Religion & Theology* 8 (2): 120–25.

Williams, Rowan. *Holy Living.* London: Bloomsbury Publishing, 2018.

———. "Language Reality and Desire." *Literature and Theology* 3.2 (July 1989): 138–50.

———. *On Augustine.* London: Bloomsbury Publishing, 2016.

Wittgenstein, Ludwig. *Philosophical Investigations: the German text, with a revised English translation.* Translated by G.E.M. Anscombe. Malden, MA: Blackwell, 2001.

INDEX OF NAMES AND SUBJECTS

Adnès, Pierre, xxxiii, xxxvii, 134n35

agit cum dicit (*de doctrina christiana*
4.15.32), 20n56, 21–25, 48, 99, 183;
Agere and *dicere*, 22

agricola, 81

Ambrose, xxxii, xlii, xlv, 42–43, 52,
59–69, 79, 102, 123, 139, 183

amen, 142–44, 154–55

Antoninus, 5, 7–11, 32–38, 41, 74,
185–86

argumentatio, xxxi, 130

artes liberales, 42, 69, 94, 97, 99

Austin, J. L., xlii, 11, 13–17,

authority (*auctores; auctoritas*), 23, 46, 56,
94, 96–97, 100–101, 112

barbarism, 46, 96, 103, 105, 107–9,
111–12, 184

Baumann, Notker, xxxvii–xxxviii

beata vita, 25, 121, 148, 158, 160, 185

bonus vir dicendi peritus, 42, 53

Brown, Peter, xxv–xxvii, 5, 17n46,
19n52, 39n1, 43n17, 44n19, 62n76,
72n3, 73n7, 74n15, 75n25, 76, 78–80,
103n34, 120

Cameron, Averil, xxv–xxvii, 19

Cameron, Michael, xxviii, 61n75, 102,
141–43, 156, 161, 164

captatio benevolentiae, 133–34, 144

caritas, xxv, 164–65, 175–76

Cary, Phillip, 13n33, 17n46, 18

cathedra, 8, 10, 20, 35, 37, 41, 63–64,
75, 138; *cathedra moysi*, 10; *cathedra
mendacii*, 10, 40, 139; *cathedra caelestia*,
9; *cathedra in caelo*, 8, 136; *cathedra
Christi*, 11, 17, 26–27, 29–30, 37, 41,
46, 65, 94, 126, 139, 145

Cavadini, John, 4, 64n82, 72n3, 76n31,
79n46, 83–84, 89

Chretien, John-Louis, 13n34, 42n11, 138

Christology, xxvi, xlv, 95–97, 175; *forma
servi*, xxiv, xxxiv, xlv–xlvi, 9, 95, 113,
120, 145, 173, 175, 177; *forma dei*,
xxiv, xxxiv, xlv–xlvi, 9, 95, 120, 145,
173, 175, 177

Cicero (Marcus Tullius Cicero), xxix,
xxxi–xxxii, xxxvi–xxxvii, xlii–xliii,
xlv, 19n51, 22–25, 27, 31, 41–43, 46,
48–59, 61, 65, 68, 70, 71, 76, 97, 98,
102, 106, 130–31, 151–53, 155, 157,
163, 167, 178, 183